India Emerging

From Policy Paralysis to Hyper Economics

India Emerging

From Policy Paralysis to Hyper Economics

Sandip Sen and Aarohi Sen

BLOOMSBURY
NEW DELHI • LONDON • OXFORD • NEW YORK • SYDNEY

BLOOMSBURY INDIA
Bloomsbury Publishing India Pvt. Ltd
Second Floor, LSC Building No. 4, DDA Complex, Pocket C – 6 & 7,
Vasant Kunj, New Delhi 110070

BLOOMSBURY, BLOOMSBURY INDIA and the Diana logo are trademarks of
Bloomsbury Publishing Plc

First published in India 2019
This export edition published in 2020

ISBN: TPB: 978-93-87457-93-5 eBook: 978-93-87457-94-2

Typeset in Manipal Digital

Bloomsbury Publishing Plc makes every effort to ensure that the papers used in the manufacture of our books are natural, recyclable products made from wood grown in well-managed forests. Our manufacturing processes conform to the environmental regulations of the country of origin

This book is dedicated to
a new India that is efficient, compassionate,
sustainable and free from doles and corruption.

CONTENTS

Acknowledgements

I thank my parents, late Indira and Ajoy Sen, for guiding me through my formative years. Especially my father whose grit, determination and never-say-die attitude perhaps rubbed off a little on me. I am thankful to my wife Suparna, my son Aarohi and my daughter-in-law Priyanka, my sisters Papri Sri Raman and Arundhaty Nayar, and my brother-in-law Raj Nayar for consistently supporting me as I navigate the world of journalism and authorship. I also thank my brother-in-law late J. Sri Raman for introducing me to the world of journalism a few decades ago.

I thank my son Aarohi for co-authoring *India Emerging: From Policy Paralysis to Hyper Economics* and giving valuable inputs. He has also been instrumental in using his analytical skills for creating charts and graphs used in the book. I also thank my sister Papri for painstakingly editing the draft before submission to the publisher and also for giving several inputs that enriched the manuscript. I also thank my friends, colleagues and batchmates at school, college and fellow Indian Institute of Technology (IIT) alumni for encouraging me and providing me with extensive industry information.

I thank the publisher and the editors at Bloomsbury Publishing who have edited and published the book. I also thank editors of several publications like *Business Standard, DNA India, Down to Earth, The Economic Times, Financial Express, Hindustan Times, The Hindu Business Line, The Indian Express, Indian Printer and Publisher, Observer Research Foundation, Pragati, TerraGreen, The Times of India* and *Woman's Era,* among others, for having published my writings.

I also thank dozens of friends and well-wishers who gave me valuable insights and information to research and write *India Emerging*.

—Sandip Sen

I owe the opportunity to write this book to my father and mentor, Sandip Sen. I may not share his relentless positivity and unshakeable grit, but I continue to be awed by it. Thank you, Dad!

—Aarohi Sen

Author's Note

India Emerging: From Policy Paralysis to Hyper Economics is a story of our times—a story of developmental politics. It is a story of how India is changing and learning through its mistakes. It is a story of successes and failures. It is a story of an economic revival in bits and pieces. It is a story of risks taken without astute risk management. Some of those have succeeded, some backfired.

India Emerging is a sequel to my first book in the series, *Neta, Babu and Subsidy: Economic Roundup 2000 to 2014*, which was published in February 2014. It was an effort to show the economic decision-making during UPA (United Progressive Alliance) I and UPA II and measure the performance against the economic data during the Vajpayee era.

This book is an attempt to document—against data from the past—the economic decision-making during the four years of the National Democratic Alliance (NDA) government led by Prime Minister (PM) Narendra Modi. Like in the previous book, *India Emerging* also visually demonstrates the state of various sectors of the economy. But, the story this time is much deeper than what mere graphs or statistics can portray—because it is a story of change, a story of an emerging nation on a learning curve. A nation that has swung from policy paralysis to hyper economics. A nation that does not always get things right because of lack of knowledge, capital, technology, discipline, systems, structuring, conditioning and many other causes that separate the emerging from matured economies.

All data quoted in the book are from authentic sources in the public domain, including Reserve Bank of India (RBI), International Monetary Fund (IMF), ministry annual reports, public and private institutions and publications of repute. The details and references of data sources used are provided in the bibliography. Whereas all graphs in the book have been plotted by us, the data used for them are taken from the websites of public institutions as mentioned in individual graphs.

The book is also a story of a grassroots leader who tries to grapple with the problems of an emerging economy and bring reforms viewed from his perspective. A perspective that is bold but risky. It is innovative and experimental but not what you can always call prudent. Like all experimental approaches, it succeeds in bits and pieces. Where it succeeds, it disrupts and creates new horizons and endless opportunities. Where it fails, it wastes time and money—resources India cannot afford to waste. Since it is the taxpayer's money at stake, not everyone is amused by his style of operation and decision-making.

PM Modi has lent a new experimental approach to modern-day democratic politics. You can call it risky, but it is how and why entrepreneurs succeed or fail. Once selected to lead the Bharatiya Janata Party (BJP), he ensured that its election campaign was aggressively positioned as the vote for 'Modi *sarkar*' and not the 'NDA *sarkar*'. It was risky because it only motivated the opposition parties to attack him personally. The Congress positioned its campaign *against Modi*—not against the NDA. It tried to paint him as a dictator who is communal and megalomaniac. He did not respond to Congress' jibes on the Godhra riots. Like a man on a mission, he just kept on selling his dream—the Gujarat model of good governance—during the election campaign.

Surprisingly, he did not even share his concerns with the people of India about the distraught state of the economy. Rather, he needlessly made claims of '*achhe din*' (good days ahead) that he would find impossible to deliver in one term. As soon as Modi came to power, he abandoned the conventional way of incremental but time-tested reforms that Indian politicians normally undertake, often, just to tell the voter, 'Here is your candyfloss'. Instead, Modi started taking bold risks, some of which worked and some of which boomeranged. As a result, in the last four years, both his worshippers and detractors grew in number.

While demonetisation did not meet its goals and created a nationwide cash crisis, the *Jan Dhan* account provided banking facilities and new opportunities to 300 million people. While the implementation of Goods and Services Tax (GST) was laborious and far from perfect, the Stressed

Asset Insolvency Act and resolution mechanism was a much-needed reform that will help clean up the banks' non-performing assets (NPAs) and make them healthy. A lot of work has been done in diverse areas including streamlining power supplies to cities as well as rural areas, but the environment and pollution concerns have also risen meteorically. Modi cannot be faulted for inaction, but his hyper-active economics stretched the resources of a developing economy. Besides, there were one too many initiatives and they, at times, remained incomplete and open to criticism.

Four years into his term, Narendra Modi has shown that he is clearly no magician. Although the economy is arguably in better shape, we are far away from double-digit growth, low inflation, low interest rates and low unemployment. Much as he may try and achieve, *achhe din* is still a distant dream.

My apologies to all Modi lovers and Modi haters, but it is India which is more important than political ideology and leaders.

—Sandip Sen

Introduction

This book attempts to chronicle economic decision-making in India and its effect on society during the first four years of the Narendra Modi government (2014–2018). Our previous analysis, four years ago, scrutinised the period from 2004–2014 under Manmohan Singh.

We start this book with a discourse on the economy before and after liberalisation. We analyse some of the major economic decisions taken by PMs Jawaharlal Nehru, Lal Bahadur Shastri and Indira Gandhi. This was a very critical period that has to be discussed as several laws with deep-rooted economic implications were formulated then. They are being revisited now.

There is one more reason why a discussion about the past is extremely relevant. Ever since 2014, the banking sector has been witnessing some major changes. This is something that has not happened in the past 50 years. It is the experiment with the banking sector that makes this government and the government under Indira Gandhi 50 years ago so different from any other government that India has witnessed since independence.

Bringing banking to the masses was first attempted by Indira Gandhi 50 years ago. It was unlike most reforms that traditional economists push for. It was something that Indira Gandhi started initially and has been taken to the next level by PM Narendra Modi. Both were great experimental initiatives that changed the destiny of millions, but also put undue stress on the banking sector. These decisions will be debated by economists endlessly in the coming decades.

The story around *Jan Dhan* accounts, demonetisation, digital payment initiatives, Unified Payments Interface (UPI), banking sector reforms, the bankruptcy law, the declaration of stressed assets, rising NPAs, the resolution mechanisms, direct payment of subsidies through bank accounts, loans by Micro Units Development and Refinance Agency Ltd (MUDRA loans), farm loan waiver—all point out the fact that banks are the core area around which the Modi government intends to carry out its economic policies. Many of the above are game-changing solutions. For every failed execution like demonetisation, there were two success stories like UPI and quick resolution of stressed assets. The failures have had an immediate short-term impact, unlike the successes that are long term.

The banking sector story is not the only plus point of the Modi government and the faulty execution of demonetisation not its sole failure. Even before the effects of demonetisation had subsided, the long-pending GST bill was tabled in the parliament in July 2017, again tying-up the economic activity in knots. Conceived in 2002, GST bill took 15 long years to be implemented.

The GST bill, when finally launched, was found unusually complex, structurally faulty and multi-tiered. Tax slabs were high and burdened the manufacturing sector, hurting economic growth. It has been amended time and again for over a year. To add to the confusion and to the already difficult situation, the E-Way bill was introduced in April 2018 that further compounded the problems. The revenue secretary admitted in June 2018 that more simplification is due and a new avatar of the GST could unfold before the polls.

After focusing on banking and GST, this story moves on to the energy sector where the three areas of coal, oil and renewable energy are dealt with individually. All these areas had their own challenges and problems to be solved.

The coal sector saw some major initiatives to ease supply chain bottlenecks, but though supply positions have improved, comfort levels have still not been achieved. Even today, coal supplies need to be micromanaged to ensure steady and seamless functioning of industries and power plants across the nation.

In the oil and natural gas sector, global prices plummeted. For three years oil prices remained subdued, yet India missed the opportunity to build its oil reserves and oil sector infrastructure—storage tanks, oil pipelines and natural gas terminals. Also, the punitive taxes levied on oil imports hurt the economy and the common man needlessly. High taxes on petroleum products, particularly diesel, has created both anxiety and anger amongst the electorate.

The renewable energy sector was, however, a winner. Major risks were taken—all paid off. It was an exemplary work that has critical implication on India's energy security. Full credit goes to the government for not only expanding the renewable energy footprint and creating scales that helped reduce its cost but also for taking the initiative to take it to the remote corners of rural India.

After the energy sector, the story moves to the manufacturing sector where the Modi government announced the Make in India initiative. We visit three critical areas here that completes the sectoral review and include mining, infrastructure and manufacturing.

The mining sector has indeed witnessed policy paralysis and inaction from the Modi government as well as the states. Faulty policies of the past decade have continued without redressal. Due to this, legal mining has receded and illegal mining has been on the rise. Apart from coal and iron ore, mining witnessed no major initiative by the Modi government. As a result, the domestic industry lost billions and the import cost of raw materials mounted.

The infrastructure sector performed far better. It was not only roads, railways and airports around the metros that were expanded—even India's hinterland saw major initiatives to the credit of both centre as well as state governments. Even basic infrastructure like rural electrification, water management and education and health centres saw improvement.

Still, Make in India did not quite take-off. Manufacturing is at crossroads due to various reasons but low demand is certainly not one of them. Much is needed to be done to reposition India as a manufacturing major. Bringing telecom manufacturing to India is being attempted but needs to be sped up. Lack of affordable finance and tax regime instability are some of the issues that have to be addressed.

From banking and industry sector, the storyline moves to food and agriculture. This section is key to Indian politics because it affects a large segment of voters. Despite several initiatives taken by the government, the kitchen has been under siege and farmers under the pump during the first four years of Modi rule. This has been especially evident during the election period and has affected the outcomes of several state elections including those of Delhi, Bihar and Gujarat. We believe that bringing smiles back to the kitchen and to farmers' homes will be the key to success in the 2019 elections.

The Modi government has taken several measures to reduce farm price volatility. This included income tax raids carried out on hoarders and black marketeers. But, efforts to check rising prices have been only partly successful. Also, food price volatility has been more visible during elections.

Agriculture is another area where there has been a lot of work done by the Modi government, though not all in the right direction. Importantly, it has not been enough to mitigate distress and poverty in the agriculture sector. Big-ticket measures like raising Minimum Support Price (MSP) of crops do not reduce poverty among marginal farmers in poor states. This is because the Food Corporation of India (FCI) procurement has been traditionally limited to rich farmers of rich states. Agriculture has many issues including water scarcity, floods, climate change, crop nutrients, pesticides, marketing, wastage and pricing. Each must be attended to separately to help farmers. Farm loan waivers are meagre and not enough to dispel distress.

From the food and farm sector, the story now takes a look at Mahatma Gandhi National Rural Employment Guarantee Act (MGNREGA) and *Swachh Bharat* Mission (SBM) under social sectors. Both schemes have seen a humongous amount of money invested and questionable results. This despite the fact that they have both been the top priority of the two most important political leaders. Congress President Sonia Gandhi personally invested her time and attention towards MGNREGA and PM Modi personally monitored SBM. Still, results of both the flagship projects are far from satisfactory.

The employment generation sector showed mixed results. Whereas jobs were created, the number of educated unemployed rose. This is natural for an emerging economy where millions are getting educated and becoming graduates every year. But, as no job data has been produced for over a decade, the political slugfest over unemployment continued. Entrepreneurship, meanwhile, continued to flourish and the unicorns grew with the arrival of global technology and capital.

Like in other fields, telecommunication showed a promise despite several pitfalls. The Modi government has been proactive for the growth of the sector. The intent was evident when the long-pending spectrum auction issue was resolved within a year of the government taking office. Auction of the spectrum was conducted both transparently and speedily during the next few years. Soon, digital India became a reality and many of the three-tier cities across India started receiving not only mobile services but also dependable internet connectivity.

The consumption of data has been phenomenal in the last four years. With 400 million active smartphone users, India has witnessed the highest mobile data consumption during this period. This, even though it ranked a poor 109th in mobile download speed. This clearly shows that, like in every other sector, there is demand but no matching service. Despite the investments in telecom infrastructure, the quality of services to quench the customer demand is indeed pretty ordinary. Call drops continue to rise despite the best efforts of the regulator and the consumer continues to suffer.

The Information Technology (IT) sector is witnessing global headwinds. President Donald Trump's insistence on jobs for Americans has resulted in a reduction of the Indian workforce employed as contractual labour on United States' (US) projects. But, there are opportunities in the domestic sector that have opened up largely because of the increased activity in the banking and telecom sector. With entrepreneurship picking up and unicorns growing in business opportunities in India, the Indian IT worker should be able to make up for the overseas losses.

This comprehensively sums up the story of *India Emerging*. India is a nation with huge demand but one that lacks high-quality services. Be it agriculture, manufacturing or other services, the Indian economy is still a work in progress and its political leadership, its bureaucracy, its business class and its citizens are still on a learning curve, searching for ways to get it right.

Part I

Early Development

CHAPTER 1

India Before the Millennium:
Only Indira Gandhi Was Disruptive

Though change is inevitable, humans do not like it. The natural tendency is to stall change and let the status quo persist. Economic reforms necessitate major changes. They are usually not popular measures. In most cases, they take place to mitigate economic distress. They are seldom voluntary and are mostly forced by circumstances.

The story of forced reforms is not unique to India. It is a worldwide phenomenon. The banking reforms after the Great Depression in 1942 and after the Housing Mortgage Crisis of 2008 in the US show that the trend is universal. Greece, Argentina, Italy and several other states have done it reluctantly. Humans have this tendency to 'leave well alone' as long as it is possible. They tend to overlook the early warning systems, especially in a financial crisis. It is partly due to negligence and partly due to vested interests that a financial crisis occurs. Markets correct such inefficiencies and provide a reality check. They do it either by driving down the currency market or the stock market or both.

The Game Changers

Not all politicians act belatedly. There are a few who proactively act on gut feeling. They do not take feedback from economists. They take feedback from the streets. They are charismatic leaders, strong and gutsy, who disrupt normalcy and the status quo. The changes they make are far-reaching. They have a stunning impact for good or for worse.

Typically, they do not pause after making one change. They keep on at it continuously with an ardent desire of changing the entire ecosystem. Economists rarely agree with them. Markets swing with approval or rejection of their policies, creating volatility. They throw caution to the wind and make disruptive changes that most economists even shudder to think about. Voters love them or hate them but can never ignore them.

They practise street economics or simple 'streetonomics' as we call it in this book. They bring solutions and judgements from the marketplace that are volatile and disruptive. They stop social upheaval like in the Arab Springs because they anticipate distress and act. Before the protests for political change start as in Brazil, Argentina and Greece, they create their own brand of turbulence. They, at times, cause immense prosperity for future decades as seen in the case of Margaret Thatcher or Ronald Reagan or Deng Xiaoping. But, there are fallen heroes too, like Gorbachev whom we tend to forget.

They simply shake up the sluggish system before it can go into deep decline. They are the mavericks. They attempt something that no economic theory, science or fuzzy logic can decipher with conventional wisdom. They force reforms and changes and at times even go against the popular mood. India has been no exception. Political and social changes have happened and are happening because of economics on the street. India has had two such charismatic leaders who actively practised streetonomics, rightly or wrongly—Indira Gandhi and Narendra Modi. Not surprisingly, they have taken decisions that have been both good and bad for the economy.

1962, 1965 and 1971 Wars Weakened the Indian Economy

The rupee was pegged to the British pound for nearly three decades, starting from independence. There were two devaluations that happened to the Indian rupee in that period, both during Indira Gandhi's rule in 1966 and in 1973. The devaluation of the currency had a lot to do with the economic brunt of the wars. Soon after the Chinese war of 1962, Pakistan began to sense its opportunities in Jammu and Kashmir. Nehru died in May 1964 and his successor was the frail and diminutive Lal Bahadur Shastri, widely known as a man of peace. The India-Pakistan (Indo-Pak) war that started with border skirmishes from April finally broke out in August 1965 following Pakistan's Operation Gibraltar in Jammu and Kashmir.

It was a 22-day-long war that began with Pakistan, under President Ayub Khan, sending 30,000 insurgents (*mujahideen*) to liberate Jammu and Kashmir. By the time the ceasefire was called, the Indian army despite some setbacks in Akhnoor and Rajouri, was knocking at the gates of Lahore. They were also in clear control of the strategically important Uri-Poonch bulge in Kashmir and had won three times more land area than they had lost. However, the economic cost was high and India was facing a massive food shortage.

Following the back-to-back wars of 1962 and 1965, the Indian economy had weakened substantially. The World Bank had strongly recommended rupee devaluation more than six months earlier. It had stated that unless the currency was devalued, India would not get any more foreign credit or aid. At that time, India was not self-sufficient in food production and was highly dependent on aid. Besides, it was going through a drought and low-crop output.

The devaluation decision had already been taken by Prime Minister Shastri. World Bank and the IMF had already been informed of the date. T.T. Krishnamachari, the finance minister, had also been replaced in December 1965, reportedly due to his continued and unrelenting opposition to the devaluation. Unfortunately, as PM Shastri died in Tashkent, implementing the difficult decision was left to the new incumbent Indira Gandhi. In June 1966, soon after Indira Gandhi assumed office, she was forced to devalue the Indian rupee by a massive 57.4%. Her enemies, both in the opposition as well as in the Congress, were many. The 'syndicate' or the old guards of the Congress party led by Morarji Desai did not take kindly to her elevation as PM. They made it appear as if devaluation was her fault and the opposition in the parliament was massive.

Rupee Devaluations Made Indira Distrust the West

On 6 June 1966, the Indian rupee was devalued from ₹4.76 to ₹7.50 to a US dollar. That year, India was facing drought and famine.

Indira Gandhi told parliament on the assurance of the World Bank that the devaluation was to get quicker aid. However, after devaluation, the aid givers dithered and dallied. Apart from emergency food shipment of 16 million tonnes of wheat from the US under Public Law (PL) 480, nothing else arrived.

Those days, US politically supported Pakistan while Russia supported India. US funded and controlled most of the World Bank relief projects. India's relations with the US were strained as it relied heavily on arms from Russia during the 1965 war. Aid to India was around ₹819 crore (₹8.19 billion) in 1965. This aid was cut off after India's war with Pakistan and resumed only in 1967. Despite the devaluation and the promise made by World Bank, the aid was held back by over 18 months.

That made Indira Gandhi distrust the western governments all the more. She decided to go for Russian aid and imports from Russia against rupee payment. These twin moves of devaluation and reduction in dollar imports helped improve India's balance of payments. Exports that had been nearly non-existent during the first two decades after independence rose while imports tapered down. The then current account deficit was lower and so was the import bill. Though the 1971 war created conditions for yet another devaluation, the situation was better than before. India had become more self-reliant and the need to import reduced during the 1970s.

Bank Nationalisation, Not Only for Political Gains

When Indira Gandhi came to power in 1967, the first political battle she had to fight was within the Congress party. The senior Congress leaders of the syndicate led by Morarji Desai challenged Indira Gandhi. After the showdown and Indira Gandhi's victory, a negotiated settlement followed in which Morarji Desai became the deputy PM.

Indira Gandhi believed that Morarji Desai, the then finance minister and deputy PM, had the support of business tycoons. Hence, she distrusted industry barons. She also believed that the Russian model of socialism could help her deliver her election slogan, '*Garibi Hatao*'.

Those days, commercial banks across India were owned by India's business barons. The Birlas owned the UCO Bank—formerly United

Commercial Bank, the Chettiars controlled the Indian Bank, the Pais held a majority stake in the Canara Bank and Syndicate Bank. The 14 big private-sector banks that were nationalised in 1969 held nearly 77% of the assets and accounted for the majority of the banking transactions across India. But, they somehow failed to grow outside the big urban city centres.

Also, as the major investments under the Nehruvian model were in the public sector, the private-sector banks had limited exposure to industrial growth. Those days, private-sector banks expanded credit slowly. Despite this, they displayed the propensity to fail. There were 361 cases of private bank failures in the first decade after independence where depositors had lost their money.

The Imperial Bank had been nationalised way back in 1955. It was renamed as State Bank of India (SBI) and was the largest bank owned by the government of India. It had grown much faster than the private-sector banks and had moved into India's hinterland. Not only had it addressed the issue of managing rapid expansion but had also started lending to the small and medium sector that was at its infancy. The left parties, which were powerful those days, persistently called for nationalisation of other banks but the Congress party old guard and Finance Minister Morarji Desai opposed it tooth and nail.

Bank Nationalisation Spurred Customer Base and Economic Growth

On 19 July 1969, Indira Gandhi issued the Banking Companies (Acquisition and Transfer of Undertakings) Ordinance that transferred assets of 14 biggest private-sector banks to the government of India. She also took charge of the finance ministry that forced Morarji Desai to resign and he was left with no portfolio.

The growth of the banking sector was spectacular after its nationalisation. Though modern-day economists feel that the 1969 nationalisation of banks was one of India's biggest economic blunders, it was not so. Before bank nationalisation, in the first 20 years of independence, India had less than 10,000 bank branches. There were just 1,443 branches in rural India where 70% of the population lived at that time. A decade after nationalisation, the number of urban bank branches had grown fourfold to 32,219 and rural bank branches had increased tenfold to 14,171.

The aggregate deposits of ₹4,822 crore (₹48.22 billion) during the first two decades after independence had languished as had the advances of ₹3,467 crore (₹34.67 billion). In the decade after bank nationalisation they more than doubled. By 1991, before Narasimha Rao's liberalisation, the aggregate deposits of the banking sector had grown to ₹2,19,539 crore (₹2.19 trillion) and the advances had jumped to ₹1,33,745 crore (₹1.33 trillion). Even before liberalisation, the calculated Trend Growth Rate (TGR) was 17.6% in aggregate deposits and 16.8% for advances, which is phenomenal by any standard.

Priority Lending by Nationalised Banks Revived Farm Sector

The nationalised banks catered to priority lending to small and medium industries and the agriculture sector. Pandit Nehru's stress after independence was more on industrial growth than on agricultural growth. Before nationalisation, just 2.2% of the credit went to the farm sector, as a result of which there was no capital infusion in agriculture. This ensured low capital flow to farms, falling domestic prices and reduced acreage. By the end of the first decade, India started experiencing a shortage of food. To avoid starvation, the Nehru government signed the PL 480 in 1957 that permitted concessional wheat imports from the US under rupee payment.

During the early 1960s, India was predominantly becoming dependent on foreign aid and the PL 480 Food for Peace aid programme of the US government. The US under President Lyndon B. Johnson from 1963 to 1969 started tweaking the terms of PL 480 to garner India's support for US's war in Vietnam. This made imports difficult. Soon queues at ration shops for monthly quotas of wheat and rice in India reached a peak.

It was the bigger size of US wheat that we waited for at the ration shops. The high-yielding varieties of Indian wheat and hybrid rice had just begun to arrive at the markets but in small quantities.

The superior sharbati wheat of Madhya Pradesh was far more expensive by comparison and was not distributed by fair price shops.

Despite the white revolution during Lal Bahadur Shastri's time that started off National Dairy Development Board (NDDB) and led to milk self-sufficiency, India's agricultural output continued to suffer. This shortage only accelerated during the late 1960s. Indira Gandhi quickly realised that the demand for agriculture capital had grown. After the first green revolution started producing high-yielding varieties, farmers were ready to invest but private banks were not ready to lend. Farm credit needed to be ramped up if India were to become self-reliant in food production. Bank nationalisation and priority lending to the agriculture sector provided the solution.

After initial hiccups in the early stages, the growth in the agriculture sector picked up as nationalised banks started to fund crops, fertiliser and farm equipment. After this, there was no looking back—wheat production crossed 60 million tonnes per annum in 10 years' time.

Not all Nationalisations Benefited the Economy

The success of bank nationalisation and the wide public support it received prompted Indira Gandhi to turn the screws on the private sector. She started to believe that controlling the private sector would yield better wealth distribution. During her second term in 1971, she took the bold step of nationalising coal, steel, petroleum refining, cotton and insurance industries.

The nationalisation of the coal industry was widely welcomed by one and all. This was because coal mining was largely underground those days and extremely hazardous. The private-sector mine owners did not pay any heed to workers' safety. Profit maximisation was the motive and incidents of miner exploitation and mining accidents were increasing. Besides, the investments that were needed to be done to mechanise mining operations and make them safe were possible only at a large scale. Indira Gandhi immediately got approval from both people and the parliament when she took the bold decision to nationalise coal mining.

This made Indira Gandhi feel that nationalisation was the cure for all ills. The government started taking over other industries, especially those where the workers' union was strong and inefficiencies were high. The remaining private-sector enterprises were put under strict statutory control. You could not raise the price of products without consent. You could not expand the business without a licence. You could not even increase capital without permission. In short, to invest your money into your own company, you needed government permission, which was not easily forthcoming.

Though the demand was there, manufacturers were not permitted to produce goods more than the licensed capacities. Expansion was not permitted and during the 1970s and 1980s, the waitlist for Bajaj scooters went up to 20 years and that of Fiat cars up to 10 years. Indian manufacturing stagnated despite consumer demand. That was when Deng Xiaoping, the then chairman of Chinese People's Political Consultative Conference, started to unleash massive reforms in China that encouraged private-sector expansion. It was a period when the Indian private sector suffered stunted growth.

Birth of Inspector Raj That Created a Parallel Economy

While strict licensing norms ensured the stunted growth of the private sector, high excise duty, sales tax and customs duty ensured the creation of a parallel economy. While the norms were strict and tax rates were high, you could circumvent all rules by paying a monthly bribe. A part of the bribe given to the inspector, officer or the department concerned would be funnelled to political masters.

Soon politicians and bureaucrats started devising restrictive laws that would increase their control. This way their private wealth and corruption skyrocketed.

Even in the newly-created public sectors, productivity was on the wane as political and bureaucratic interference grew. After nationalisation of the coal industry, coal mafias started taking over labour unions. Soon they controlled outsourced activities such as transportation of coal from mining companies like Bharat Coking Coal Ltd and massive pilferage started. Corruption rose and productivity in coal mines started to drop.

The booming cement industry in the private sector had stopped investing. So did steel, copper and aluminium plants. The textile industry, including the famous mills of Mumbai, all went into losses during the

1970s. Leaders like Bal Thackeray and George Fernandes who opposed Indira Gandhi, followed her path of private-sector bashing. India's licence permit raj was by now infamous worldwide and a deterrent to investors.

The government took over several sick industries but organisations like Cement Corporation of India (CCI), National Textile Corporation (NTC), Fertilizer Corporation of India and Hindustan Copper Ltd (HCL) have all become unmitigated disasters. They consumed more public wealth than what they created over the years. They piled up enormous losses and pushed scarce public resources into areas where the government had no reason to be.

On 24 September 1975, the historical linking of the Indian rupee to the British pound was broken. The rupee became a floating currency that was linked to a basket of currencies of India's major trading partners. By 1979, Food Corporation of India's godowns were overflowing and India had no need to import rice or wheat. Though inflation had gone double digit again in the early 1990s, the food shortages in India had happily disappeared. The rupee downslide, however, continued. By 1990, the rupee had slumped and was traded at ₹17.50 to a dollar, and by 1995 it was traded at ₹32.50 to a dollar.

Indira Gandhi came back to power thrice between 1966 and 1984, and she did not change her course before or after the emergency. When she was assassinated, her son Rajiv Gandhi was elected by the party to the post of PM. Rajiv Gandhi tried to open the Indian industry to competition by making imports easier. He brought in computerisation and the automaker Suzuki but did not do much to unshackle the domestic industry. However, the socialist legacy created by Indira Gandhi found diehard followers even amongst the opposition. Not only Rajiv Gandhi but V. P. Singh and Chandra Shekhar, PMs after him, continued in the same path and forgot to liberalise India's restrictive domestic economic policies.

The First Economic Reforms of 1991 Were Forced

The story of the Indian economy shows a continuous decline during the 1980s. Rajiv Gandhi (PM from 1984 to 1989) took over from Indira Gandhi. He was followed by V. P. Singh (PM from 1989 to 1990). In 1991, after the disastrous economic management by successive governments, India's foreign debt skyrocketed. The current account deficit (CAD) rose from ₹11,350 crore (₹113.50 billion) in 1989–90 to ₹17,350 crore (₹173.50 billion) in 1990–1991. It was a big and unprecedented leap from 2.3% to 3.1% of the Gross Domestic Product (GDP). The foreign exchange reserves slumped by over 50% from ₹5,277 crore (₹52.27 billion) in December 1989 to ₹2,152 crore (₹21.52 billion) a year later.

The rupee slide did not happen overnight. Though PM Chandra Shekhar was blamed for everything that went wrong, the rot had started much earlier. The currency took an unprecedented downturn during the 1980s when Rajiv Gandhi, V. P. Singh and Chandra Shekhar were PMs. Noted economist Arvind Panagariya, in an IMF conference on India and China held at New Delhi in November 2003, talked about the fragility of growth during the 1980s. He said that between 1977–1978 and 1987–1988 the average growth rate was just 4.1%.

Surprisingly, the growth remained pedestrian despite Rajiv Gandhi's piecemeal efforts to open up the economy to imports. Most economists agree that the GDP growth possibly remained feeble because domestic delicensing was ignored. The private-sector capital formation remained at 4.5% of the GDP during the 1980s. Meanwhile, imports were liberalised to usher in foreign capital. Hence, the then CAD began rising and foreign exchange reserves started falling steadily.

The Balance of Payments Crisis and the Return of the Congress

When Chandra Shekhar's minority government supported by Congress (Indira), otherwise known as Congress (I), took oath in November 1990, all political parties started preparing for polls. Chandra Shekhar, who split from Janata Dal to create the Janata Dal (Secular, JDS), had only 60 members while Congress (I) that supported it had 211 members. It was a case of the cart pulling the horse as far as decision-making in the Prime Minister's Office (PMO) in South Block was concerned.

The economy was already in dire straits. Chandra Shekhar knew about this as everyone else. But, his ambition to be PM made him throw caution to the winds. A couple of wrong moves by the inexperienced government of Chandra Shekhar soon after he took office affected the balance of payments (BOP) further. Inflation quickly rose and along with that rose public dissatisfaction and panic.

Even while supporting it from outside, Congress (I) started blaming Chandra Shekhar's government for economic mismanagement, knowing that fresh elections were around the corner. This helped them prove to the electorate that it was not wise to trust any other party except Congress (I) to rule India. It was just a matter of time and it was up to them to pull the plug. The BJP, which had withdrawn support to V. P. Singh earlier, also started projecting themselves as the only credible face of the opposition. But, its sway over voters had waned.

Narasimha Rao: Preparing for a Political Exile

Rajiv Gandhi was fairly sure of riding back to power when the elections were announced in early 1991. Surprisingly, he did not give a ticket to P. V. Narasimha Rao who had over 20 years of cabinet experience under Indira Gandhi and Rajiv Gandhi. According to his biographer Vinay Sitapati, the 69-year-old Rao was getting ready for a political exile. Rao wrote in his diary: '26 April 1991. At 3.00 pm today, a gap arrived in my legislative career for the first time in 34 years. I am feeling extremely dejected.'

Little did Rao know that fate had destined him for greater glory. That Rajiv Gandhi would be assassinated in May 1991 during an election campaign rally at Sriperumbudur. That Rajiv Gandhi's widow Sonia Gandhi would refuse to take his place to become the PM. That Congress would look forward to a new model of governance under Sonia Gandhi. That they would select a non-ambitious Congressman like him to be at the helm as the stopgap PM. That he would score higher in Sonia Gandhi's trust factor than other candidates like Pranab Mukherjee or Manmohan Singh. That he, an economic greenhorn, would be ultimately selected to lead the nation at the time of a grave economic crisis.

Twin Devaluation and a Bold Budget of 1991 Paid Dividend

Like most Congressmen of the 1960s and 1970s, Narasimha Rao was a socialist at heart. He had little option but to devalue the currency to avoid a debt default. But, what he did was way beyond what was needed. He devalued the currency not once but twice in a span of 48 hours.

Narasimha Rao became PM on 21 June with Manmohan Singh as his finance minister. He unleashed the first set of much-need economic reforms within the first fortnight, unprecedentedly. It showed great intent for a nation known for meandering.

The first devaluation of 7% to 9% took place on 1 July 1991. Before the markets could react to the news and start driving the rupee down in real earnest, the second devaluation of around 11% was announced on 3 July. Both devaluations were small. Much smaller than the massive devaluation of 1966 as done by Indira Gandhi. But, they showed intent. This gave punters a clear signal that the Indian government would do whatever is needed to turn the tide. That even multiple devaluations were on cards. The rupee's downward slide that had been going on for nearly five years quickly stuttered and was arrested, at least temporarily.

Trade liberalisation and delicensing followed in quick succession. A new-look budget was presented that was reportedly different from Manmohan Singh's original draft presented to the PM. At the behest of Narasimha Rao, the budget was redrafted ushering in the first wave of liberalisation. The reforms ushered in both short-term and long-term measures. It started to dismantle the licence raj that Indira Gandhi had unleashed in the 1970s and 1980s under the influence of socialist rulers of Russia.

At Ground Level, Rao Took Licence Raj by the Horns

The major steps taken by Narasimha Rao as a rearguard action were effective in abolishing the draconian rule of industrial licensing. Except for a few industries that were hazardous, environmentally polluting or a security risk, no licences were officially needed. But in India, abolishing of licensing and inspector raj is easier said than done because every department of the government of India has restrictive laws in their manuals written in thousands of ways.

So, maybe you had done away with one licensing law, but there were over a 100 other permissions to be taken. I remember the Noida authority giving land in the 1980s and 1990s on a single window clearance basis. You were given to understand, after filling up lengthy forms before allotment, that this was a 'single-point clearance' for setting up your industry. However, after allotment of land, you found out that over a 100 permissions were still needed before you got the completion certificate of your building. Electricity, water, sewerage, pollution, plot-size verification—you name it and there was a rule book thrown at you. And you could bypass every rule if you agreed to pay a bribe. I am told that this still exists.

Delicensing is a myth in India because we do not move the army of inspectors we created during the 1970s and 1980s to more productive pursuits. Those posts still exist in all government offices—both in the state as well as the central government. Surprisingly, these inspectors still get hired by the hundreds. Narasimha Rao gave a clear-cut message that inspector raj was over. He chose to keep silent against complaints by trade unions and activists while letting business and industry grow. During the ten years between Rao and Vajpayee, the economy flourished and politics of agitation saw a decline. Unfortunately, many of them returned after the UPA government headed by Manmohan Singh took charge a decade later, supported by a new brigade of social activists who were always ready to confront and stop any industrial development and mining activity.

Vajpayee Built on Rao's Legacy

Atal Bihari Vajpayee took advantage of the favourable mood towards liberalisation and consolidated the gains. He removed the shackles on four important sectors of the economy. The road-building sector in India was languishing at that time. Vajpayee started the *Pradhan Mantri Gram Sadak Yojana* (PMGSY) to connect 1.7 lakh villages in India with all-weather roads. In the late 1990s, village roads in India were largely dust tracks. Work on PMGSY put substantial development funds to be used in rural infrastructure. It has been taken up by successive governments but the exercise is massive, and it is expected to be completed by 2019.

The connectivity of most cities was through two-lane roads during the Vajpayee rule and only small patches of four-lanes had been done on the Grand Trunk Road built by Sher Shah Suri in the sixteenth century. In the year 2001, Vajpayee launched the Golden Quadrilateral project, the first national highway development project under National Highways Authority of India (NHAI) that proposed to connect the four major metros—Delhi, Kolkata, Chennai and Mumbai—through four-lane/six-lane highways. The 5,846-kilometre (km) project that started in 2001 was eventually completed in 2012.

The Centre for Monitoring Indian Economy data shows that India had just 1,576 km of multi-laned highway in the financial year ending March 1998. When Vajpayee was voted out of power in 2004, over 6,000 km of highways had been built. He also energised the construction boom in the housing sector by making interests paid on housing loans exempt from income tax. This was a huge incentive for the salaried class who had just started investing in the first private-sector housing boom witnessed in the country. The construction industry's share in employment went up to as much as 15% during the last year of the Vajpayee rule.

Another of Vajpayee's key initiatives was the liberalisation of the telecom sector and building on the foundation created by Rao. The mobile phone revolution that was ushered in during the Rao rule in 1995 was rejuvenated by Vajpayee. In 1999, the telecom ministry moved from the licence-fee regime to a liberalised revenue-sharing structure. Though the government's telecom revenue dipped, the number of mobile handset connections that were under 10 million then, doubled year after year thereafter for the next five years.

The health sector and the education sector also benefitted under the Vajpayee rule. There was virtually an explosion of engineering and medical colleges across India during the Vajpayee rule, largely due to tax exemptions given as incentives to invest in education. The *Sarva Shiksha Abhiyan* under the Vajpayee government made education compulsory for the age group of 6 to 14 years. The hospital sector also witnessed a large flow of private funds during the Vajpayee era. This 12% year-on-year (YOY) growth was unprecedented as the growth of hospitals under the government sector had seen stagnation in the previous decade.

Managing Growth and Fiscal Discipline

When Rao came to power, the economy was in the dumps. The foreign exchange reserves had dropped precariously and were just 7% of the external debt. The rupee was in a downward spiral and Rao was forced to do two quick devaluations. Rao, despite initiating the reforms, could only stem the tide. By the end of his term, the foreign exchange reserves had risen to 23% of external debt but rupee's slide had not slowed. When Rao assumed office, the rupee was at ₹19.64 to a dollar. By the time he quit in 1996, the rupee had tumbled to ₹34.35 to a dollar. There was further instability after Rao, before Vajpayee returned for his third term and steadied the ship. Figure 1.1 shows how the rupee fared better during the Vajpayee rule, better than even the UPA and the NDA regimes that followed him. Why did it fare better?

Figure 1.1: US Dollar (USD) to Indian Rupee (INR) Exchange Rate (Oct 1998 to Sept 2018)

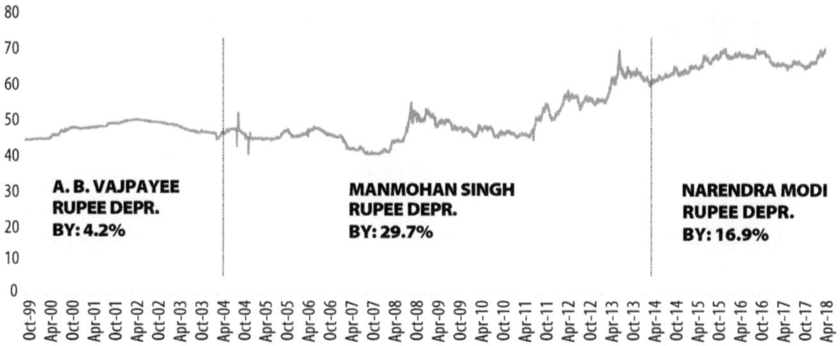

Data source: RBI

PM Vajpayee introduced the Fiscal Responsibility Act and took strong measures to ensure the same. Public-sector savings rose during his period from 0.8% of the GDP to 2.3% of the GDP. Under his rule, the disinvestment ministry was formed and Videsh Sanchar Nigam Ltd (VSNL), HCL, Bharat Aluminium Company Ltd (BALCO) and National Aluminium Company Ltd (NALCO) saw disinvestment. Air India too was on the anvil but since he was not re-elected, the proposal was not taken forward after 2004. Vajpayee built on the strong foundation laid by Rao. The fiscal deficit was low and continuously under check as India's credit ratings once again improved.

Moreover, imports under the Vajpayee regime were under control and exports grew. The telecom industry and the IT industry took off.

So, the forex reserves grew rapidly during his rule. The then CAD was reduced and the last few years of the Vajpayee rule was the only period when India was in a position of current account surplus (Figure 1.2). During the Vajpayee rule, the foreign exchange reserves, for once, rose above the external debt, the fiscal deficit started falling, the GDP growth rose over 7% and the rupee was rather steady. From October 1999 to May 2004, the rupee moved from ₹43.31 to ₹45.12—a small dip of less than 4%.

Figure 1.2: Current Account Balance (in USD Billion) (March 2000 to March 2018)

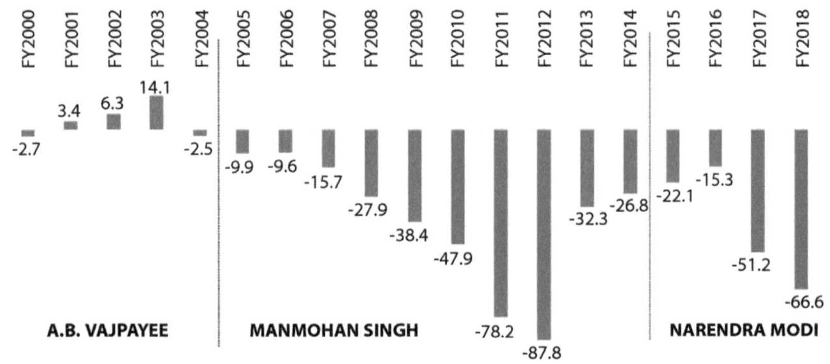

Data source: IMF and RBI

Part II

Finance and Economy

CHAPTER 2

Living Dangerously with a Troubled Legacy: The Chimera of *Achhe Din*

The BJP cruised to power in 2014 largely because the Indian voter was disillusioned with the UPA. The Manmohan Singh government had failed to deliver on several fronts, leading to court proceedings on scams, rupee crash, economic slowdown, food inflation and joblessness. The government machinery had become fully dysfunctional during the last days of the UPA. It was either no decisions or bad decisions that were taken and the opposition made no bones to play it up. The press dubbed the Manmohan Singh government as one suffering from policy paralysis.

Even before the elections, most observers knew that the UPA was a sinking ship. The Congress was also going through an organisational crisis. Manmohan Singh lacked oratory and organisational skills. Rahul Gandhi was not given the leadership role and Sonia Gandhi was ailing and past her prime. No cadres were visible at the grassroots level and state *satraps* were often not on the same page as the central leadership. Most opinion polls predicted that it would be a washout and BJP would sweep the polls. Even senior Congress ministers like P. Chidambaram and Ghulam Nabi Azad were convinced that the UPA would bite the dust and hence, they did not contest the 2014 elections.

The Unrealistic Promise of *Achhe Din*

However, surprisingly, during the election campaign of 2014, Narendra Modi did not delve into the negatives of the UPA regime. That alone could have won him the seats. Instead, he boldly went ahead and promised *'achhe din'* or good days ahead. He made promises of a new India devoid of corruption and want. He promised good governance, plentiful jobs and prosperity. He even promised to halt tax evasion and bring back black money to bank accounts of poor Indians. All those were unnecessary promises. They unwittingly raised the expectations of the people. There was already a wave in his favour, largely due to poor governance of the UPA. All he needed to do was present a true picture to the people and promise to find a way out. But, political leaders do not choose simple solutions.

Politics in India is larger than life. It is full of drama, rhetoric and more often than not, *jumla* or far-fetched promises. It always has been so, ever since the independence. Modi was no exception. He rose to the occasion like a sphinx and promised much more than he could deliver in one term. People were awestruck. They said, 'Here is a messiah who can turn things around in a jiffy.' Modi had already built a good reputation as the chief minister of Gujarat for three successive terms. He was known for his integrity and hard work. The BJP went on an overdrive projecting him as a miracle man—one who would bring good days to the people of a nation that was desperate for a change in governance.

The Understated Achievements of the Early Days

After winning the elections, they set about the task in right earnest. The two quickest and most difficult decisions they took in the first year itself was to set right the long-pending e-auction of coal and telecom spectrum. The matter had lingered on during the UPA rule without resolution. Following the unravelling of the licensing scams and the cancellation of licences by the Supreme Court (SC), spectrum allocation had come to a halt—so did coal block allocation. The auctioning process that was opaque for more than two decades now saw transparent methods of procurement in the first year of formation of the NDA government.

During the year 2008, the UPA government had issued 122 second-generation (2G) telecom licences in the 2G spectrum on a first-come-first-serve basis at 2001 prices. Among the beneficiaries were Swan and Unitech group companies—both of which were companies without prior experience. In the year 2010, the Comptroller and Auditor General

(CAG) of India opined that allocation of these licences was arbitrary and made to corporations that were not eligible to bid. It further stated that the arbitrary allocations had caused a loss of ₹1.76 trillion, that is, ₹1.76 lakh crore to the exchequer. Following this observation, there was an uproar in the parliament and a Public Interest Litigation (PIL) was filed in the SC for cancellation of these licences. In February 2012, SC declared the allocation of spectrum as unconstitutional and arbitrary and cancelled all 122 licences issued by the then telecom minister A. Raja in 2008.

With the spectrum licences issued after 2008 cancelled and no fresh licences being issued, the fast-growing telecom sector started choking at the time of peak growth. India needed new technology and transparent auctioning process. In 2012, the UPA government conducted an auction that was officially declared a flop as bids above minimum reserve price were not received. In February 2014—during the last days of the UPA—an auction for part of the 2G spectrum yielded around ₹60,000 crore (₹600 billion). After the Modi government came to power, they decided to free up large chunks of spectrum and devised an open bidding mechanism to get the best prices. The 19-day bidding battle in February 2015 saw Vodafone bid for spectrum worth ₹34,500 crore, while Idea bid ₹28,000 crore and Airtel ₹27,500 crore. The ₹1.1 lakh crore (₹1.1 trillion) auction of airwaves proved that the CAG had rightly pointed out that transparent bidding could generate trillions of rupees in revenue for the exchequer.

The coal block auctions were not much different from the spectrum auctions. Here also, notional losses of trillions had been reported by the CAG. Here too, a transparent bidding mechanism was needed. Whereas the spectrum auctions would bring immediate relief to the telecommunication companies (telcos) and consumers, the coal block auctions would yield returns in the long-term.

Coal in India is largely mined in the public sector. As a result of this, coal mining is largely inefficient. The operation is primarily a surface mining operation where investment and risks are low. Privatised coal mining has been an objective of several governments since liberalisation in 1991—but the method of issuance of licences has been questionable. CAG in the year 2012 had reported that an estimated ₹1.86 lakh crore (₹1.86 trillion) of licensing fees could have been lost due to irregularities in allocation. The 193 coal mine licences that were under the CAG scanner were issued between 1993 and 2008.

Following this, the SC cancelled all of 214 coal mine licences issued without opening the bidding. It also asked the government to devise a transparent mechanism for coal block auction in September 2014. The SC had made a similar request to the Manmohan Singh government in 2012. The Modi government rose to the task and not only devised an electronic bidding mechanism within months but successfully conducted the auction. The 34 blocks that went through e-auction by February 2015 fetched the three eastern states of Odisha, West Bengal and Jharkhand a mind-boggling ₹2.1 trillion in licence fees to be paid in a 30-year span. This proved the CAG right once again—that the mining licences were indeed undervalued. A sixth of the mining blocks had yielded more than the number of notional losses estimated by the CAG.

The Cleansing That Did Not Happen

The coal block and the spectrum licences were not the only problems that needed to be sorted out by the Modi government. There were dozens of other concerns. Modi himself knew about some of the legacy problems that he had inherited from the UPA. Speaking to Rahul Joshi of Network18 in a nationally televised interview two years after he assumed office, Modi said, 'Perhaps I should have published a white paper on the poor state of the economy that I inherited from UPA II.' But, Modi did no such thing. As a matter of fact, he has shown remarkable reluctance to investigate or punish those who had indulged in corruption before 2014.

The 2G scam, the Commonwealth Games (CWG) scam and the Coalgate scam have not seen any rigorous follow-up by investigation agencies. Several other import scams that have happened during the past decade have not been probed. The fertiliser import scam and the mining scams are some that have been dealt with in the previous book of this series *Neta, Babu and Subsidy: Economic Roundup 2000 to 2014.* Some of the scams that started during the UPA have continued at a low-key level during the NDA, and public-sector banks (PSBs) bore the losses. Besides, there has been no agility shown to stop clever businessmen like Vijay Mallya or Nirav Modi escape the country after cheating PSBs.

As a matter of fact, it is widely believed that both businessmen who were close to the UPA and the NDA governments have been told to flee India. This feeling is unsubstantiated, but it exists. Many other scamsters are leaving India. They had been making billions during the UPA rule. Now they are being allowed to flee. The NDA will not allow scams to happen. But, since all political parties have been funded by these corrupt fugitive billionaires, they are being let off and told to go. Meanwhile, India achieved the dubious distinction of a nation where the highest numbers of High Net Worth Individuals (HNWI) are leaving the country.

True, the Modi government is not involved in any scam. But, it is still unclear to the citizen why Modi is reluctant to probe into financial irregularities of the previous government.

Even the CBI probes into the 2G scam, Coalgate scam and CWG scam that were initiated previously are today toothless. The agency even dropped charges against the then telecom minister A. Raja and M. Kanimozhi, daughter of Dravida Munnetra Kazhagam (DMK) supremo M. Karunanidhi, in the 2G case citing lack of evidence in 2018. Perhaps Modi does not want to set the precedent of jailing politicians. Perhaps he does not want to send investors away by laying bare the state of the economy. Maybe he does not want to upset the bureaucrats who were involved in the scams as much as the UPA politicians.

Whatever be the reason, it has ensured that the rotten apples stay in the system. They could be dormant under the watchful eyes of the PMO but are still to be purged. They could also, however, come back to haunt and prove to be the proverbial Trojan horse. It is a reason why scams and irregularities may keep happening even now despite a clean record of the ministers in the NDA. The fact that scamsters are being permitted to flee India is not acceptable to most Indian citizens and taxpayers.

Aadhaar, Permanent Account Number (PAN) Card and Bank Account Linking Tightens the Noose

It is not that the systems are not being tightened. Ever since the Modi government came to power there has been a concentrated effort to connect a person to all his bank accounts. The Aadhaar card, a programme started by the Manmohan Singh ministry, was incomplete and directionless during the UPA rule. The Modi government seized the initiative with both hands and removed the bottlenecks and launched Aadhaar with much fanfare. Aadhaar was pushed with a missionary flavour and became the mantra from residential identification to terrorist detection. Paradoxically, the Congress party which had conceived the project started opposing it while the BJP that initially had reservations when the Congress conceived it, started owning it.

Once the Aadhaar number was allotted, the subsidies for cooking gas and for food to the poor were all transferred to the bank accounts of beneficiaries. Aadhaar also had several other uses—it enabled the introduction of biometric attendance in government offices. It was a big step to ensure security as well as infuse discipline in the staff. In 2015, the IT department asked banks to link all accounts on basis of PAN numbers. This ensured that the IT department and banks had access to all accounts of a single PAN card holder. It helped banks track individual loan defaulters through credit rating and the IT department check *benami* account holders who held incognito accounts in false names.

But, within a year, it was discovered that *benami* account holders had multiple PAN accounts. Hence, the government wanted the biometric Aadhaar cards to get linked with bank accounts. Soon, banks issued circulars and got most account holders to add Aadhaar number to their accounts. RBI has clarified that for large account holders, this linkage is mandatory under the Prevention of Money Laundering Law enacted in 2017. This happened at a time when activists started opposing the move to make Aadhaar compulsory in the SC as it violated privacy. Less than 1% Indians today have resisted the linking of bank accounts with Aadhaar. But, political activists backed by civil society groups continue to claim that it violates privacy. The SC in a 2018 verdict ordered banks to stop using Aadhaar as a verification tool but permitted the government to use it to give subsidies or payments from the national exchequer. It also permitted the linking of PAN to Aadhaar by the IT department.

Crying wolf that Unique Identification Authority of India (UIDAI), the agency that issues the Aadhaar card, wants to violate privacy, activists had petitioned the courts and taken the battle to social media. In August 2018, a French ethical hacker, Elliot Alderson created a national uproar by tweeting that the UIDAI had inserted an Aadhaar helpline number in users' mobile phones. The matter was discussed on television channels, social media and the Indian parliament for two days despite UIDAI's denial. Finally, Google came up with the admission that it had inadvertently inserted the helpline number in people's phones, and the controversy subsided.

I wrote an op-ed piece for *DNA India* the following week explaining that UIDAI does not have the necessary technical competence to intrude into people's phones or stop others from doing so. It is merely an agency that issues the Aadhaar number, which is like a social security number. The only three agencies that can intrude into a user's mobile phone are mobile phone makers like Samsung, its software makers like Google Android and the service providers like Airtel. So, the controversy around UIDAI trying to violate users' privacy is an argument that needs no serious consideration.

The Aadhaar issue is sub judice and will remain so for the next few years as the government as well as activists appeal against the verdict. Any judgement will be challenged and appealed against. Meanwhile, the courts may not give respite to the government by permitting bank account and Aadhaar card linking. This is because a large number of arguments of privacy violation extended by lawyers make the courts suspicious of the government's intent. So, the problem is twofold. Firstly, violators under *benami* accounts are not being proceeded against in earnest by the government. Secondly, the courts are not convinced that Aadhaar*'s* biometric connectivity is needed to get all bank account linking done and *benami* account holders identified.

Discovery of Stressed Assets Begins

One of the biggest reforms in the banking sector has been the laws enacted to discover and resolve stressed assets. Bad debts still happen and will keep happening because bad apples remain in the system. Those bad apples are not restricted to Nirav Modi and Vijay Mallya. There are thousands of others. In 2015, when bankers were instructed to tighten the system and some bank account connectivity began to take real effect, bank defaults started to surface. Bad debts that were lying buried in bank books for decades started getting connected and began bursting forth like fountains on a celebratory night.

The heat was on but no action was taken to purge the system. Perhaps the laws and the enforcement machinery were not geared up to act. Over 23,000 millionaires have officially left India since 2014 and several thousand of them are suspected to be people with *benami* accounts. There were many good apples too who left. That does not make India a favoured investment destination. Critics of the government say that since the highest exit destination is Dubai, it is Muslims in the beef and leather trade who are leaving due to religious discrimination. Some allegations may indeed be true. There has been a lot of pressure by *gau rakshaks* on those engaged in the leather and beef trade. This feeling of discrimination is something that the Modi government would not want to project. So, the Modi government is caught in a Catch-22 situation—should it take strict action against *gau rakshaks* and protect the multibillion-dollar leather industry? Should it slap an exit tax on the HNWI's withdrawing operations from India like the US does? Or should it go slow on tightening the noose?

Non-performing loans were just 4.2% in the year ending 2014 during the UPA rule. The number jumped to 5.88% in 2014–2015 once the inter-bank connectivity took place and Credit Information Bureau (India) Ltd (CIBIL) credit rating and Credit Analysis and Research (CARE) ratings became more meaningful. Before RBI Governor Raghuram Rajan completed his term in 2015, he was able to enforce the mechanism to declare stressed assets by banks. It was a reform he could not do during the UPA rule. By March 2016, bad loans had soared to a mammoth 9.18% and the names of big defaulters started surfacing. CARE ratings showed gross NPAs of state-owned banks rose by 56.4% to ₹6.15 trillion in the year 2015–2016 and they kept soaring.

In May 2016, India introduced the Insolvency and Bankruptcy Code (IBC), creating a single law for a quick insolvency and bankruptcy resolution. Soon, Jaypee and Unitech groups who were among India's largest real-estate developers declared themselves insolvent. So did Essar Steel and Bhushan Steel. Within the next one year, these companies went bankrupt and were put on the block. In India, it normally takes four years to declare a company insolvent as against two years in the US or China. The IBC helps reduce this time. But, there are many more who are waiting to go under the block. Most of these companies are in real-estate, steel, energy and retail sectors, and the loans that went bad have mostly been given during UPA II, between 2008 and 2013.

The tightening of banking norms and the framing of the IBC had two effects. By 2017, bad loans had soared to ₹9.5 trillion, which was 8.6% of the total loans given as per IMF data. So, the heat was on defaulters. A large number of HNWI who were on the default list started moving outside India. But still, the government refuses to dig real dirt. It refuses to take action against scamsters. It fails to punish the politicians, the bureaucrats, the auditors, the regulators and the businessmen who have looted the nation. Perhaps it does not have the bandwidth or the willpower to do so. Only time will tell.

Pushing Growth at a Cost

There is a huge ongoing debate raging in the country today as the 2019 elections arrive. The UPA claims that the economy fared better under them. In August 2018, P. Chidambaram in a press conference stated that the UPA was the only government after independence to have given double-digit growth for two years. The NDA under the Modi government claims that the economy has fared better under them. Arun Jaitley claims that for the first time under the Modi government India has witnessed the highest GDP growth rate in the world, even ahead of China, for two successive years.

So, we decided to test these growth numbers and see in what circumstances they were achieved. We also did a comparison of three successive governments that have taken office since 2000 and compared a few fundamentals. First, we considered the GDP growth of the three—the Vajpayee regime, the Manmohan Singh regime and the Narendra Modi regime. Figure 2.1 gives the data from RBI and IMF. We found that the highest growth rate amongst the three regimes was during the UPA and also that during its rule, the growth had crossed the double-digit mark *once* in 2010 (not twice). This was indeed strange because it was immediately after the global stock market crash in September 2008. So, we decided to investigate how that had happened. We also decided to look at the fundamentals of the three regimes and the fiscal discipline adopted during each period.

Figure 2.1: Percentage GDP Growth and Fiscal Deficit (March 2000 to March 2018)

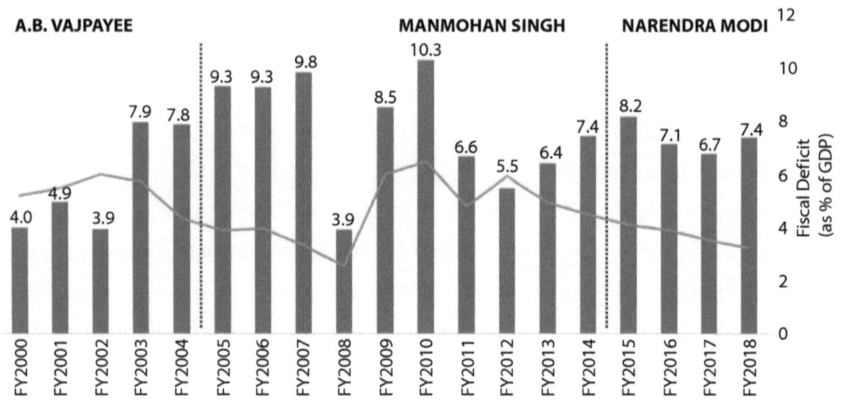

Data source: RBI and IMF

The set of charts gives the composite visual story of what happened in India in the last two decades under three PMs. Figure 1.1 in Chapter 1 gives the travel of the rupee that was the effect of the economic decisions taken. The unprecedented rupee plunge in 2013 and the dipping rupee in the second quarter of 2018 show weakness and investor disapproval. Figure 1.2, again in Chapter 1, shows the current account balance and the mounting CADs in 2013 and 2018 that was one of the reasons of the rupee plunge. In Figure 2.1, the GDP growth rate is given from 2000 to 2018. Also, the fiscal deficit incurred to spur growth is shown as a line curve. Volatility shows that measures taken to boost the GDP by increasing deficit in 2009 and 2010 have been unsustainable. The periods—financial year 2003 to financial year 2007 and the financial year 2014 to financial year 2018—show relatively well-managed growth where the fiscal deficit has been under control. Figure 2.2 shows the current account balance as a percentage of the GDP. It also gives an indicator of how and why the rupee plunged despite high GDP growth.

Figure 2.2: Current Account Balance as a Percentage of the GDP (March 2000 to March 2018)

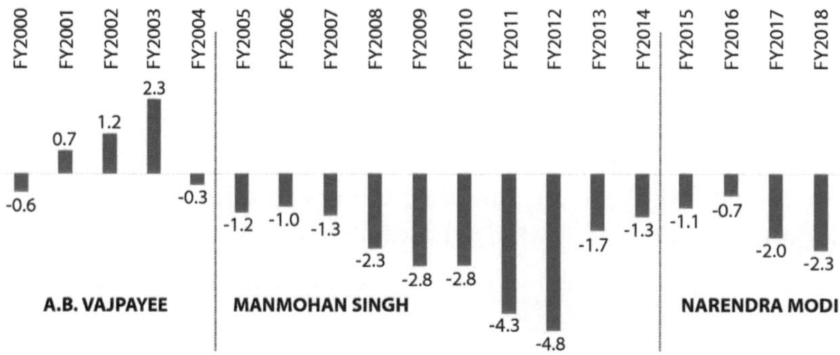

Data source: RBI and IMF

Simply speaking, global headwinds and external factors are never the only reason for a currency to dip sharply. Major structural weaknesses are often the reason why a currency succumbs to global headwinds. In this case, it was a panic reaction due to a combination of rising CAD and increasing fiscal deficit that caused the rupee to collapse, both in 2013 and 2018.

The graphs have a story to tell future politicians. Investors will not tolerate fiscal profligacy. The voter may have to wait for five years to give their next judgement. But, the investor will not be so patient. Narasimha Rao took over the economy at a very difficult time. He had to devalue the currency twice, but thereafter he built a strong reforms-based economy. Vajpayee took over the reins from Rao and took the economy ahead. He improved growth and improved fiscal discipline. The UPA I benefitted from the same but forgot to maintain fiscal discipline. The economy became heavily dependent on imports and external debt and the CAD increased year after year. The UPA II was worse, and was dogged by scams and poor decision-making and was voted out. The rupee collapsed due to fiscal profligacy. The NDA returned and with it returned foreign investors. But, its performance has been patchy, good in parts and bad in parts. Importantly, it has not performed as per promise. So, though it has attempted big-ticket changes, the rupee is under pressure as oil prices firm up and the CAD grows.

Bringing Change in India is No Mean Task

Bringing change in India is a tall task. Voters convinced by *achhe din* slogan were in no position to gauge this during the 2014 elections. The UPA had left behind a moth-eaten economy, bad loans in thousands and scams by the dozen. The Modi-led NDA has failed to purge the system of the ills. They wanted to play it safe. They did understand that some surgery was needed to get rid of the rot. But, they did not want to do the dirty job. They also did not understand that the rebuilding of the nation would need a massive amount of skill and resource deployment. It would also need persuasive and management skills that could lead to more cooperation in parliament and less confrontation in the streets.

Modi had a very small team of trusted and experienced people. He chose to ignore the members of the Vajpayee team to avoid the generation gap. That limited the pool of the BJP. The team size to govern a state and a country was however vastly different. So, though he promised the moon and got a thumping majority in the Lok Sabha, he started with a disadvantage. He did not have enough competent people to revive an ailing economy. The voters also did not realise that Modi had himself been a victim of political tribalism for years. The Congress party and its supporters had for years subjected the Gujarat chief minister to both political witchhunt and cultural isolation. As a result, Modi harboured a trust deficit. He primarily trusted people only from the Gujarat cadre or the members and affiliates of Rashtriya Swayamsevak Sangh (RSS) for top postings.

This ultimately is becoming a bottleneck in governance. Modi is also wary of letting the process take precedence over hand-picking. So, decision-making to fill top postings has become skewed and also pretty slow. Modi does not appreciate that all loyal people are not necessarily competent and not all competent people value personal loyalty. Professionals do not believe in absolute personal loyalty. For them loyalty to the profession and not loyalty to the leader is primary. Competent people want the freedom to differ and innovate, while loyalists choose to remain subservient. That further limits his choice of ministers and bureaucracy needed for such a large nation.

As a result, despite good intentions and good ideas, the delivery has been slow and inconsistent. While the Piyush Goyals and the

Aruna Sundararajans have succeeded, the Uma Bhartis and the Hasmukh Adhias have, perhaps, not. Execution has lacked pace, the return on investment has been uneven and the economy has struggled to get off the blocks. Perhaps, Modi himself did not correctly assess the amount of work needed to be done to genuinely usher in *achhe din*. But, whatever be the reason, PM Modi will always be pulled up in posterity by critics for promises that he made but could not keep.

CHAPTER 3

Jan Dhan and Demonetisation: A Political Gain and Economic Loss

AT 8.00 pm on 16 November 2016, India's PM Narendra Modi in a seemingly innocuous broadcast to the nation announced demonetisation of higher denomination notes of ₹500 and ₹1,000. The television announcement said that in the next four hours 86% of India's circulated currency would be obsolete. The obsolete currency would be exchangeable at banks from the next day for a period of 45 days, until the year-end.

The demonetisation exercise was not successful. It did not meet its objective of unearthing black money. It caused a lot of distress both in rural and urban India. This was particularly in the unorganised sector where cash was the lifeline. The poor were the most affected as cash disappeared from the markets at one go and trickled back slowly. The government was proactive but unfortunately, it had two goals. One was to stop the black money holders deposit their cash into banks. The second was to quickly get out the new notes into circulation. It failed to do both in quick time.

The ingenuity of India's black money holders won the battle. They found out different ways to beat the system and deposited black money into banks. An RBI report of August 2018 stated that 99.3% of the demonetised currency found its way back to the banks. But, the demonetisation exercise went on to create an acute cash shortage for nearly a quarter of the financial year. It hurt the economic growth just after a good monsoon when the economy was poised to take off. So why did the Modi government attempt to do it at all?

Why Demonetisation?

Demonetisation was primarily done to reduce black money that was perceived to be held largely in cash. As per a report released by India Ratings and Research, a Fitch Group company, in December 2016, it was estimated that 12% of the currency or ₹4 lakh crore of black money would be unearthed after demonetisation. The economic cost of demonetisation as per the agency would be ₹1.5 lakh crore to check the proliferation of black money in India. With 99.3% cash finding its way to the bank, only ₹11,000 crore remained outside the system. So clearly, demonetisation failed to isolate the black money and just 0.7% remained outside the system. Though the move may not have actually succeeded, it was not that black money was absent in India. The BJP had both an economic and political logic behind the move, says a party ideologue on the condition of anonymity.

Only 1.7% of Indians paid taxes in the year ending March 2016 and most of them belonged to the salaried or service class. Businesses other than the publicly-held corporations had a very poor record of tax payment. This despite the fact that prosperity across India was growing and consumer spending was fast rising. It was obvious that people were earning more, but still not paying taxes. This meant that while the cash economy would be growing, tax collection would not.

It has been known for long that this process has created a parallel economy in India—a nation of more than one billion people. The scale of the parallel economy can only be guessed. In 2015, the Modi government brought in the Black Money Act (BMA) to check the proliferation of unaccounted money or black money. The BMA 2015 had supposedly tackled several existing loopholes in the law and was ready to tackle the black money menace both within India and abroad—that is, the stashed away money. However, strong steps were needed to flush out the existing black money from within the economy.

Though demonetisation was announced suddenly, it was planned well in advance. The plan was not properly risk-managed but it was thought out carefully at the political level. So, though it was economically unsuccessful, it was politically a winning solution. It was very much a part of the matrix to reduce inequality in society. The political message was very clear. This was an unprecedented step taken against black money moguls. It would punish those who had large unaccounted income and, hence, by inference, would help remove poverty and inequality. The exercise would take place months before the elections to India's most populous state, Uttar Pradesh (UP). It would not only deliver the pro-poor message but clean the state of unaccounted cash. The opposition would be caught flat-footed and would be forced to fight elections without the support of black money.

Avoidable Technical Glitches after Demonetisation

The sudden demonetisation created total chaos in banking operations. Two separate sets of operations were imposed on the already strained banking system. One was the withdrawal of all the high-denomination currency within 45 days. The second was the replacement by new high-denomination notes to maintain liquidity in the economy. The dual operation resulted in long serpentine queues outside banks. Reportedly, 23 people even died in the queues waiting for cash. Meanwhile, citizens were left high and dry without liquidity for their daily necessities. That this happened during the festive and wedding season added to their woes.

Demonetisation suddenly drained the cash-driven Indian economy, causing acute hardships both in households as well as in the business sector. The unorganised sector that employs the maximum number of daily wage labourers, all of whom are paid in cash, was the most distressed. This was because India—before demonetisation—was a society that was driven entirely by cash.

As per a December 2016 report issued by MasterCard Advisor measuring progress towards a cashless society, India had 98% cash transactions and just 2% digital or cashless transactions before demonetisation. By comparison, the cashless transactions in China were 10%, in Japan 14%, in Germany 33%, in the US 45%, in the United Kingdom (UK) 52%, in France 59% and in Singapore 61%. Apart from flushing out black money, demonetisation was a forced measure to push the Indian economy towards digital transactions.

Two Unforeseen Challenges That Made Demonetisation More Painful

Demonetisation meant replacement of the old ₹1,000 and ₹500 notes by new currency notes of ₹2,000 and ₹500 that were distinctly different in size.

The new notes to be issued by the RBI in lieu of the withdrawn currency notes could not be delivered by Automated Teller Machines (ATM) without recalibration. There were two lakh ATMs operating across the country that needed their cassettes changed to hold the new notes and their recalibration thereafter.

According to NCR Corporation Ltd (originally National Cash Register), which holds nearly 50% of the market share of India-installed ATMs, they were caught unaware by the demonetisation decision. The governor and the deputy governors at RBI missed informing the political leadership of the technicalities and the risk involved. It was a top-secret political decision, probably that is why NCR Corporation—a US-based multinational—was kept in the dark. Hence, it took them six to eight weeks to replace the ATM cassettes and recalibrate them. During this period, the new denomination notes at 1.2 lakh banks across India were paid out to consumers by bank cashiers. The recalibration of ATMs thus slowed down the flow of liquidity back into the economy.

Things got worse because those who had black money got *Jan Dhan* account holders to convert the cash on their behalf in lieu of a paltry payment. The poor acted as cash mules to convert black money of the rich into white money. They deposited large sums of cash in some *Jan Dhan* accounts and also withdrew the permissible amounts. As a result, the queues at banks got longer and business and economic spending saw a sharp slowdown. This was the second risk that was neither anticipated nor mitigated.

While the RBI and the government kept changing deposit and withdrawal rules almost every week to stop money laundering through cash mules, it continued to happen. Thus, the little liquidity that was there was cornered by the haves while the have-nots bore the brunt of the liquidity crunch.

With hundreds of bank officials conniving with the perpetuators of black money, the entire exercise of demonetisation was well and truly sabotaged. Bank officials connived with black money holders to deal a body blow to demonetisation. This was the third risk that was not managed adequately. As a result, over 99% of the demonetised currency got redeposited in the banks. Black money was converted to white in a matter of only 45 days. This prompted the opposition to assert that demonetisation was an expensive and needless exercise that failed.

Number Crunching Was Needed to Mitigate Demonetisation Risk

The stated objective of demonetisation could have been less painful and more successful, had the number crunching been done before the actual exercise. The revenue officers at the finance ministry and the RBI and India's politicians as well as *babus* are perhaps unaware that in developed nations, risk analysis and mitigation of risk are important parts of every political and administrative move today.

A basic number crunching exercise would have detailed the risks associated with replacing ₹4,000 billion in currency notes in a six-week period. It meant the replacement of 150 million high-denomination bank notes each working day. This itself was a stupendous exercise, given the fact that normally, the banking transactions in India on an average day handle just around 30 million high-denomination notes. Due to poor planning and execution the demonetisation exercise caused a lot of hardship—especially for the poor in the unorganised sector who were entirely dependent on their daily wages in cash.

Had the exercise of printing notes and calibrating ATMs been pre-planned and organised in advance, the ATMs would have been functional and flow of new notes well planned. This could have been synchronised just before demonetisation as a technical solution. Most probably, it would not have made any significant difference because the time of the announcement would still have been unknown. The number crunching clearly shows that the sudden 8.00 pm prime-time announcement with a four-hour notice would have been equally effective even if people suspected a new currency inflow months ahead.

Politically, Demonetisation Was a Success

Economically, demonetisation was a loss-making exercise. As per an RBI annual report of 2016–2017 released in August 2017, the cost of printing notes in the financial year 2016–2017 doubled to ₹7,965 crore (₹796.5 million) as against ₹3,421 crore (₹342.1 million) the previous year. This meant that the printing cost had more than doubled due to demonetisation. It also said 7,62,000 counterfeit notes were forfeited in the financial year 2016–2017, as against 6,32,000 notes in the previous year.

Despite the hardship caused by demonetisation, it was a popular decision amongst the masses. As per a Nikkei Asian Review sample survey of the rural poor conducted during December 2016 and January 2017, 73% said that the note ban had affected their life and work, yet 54% voiced their support for it. The opposition did keep bashing demonetisation in the parliament and in the streets but it failed to get public support, at least initially.

Television channels showed the footage of long queues repeatedly but most people standing in those serpentine queues braving the hardship surprisingly spoke in the favour of demonetisation. They clearly said that the pain was worthwhile because it was for a long-term gain to cleanse the Indian economy of black money. The support was especially strong amongst the have-nots or the poor who had no stash of high-denomination notes and hence nothing to lose.

The Congress and the left parties, however, misread the widespread support that demonetisation received and made it an election issue in the UP elections. Leader after leader, be it the then UP chief minister, Akhilesh Yadav of Samajwadi Party, or the then Congress vice president, Rahul Gandhi, or the previous chief minister, Mayawati of the Bahujan Samaj Party, spoke for hours on the ill effects of demonetisation. They made it look as if it was the prime issue for the assembly polls in UP. Understandably, they were surprised when BJP won more than 300 of the 403 assembly seats. The BJP's political gamble on demonetisation paid off at least for the UP elections. Some looked at it as a short-term gain. This is because demonetisation would return to haunt and assembly elections are an entirely different ball game than general elections in India. The discussion on demonetisation would not fade away and would be once again under scrutiny during the next general elections.

The Social Equity Appeal for Politicians

Demonetisation was presumably conducted to achieve social equity. More than 80% of the people who suffered were poor. But, they still supported the move despite its economic costs. Demonetisation was neither a one-off measure nor a quick fix to curb black money. India has long been suffering from the dual impact of black money and low-tax collections.

The difference of income between the rich and the poor of the country has been growing since its independence 70 years ago. While the creamy layer of the top 5% of India's 1.2 billion population has been splurging and living an opulent and extravagant lifestyle, the bottom 22% with nearly 276 million people have been living below the official poverty line, mostly in pitiable conditions.

Achieving social equity presumably gets votes and hence the Indian politicians swear by it. But, it is easier said than done. The UPA lost the elections in 2014 trying to achieve it. Theoretically, it means reducing the gap between the rich and the poor. This gap has been growing not only in India but also globally. It is commonly perceived that the rich have been evading taxes or paying less taxes than what they should. There is some truth to the argument. The rise and rise of offshore companies worldwide has facilitated the phenomenon of legal tax evasion.

The method of empowering the poor through redistribution of wealth within a legal framework is usually difficult. It is usually done either through subsidies where pilferage has been rampant or through cash or gifts for votes. Whereas cash for votes is a well-tried method to win elections, it could be easily termed 'illegal' by the Election Commission, the authority that conducts the elections. A new method to empower and enrich the poor has been long overdue.

A method where the source of money, the reason for distribution as well as the method of disbursal must be authentic and foolproof. The Narendra Modi government is possibly taking the first baby steps to explore these avenues. These will be unconventional methods and some efforts will succeed and some will fail. But, like an entrepreneur at a start-up, Modi, it seems, will keep trying.

Besides, the challenge is not only to give away money as doles. It is to ensure the empowerment of the poor through practices that increase their income. Like providing banking services at their doorstep. Giving loans and financial support, insurance and deposit facilities to the poor. These and several other measures that are being currently taken could empower the poor. But, they are fraught with risk. Risks like collateral-free loans and zero-balance accounts have a high cost. The annual GDP growth and the tax accruals should be able to bear the cost of such social initiatives.

The *Jan Dhan* Accounts Were the First Steps in Creating a Social Equity Matrix

Soon after he assumed office in 2014, PM Narendra Modi introduced the *Pradhan Mantri Jan Dhan Yojana* (PMJDY). It permitted all citizens of India with Aadhaar identification to open zero-balance *Jan Dhan* bank accounts. More than a quarter of the Indian population benefitted from this exercise. In hindsight, it was possibly the first step of an elaborate matrix that was evolving to bring about some equality between the haves and the have-nots.

The government told the parliament during the 2017–2018 budget session that as of 20 December 2017, of the 31 crore (310 million) PMJDY accounts opened, only 24.64 crore (246.4 million) were active with transactions during the last 24 months. The bank accounts have helped the economically weaker section (EWS). But initially, it helped only those who had some amount of liquidity.

Banking the unbanked is an extremely powerful solution to win popularity and votes. The politically savvy Indira Gandhi will always be revered by India's middle class, especially in rural India, for nationalising banks. Though nationalisation in the 1960s was contrary to the liberalisation of the 1990s, it brought magical growth to the banking industry and helped expand the economy.

After nationalisation, the number of urban bank branches grew fourfold in the next two decades and rural branches went up 10 times. The aggregate deposits and advances rose by 40 times and the number of account holders went up by a 100 times. This endeared Indira Gandhi to the masses like no other leader during the post-independence period. She remained popular with the poor despite the draconian days of emergency and the restrictive inspector raj unleashed during her rule.

The focus of PM Modi on banking the unbanked was apparent from the day he came to power. He realised that banks in India operated for the educated middle class and not for the uneducated poor. Banking services in India were for those who had permanent addresses and who could maintain a minimum balance. Banking, especially in the private sector, was for middle and upper classes, and not for the masses. That was the position before 2014.

The poor had no permanent address, no PAN and not enough surplus to keep a comfortable minimum balance as mandated by most banks. Within months of coming to power, PM Modi announced on 15 August 2014 that every Indian having an Aadhaar card would be permitted to open a zero-balance *Jan Dhan* account. Before the month was over, 18 million accounts were opened under the PMJDY scheme. That was a Guinness Book World Record.

The relentless pressure on the banks to open *Jan Dhan* accounts for banking India's unbanked millions has yielded results. According to PricewaterhouseCoopers (PwC), India's unbanked population drastically dropped from 557 million (44%) in 2011 to 233 million (18%) in 2015. On 27 August 2017, PM announced that 300 million accounts have been opened in the first three years of PMJDY and already have ₹65,000 crore (₹650 billion) deposited in them. From the above statistics we can infer that whereas 24 million bank accounts were opened in the 2011–2014 period, the next three years saw the addition of 300 million bank accounts.

Even if 25% of the accounts have zero balance, as reported by the financial press, the numbers are impressive. It means that 225 million functional *Jan Dhan* accounts have been opened in the last three years and the average balance in each account is over ₹2,800. This is no mean achievement for a nation where opening a bank account has been largely possible for the privileged middle class not so long ago.

Reaching Professor Prahalad's Bottom of the Pyramid

Professor C. K. Prahalad, the author and management guru who propounded the theory of fortune at the bottom of the pyramid, would have been extremely happy with this mass-banking experiment. He believed that empowering India's millions of poor people with banking and market-driven initiatives was the key to poverty removal. While finishing his school and college during the 1960s in Chennai, he was deeply affected by the poverty he saw around him. That was before he went to Harvard to study management.

One of the sharpest minds in economic theory, Professor Prahalad, the author of *Fortune at the Bottom of The Pyramid: Eradicating Poverty Through Profits* would often say, 'Think about where you would want to be 20 years later and then "fold the future" into present-day activity.' He was always decades ahead of time. When he first propounded the theory of the bottom of the pyramid, India was still hoping that socialism would deliver. Prahalad wanted to return to India from the US and teach. He repeatedly attempted to do so till the 1980s. However, those were the days of nationalisation under Indira Gandhi. After a two-year stint at Indian Institute of Management (IIM) Ahmedabad in the 1980s, he found no takers for his free-market economic theory for the poor. He soon went back to the US and resumed teaching and consulting at the University of Michigan.

In the introductory chapter of *Next Generation Business Strategies for the Base of the Pyramid*,[1] Prahalad wrote, 'The total market for credit in rural India is ₹15,000 billion (now mostly done by moneylenders at 100% interest rate maybe). The banks have just scratched the surface with ₹40 billion. Even if the organised sector only got to ₹10,000 billion and reduced the interest rate from 100% to 20%, you can calculate the income generated for the poor.'

No politician or economist in India delved on the issue of empowering the population with banking facilities as Indira Gandhi or Narendra Modi did. The PSBs were created by Indira Gandhi with an exclusive purpose of taking banking to the unorganised sector and the rural population. They had been relegated to the background after the advent of private-sector banks at the turn of the century.

Direct Infusion of Subsidies into Bank Accounts

Nobody knows how the social equity matrix will unfold but the second step was to get those *Jan Dhan* bank accounts activated with a cash infusion. India has been spending heavily on subsidies for the last 30 years, a large part of which never reached the real beneficiaries. It is alleged that unscrupulous politicians and bureaucrats often siphoned off the treasury money allocated for subsidies to the poor. My previous book, *Neta, Babu and Subsidy*, distinctly quantifies the huge growth of subsidies (as shown in Figure 3.1) that took place during the last decade. One of the principal subsidies that witnessed massive corruption in distribution was the petroleum subsidies for kerosene, cooking gas, petrol and diesel.

Figure 3.1: Subsidies as a Percentage of the GDP (2005 to 2018)

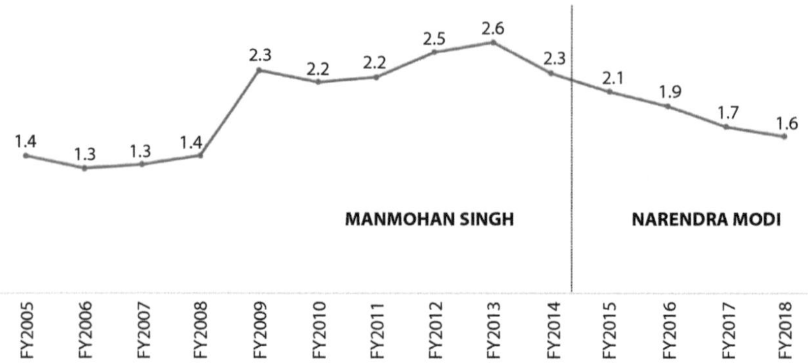

Data source: IMF

The BJP government under PM Vajpayee had reduced the petroleum subsidies to a bare minimum by 2003. Subsidies on petrol and diesel had been eliminated and the only subsidies that remained were on kerosene and cooking gas. However, one of the first things the UPA government under PM Manmohan Singh did after assuming power was to restart the subsidies on petroleum products. It helped the UPA build the image that it was pro-poor and gave subsidies to the common citizen to keep living costs down.

Petroleum subsidies jumped 30-fold during the UPA decade from ₹5,430 crore (₹54.3 billion) in 2002–2003 to ₹1,60,000 crore (₹1,600 billion) in 2012–2013. Fertiliser subsidies rose sixfold from ₹12,695 crore (₹126.95 billion) to over ₹80,000 crore (₹800 billion) in 2012–2013 and even imported fertilisers were subsidised to the tune of ₹13,800 crore (₹138 billion). The Modi government took several important steps to cut the subsidies and also plug the leakages. First, the subsidies on petrol and diesel were stopped. This was helped by the fact that global oil prices had slumped in 2014 and remained low till 2017. Hence, the price of petrol and diesel, without subsidies, did not pinch the consumer as much. The food and fertiliser subsidies have also reduced. Importantly, the subsidies were well directed to the beneficiaries' banks.

The Aadhaar card or the unique identification system was conceived by the UPA government. However, it was in shambles with plenty of glitches and issues at the implementation level. The issues were tackled on a priority basis and the system was made functional after the Modi government took control. By the end of 2014, all bank accounts were connected to Aadhaar numbers. This made Aadhaar a single-point identification for the banking system. It also made the distribution of subsidies possible through the banking system. That included the newly empowered PMJDY account holders whose bank accounts could directly benefit from the monthly trickle of subsidy cash flow.

The transfer of cooking gas subsidies directly into bank accounts started the process of providing cash to the zero-balance bank accounts. A few ₹100 were deposited directly into all bank accounts, including the 240 million (24 crore) *Jan Dhan* accounts, every month. That was a beginning. Soon, the subsidies became well directed and the cost to exchequer started reducing.

The subsidies directly paid into the beneficiaries' banks ensured that the zero-balance *Jan Dhan* accounts also started getting some funds from payments given by the government. This was the second major step of this matrix by which the poor were brought into the banking mainstream and found cash subsidies directly deposited in their accounts.

MUDRA: Unsecured Loans to the Poor

As India goes through this experimental phase of economic reforms like demonetisation, digitisation of payment and the one-nation-one-tax regime in Goods and Service Tax Network (GSTN), there will be a lot of pain and little gain initially. These are long-term measures and some will work and some will not. The jury will be out 5 to 10 years later on the need for change and the process adopted. Just like the need to nationalise banks in the 1960s is still debated today, so will be these changes.

If opening the *Jan Dhan* accounts was the first step of the social equity experiment, putting subsidy money into those accounts was the second step. Similarly, if demonetisation was the third step, then the MUDRA loan experiment was the fourth step to bring about social equity.

This fourth initiative to reduce the disparity between the rich and the poor was also very important. It is another social initiative that the Modi government is attempting. It gives unsecured loans to the EWS through the MUDRA scheme. It is too early to predict if it will be an economic success or a disaster; if it will lead to economic recovery or yet another spate of bad loans. But, the BJP government says that by 31 March 2018, the MUDRA banking scheme had issued collateral-free loans to 115 million (11.5 crore) people amongst the EWS.

In short, the people who could not open bank accounts due to procedural complexities before the *Jan Dhan* account was introduced in 2014 were now getting collateral-free loans. This was a new method of legally empowering the poor instead of distributing cash during elections. How much of that loan will be repaid and how much of it has to be ultimately written off by the banks is something we will know in the future. But, the Aadhaar connectivity to the banking system goes a long way to ensure that fake account loans and misuse of this facility will be less. Only time will tell whether it can withstand judicial scrutiny after activist pressure. It is also yet to be determined if it is a robust system of empowering the poor.

This is because the jury is usually programmed to think and act conventionally. They abhor turmoil that streetonomics usually brings about. They can never reconcile with the politics or economics of leaders like Indira Gandhi or Narendra Modi. They love steady, organised progress and incremental risk-free change. They want economic reforms but the type brought in by Narasimha Rao and continued by Atal Bihari Vajpayee.

Narendra Modi's arrival with 300 Lok Sabha seats in 2014 meant that disruptive changes were about to happen. He promised the moon to an electorate disillusioned by corruption and inefficiency. This was despite knowing that the economy was in dire straits when he took charge. It was a gamble to ensure that despondency did not spread far and wide, looking at the poor state of the Indian economy. There was no question that he wanted to bring about a major change in both the society and in the governance. The key question was—would he deliver?

It is apparent now that the Modi government will behave differently than its predecessors. Unlike in the Sonia Gandhi-Manmohan Singh rule of the last decade, things will not be allowed to drift. There will be mistakes due to inexperience but, graft will not rise and policy paralysis will not set in. Nor will the change be orderly and gentle like during the rule of P. V. Narasimha Rao or Atal Bihari Vajpayee. Rather like in

Indira Gandhi's time, a lot of effort will be made to continuously change the status quo. Apart from the nationalisation of banks and coal mines, none of Indira Gandhi's economic initiative paid off in the long run. It is too early to say if the moves PM Modi makes will benefit the economy. Disruptive changes will take place that could change the destiny of the nation and its people. Whether it will be for good or bad is for the future generations to judge.

Will the Kitty Turn Digital?

After demonetisation, the debit card usage reportedly jumped by 18% to account for 60% of the total transaction value. The government also introduced Bharat Interface for Money (BHIM) application (app) with UPI for peer-to-peer payments through smartphones while the private sector revved up their business of mobile wallets. Debit cards and credit cards are used by the educated class who have access to banking facilities.

Saving for a rainy day is in the ethos of every Indian. Indians are by nature cautious and prone to worrying about the future. Unlike Americans, they are more than willing to sacrifice present-day comforts to ensure future security. They save for themselves first and then save for their children. If they grow old and prosperous, you will find them saving even for their grandchildren. They are habitual savers and borrow only when in dire need. This is perhaps why the debit card is more popular than the credit card in India. But what about the unbanked?

According to Professor Prahalad, banking India's unbanked would be the single biggest economic reform. Surprisingly though, modern-day economists have quietly discounted the effort. This is because few realise that the unorganised sector in India saved billions of rupees each month in cash through kitties or committees. This included small shopkeepers, farmers and rural artisans, domestic helps and even housewives who did not have access to bank accounts.

Kitty or committee is an all-cash transaction based on goodwill and trust among a known group of people. It is also known as 'chit fund'. Every member of the group saves a designated amount agreed between the members every month or week. The collected cash can be taken by any member of the group by rotation. Those who want the cash early take a discounted value while those who take the cash last usually get a small premium. If there is more than one bidder for the amount in any month, then the discounts offered by the bidder decides who will take the cash. The one who gives the most discount gets the cash for that month.

The concept of a kitty or committee is simple. If I need a lump sum money first, I have to offer a discount. On a kitty of ₹10,000 the discount could be ₹1,500 in the first month. This means whoever picks up the kitty first gets only ₹8,500 cash. But, if three people want the cash in the second month, they will have to compete with each other—as a result of which the discount could be even higher than that given in the first month. Each month the contenders for the kitty reduce and so does the discount. So, if I wait for the money and pick it up last, I get a premium. Kitty is a universally popular method of community savings outside the banking system. Women, rich and poor, both in rural and urban India, use it extensively to fulfil their household shopping needs for big-ticket items like refrigerator or television. Another segment that uses kitty or committee extensively is the small business segment that essentially deals in cash. Billions of rupees each year are saved outside the banking system by India's small savers. Maybe attractive cash prizes or lottery schemes for kitty parties could induce them to turn digital.

Savings through peer communities is a subcontinental practice due to the lack of banking facilities and is not limited to India. It has now become an effective social engagement tool. What the Modi government has attempted to do is to bank the unbanked. It has given a sort of added legitimacy to kitty, though the preparatory process has gone on for over two decades. The concept of formalisation of collective informal savings, largely by women, into bankable savings was pioneered in the subcontinent by Nobel Laureate Muhammad Yunus of Bangladesh in the 1970s. The capital formed was augmented by small loans from Grameen Bank free of collaterals. The concept of a physical collateral was done away with and was substituted by trust and peer pressure from community members.

The Self-Help Group (SHG) movement started in India as a part of Rao's liberalisation when the National Bank for Agriculture and Rural Development (NABARD) realised the potential and started promoting it. Four states of South India set up autonomous organisations headed by senior bureaucrats and managed by development professionals. These small savings form the backbone of the National Rural Livelihood Mission (NRLM) and the State Rural Livelihoods Mission (SRLM), the largest poverty-alleviation programme in the world. This brought small cash savings into the economy and opened the door for the small saver to avail collateral-free bank loans. The current push will help mobilise the savings into those *Jan Dhan* accounts.

Digital Banking, UPI and Mobile Wallets

Demonetisation was followed by several digital banking initiatives. This was possibly the fifth initiative to bring small cash into the formal economy. Mobile wallets that were already active took off vertically during demonetisation. Little did any one expect that people would flock to digital payment modes in the absence of cash liquidity. Mobile wallets were merely bridging the gap between the banking system and customer. It was a niche segment that targeted a small revenue base but had a large number of customers.

Since the mobile phone was an instrument that two out of three Indian city dwellers used regularly, people took to mobile wallets like a fish to water during the cash crunch after demonetisation. The banks were overcrowded and had no facility other than debit and credit cards to facilitate payments. Here, small day-to-day payments including fund transfers to individuals up to ₹10,000 could be done through mobile wallets. Besides, overhead costs of banks were high as they had a bulky physical infrastructure cost. It was beyond them to service small customers en masse with the convenience that mobile wallets with low overhead costs could do.

UPI and BHIM app were developed after demonetisation to enable citizens to facilitate transfers of funds from one account to another seamlessly through their mobile phones. Besides, debit card usage saw a sharp upswing following demonetisation. Debit card users in India had always been numerous and had outnumbered credit card users by 25%. Debit cards accounted for only 42% of the total card spending before demonetisation but it spurt to 60% immediately after demonetisation.

UPI is a major success story. Developed by the National Payments Corporation of India in 2016, it was considered the best among 40 digital payment systems prevalent across the world by Fidelity National Information Services (FIS) in their December 2017 report. That was because it was found to be the most innovative and the most popular digital payment service among users. UPI's popularity with mobile apps has not only made banks and digital wallets adopt it but has got big names like Amazon, Ola, Uber, Paytm and WhatsApp adopting it. Though the Indian digital payment market is currently just $200 billion, UPI has been rated ahead of Swiss, British, Japanese and Chinese payment systems.

However, the trends towards digital payments have slowed down as the cash crunch disappeared. Most small shopkeepers still look out for cash earnings and have once again stopped accepting digital payments even though the government is trying its best to ensure digital compliance. Changing India's spending habits from cash to digital modes and increasing the number of taxpayers are two major challenges that any government will have to face in the coming days. But, how millions of India's unbanked people are slowly brought into its banking system will be an interesting exercise to watch nonetheless. We will have to wait for PM Modi to unfold the next layer of his social equity initiative and that could happen just before the elections of 2019.

CHAPTER 4

GST: Reform Done, Revamp Needed for a Business-Friendly Solution

A few months after demonetisation, another major reform was initiated by the Modi government. After 16 years of debate and drama, the GST was finally rolled out on 1 July 2017. GST was a single-point consumption tax. It had four goals. It aimed to replace the dozen taxes imposed at the central and state level across India. It envisioned to make the tax regime simpler. It also sought to ensure better compliance. Finally, it aimed to increase the tax base in a nation where tax evasion was rampant. Like coal auction, spectrum auction, Aadhaar and UPI digitisation, GST was another major reform that was launched by the Modi government.

GST Was Conceived to Simplify the Tax Regime

The single unified tax was first conceived in 1999. Its founder-architect was the then PM Atal Bihari Vajpayee of the BJP, who along with three ex-RBI governors and the then finance minister of West Bengal, Asim Dasgupta, initiated it. Initially, the Congress opposed it. Later, when the Congress came to power in 2004, the UPA government tried to introduce it several times but the BJP opposed it tooth and nail.

So, when the Modi government took office in 2014 and tried to table it in the House, the Congress and the left parties opposed it initially just as a tit-for-tat measure. However, good sense and public pressure prevailed. The consensus between the government and opposition was reached after protracted negotiations two years later. After Article 279A was passed in September 2016, the GST council was formed to make the decisions on behalf of the centre and the states. The GST rollout thereafter was quick and three months ahead of its year-long time frame.

Before the 2017 rollout of GST, there were five central taxes and seven state taxes. This included Central Excise Duty, Customs Duty and Service Tax levied by the central government. The tax platform also comprised seven state taxes, including Central and Local Sales Tax, Entertainment Tax and the Octroi or entry taxes. They were all presumed to have a cascading effect. It was felt that this increased the ultimate cost to the consumer. So, when GST was devised, it should have aimed to lower the ultimate burden of the consumer. Instead, tax slabs for goods and services for most items were kept around the level of the previous composite taxes.

A Modern Tax System Should Not Be an Amalgamation of the Old

The bigger problem was its architecture and the complex structuring of the GST law. For example, if you are asked to demolish the 100-year-old Sadar Bazaar market or the 50-year-old India Trade Promotion Organisation (ITPO) Pragati Maidan Exhibition Centre and build a new market or exhibition hall, would you replicate the old architecture? Would you remake those dark alleyways and winding corridors of old Delhi? Would you recreate the tiny cubicles and narrow shops with unsafe electric wiring that are hallmark of Sadar Bazaar today? Or, consider revamping the ITPO infrastructure for a modern exhibition centre, would you rebuild those high facade octagons that are elegant but consume space inefficiently such that only 10% of the 6,25,000 square metres is dedicated to display? Would you recreate 16 non-utilitarian high-ceilinged halls that keep guzzling electricity without effective cooling? Obviously not.

Similarly, if a tax system is devised in 2017, it must be modern, smart and efficient. But, the GST council and the mandarins of the North Block who had the lifetime opportunity of creating a new tax regime were not competent and equal to the task. Both the centre and the state bureaucracy are to blame. Perhaps many years of administration work has dulled their approach to problem-solving and the ability to think fresh. Not surprisingly, they used the old architecture of Central Excise Duty Act devised in 1944 as the tax model. Then they kept on adding the clauses from the dozen existing indirect tax schemes to create a complex GST architecture.

The result was a faulty and labour-intensive labyrinth of clauses. The GST council and the revenue department prepared too much documentation. The submission forms were full of glitches and needed several rounds of reworking after the GST rollout. When the problems were pointed out by industry associations and in the media, they kept on revising the clauses with amendments. They also changed tax rates and the provisions every day.

In the last quarter of 2017, I wrote a series of articles in *The Indian Express* on simplifying GST. I spoke to businessmen and industry representatives along with my friends from the Pan IIT group (it is an umbrella organisation of alumni of all IITs). Due to my past association with the industry, I was able to get several insights that showed me how projects across states had stuttered to a grinding halt as there was no clarity on invoicing and GST. One of the articles was headlined, 'Reducing Data Entries, Educating Sales Tax Officers Are Key Measures to Let Make in India Succeed'. There were several other media analysts who spoke about the complexities of GST.

The political leadership was extremely proactive. Soon, the GST council and the bureaucracy, which was initially chest-thumping about the early rollout, swung into action. The industry associations had already submitted their list of complaints before the media started highlighting the issues. Changes started to happen at increased speed. Soon it was a tax regime that swung like a gyroscope in motion. It was a bizarre comedy of errors. The very proactive bureaucrats and GSTN—the Infosys subsidiary that manages the platform—making rapid changes to improve the working, unfortunately, did not have a clue about simplification of taxes. They failed to understand the concept that PM had spelt out in the parliament—to create a 'good simple tax' regime.

Thousands of Amendments in the First 100 Days

As it is the GST Act is cumbersome with hundreds of clauses and subclauses. Initially, a few of the clauses even contradicted one another. Hence, they were changed again and the amendments were fast and furious. In October, in one of my articles in *The Indian Express* headlined, '40 Amendments in Three Months as Ease of Business Disappears, Tax Officers Arrive', I highlighted that subsection (1) section 11 of the Central GST (CGST) Act 2017 saw 40 amendments by 23 October 2017. The GST council introduced yet another rate of tax (0.5% CGST + 0.05% State GST [SGST] or 0.10% Integrated GST [IGST]) for merchant exporters with the most bizarre conditions. As a result, seven tax rates were applicable for this section namely, 0%, 0.05%, 2.5%, 6%, 9% and 14%. The difference to the revenue would be insignificant with the new tax rate. Yet, it was added.

In just a little over three months from the rollout, 40 amendments were issued to a single subclause in the new Act and tax slabs had more than doubled. Due to such thoughtless amendments, the administrative and compliance conditions had become much more difficult. If you consider the number of amendments to all the clauses and subclauses, it runs into several thousands. Now, not only should the taxpayer keep abreast of the complex GST laws but thousands of amendments notified by the GST council each month. Is this ease of business?

Facing scathing criticism, Revenue Secretary Hasmukh Adhia acknowledged in October 2017 that GST needs a rejig. But, the rejigs have been mindless amendments to the GST Act. This has made an already complicated Act even more unviable.

Niladri Biswas, heading the indirect tax division of a multinational manufacturing giant, explains the key problem with GST. He says that all the provisions and tax slabs of Value-Added Tax (VAT), Service Tax and excise duty are making a backdoor entry into GST with their complicated structures. If that happens, consequences shall be disastrous. In 2005, when VAT was introduced, there were just two tax slabs. By 2017, just before being replaced by GST, there were 17.

The Jurisdictional Tax Officer Arrives

The fortieth amendment to subclause 11 also says that the merchant exporter shall provide documents of the supplier to the jurisdictional officer. The GSTN identification number and the tax invoice number of the registered supplier, the duly signed warehouse receipt, the shipping bill and the proof of export are needed as per the amendment. This information is already available online and absolutely unnecessary. It is totally redundant. Since the government already has the consignment details of all the exported goods, why should they not refer to these documents internally?

Why should they repeatedly ask for documents since everything is already uploaded digitally in the government records? *Also, why should an exporter have to satisfy the tax officer about invoicing of the supplier?* GST was supposed to be a digital tax process, keeping the corrupt tax officers at bay. So, how and why is the tax officer making an appearance?

There are several conceptual problems apart from technical issues that GST faces. This has caused complications in business practices and has possibly shaved of half a percentage point from the GDP. It also showed that India's bureaucrats are living in bygone times and the nation has to live with their myopic vision.

GST Needs to Be Redrafted as a Simple Consumption Tax

For some strange reason, our bureaucrats and law officials who scripted the GST law in 2017 forgot the basic rule of evolution. New laws, like new buildings, must be efficient and smart and keep pace with the current-day needs and practices. GST 2017, unfortunately, missed the plot.

Getting the concept right is the first requisite of any legislation. The role of GST in the indirect tax system should first be made clear. GST is primarily a consumption tax. It should remain so. It should not be burdened with the role of doing every function in the erstwhile indirect tax system.

The problem with GST is its architecture. It is not a pure and simple consumption tax as it should have been. That would have made it business-friendly and consumer-friendly. The current GST law is a complicated amalgamation of multiple taxes that have existed in the past 70 years since independence. It has also an added burden of compliance. This makes it complex, archaic and pretty difficult for both the taxpayer as well as the tax administrators.

We have so far heard of the taxpayers' woes. The administrators' woes will start surfacing once the return matching starts. At that time refunds will be delayed, mismatches will balloon and the entries will all be subject to litigation. That is not a happy situation to have when you are creating a new tax law. We have mentioned half a dozen major drawbacks of GST below and hope that future governments take measures to address them.

GST Needs a Start-Up Solution

Complicated laws deter investors—not only foreign but Indian investors too.

More than 20,000 HNWI of Indian origin have moved out of the country since 2014. We spoke to a few Non-resident Indian (NRI) investors who are doing business in Africa, the Middle East and the US. All of them agreed that the only reason Indian investors go away from India is because we send them away.

They had expected things to change after Narendra Modi came to power and licensing corruption diminished. But, ease of business is still nowhere in sight as far as GST is concerned, despite India's improvement in the World Bank's ease-of-doing-business index. Here we had an extremely good opportunity to bring back investment to the nation. Have we lost the opportunity?

There are several other issues to be sorted. States have not made India a freeway that we had envisaged before GST. Barriers have gone officially but they still exist unofficially. Officers at the state level have not been moved from their postings. Some of the check posts have gone but not all. '*Gunda* tax' has actually grown in several places where barriers have been removed. Transporters are unhappy that the conversation that started with them has not looked at making goods movement across India simple. Transportation time has not been substantially reduced.

However, not all is lost. GST implementation has been complicated in many other nations. More than a 100 nations have GST-like laws implemented and not all of them are faultless. The Indian indirect tax laws were complex even earlier and it is no less complicated now. GST council, centre and states, the revenue department and GSTN that runs the platform are all to blame. It is a collective failure to make GST simple. Now, to make it simple, we need a dose of start-up innovation. Fortunately, the Modi government has done it before.

UPI and BHIM app were pro bono efforts by its founder Nikhil Kumar and a handful of 20+ app developers working with a start-up called India Stack. Their initial clients were FreeCharge and Flipkart before the Indian government asked them to create BHIM app post demonetisation. It was developed in three weeks flat and is the best digital payment system in the world as per a Fidelity report of 2017. A similar effort is needed to solve the GST puzzle. India needs a start-up solution and maybe an open contest to find the best answer to a simplified GST.

A New Law Must Be Modern and Quick to Implement

A new law must be modern in letter and spirit. The 2018 issue of India Development Update of the World Bank says that only four nations, out of the 115 surveyed, have four basic tax slabs like the GST in India—49 nations have a single tax slab, 28 nations have two and 34 nations have 3 tax slabs.

The onus of paying the tax and proving that he is not cheating is all on the taxpayer in GST. Repeatedly so. If he has exported a consignment and all the details are already with the customs, he has to still repeatedly file those details in all his GST returns. Why can't the government *babus* do the job of co-relation? Why cannot the government devise its own digital access system that does away with this redundancy?

Then, there are strange laws. A supplier to a merchant exporter must ensure that the merchant exporter has shipped the consignment within 90 days of purchase and must furnish the invoice details with GST returns. Why should an exporter abide by the directives of his supplier or share the invoice details of his consignment? There are hundreds of such meaningless clauses of the 1950s era that has entered the GST 2017 act. The audit trail devised to check tax evasion is repetitive and redundant. That needs to be revamped and the act needs remodelling before redrafting.

Where Is the Ease of Business?

There are two separate issues that make doing business under the GST Act a difficult proposition. The first is structural issues. Here GST is not attempting to usher in a new tax architecture of 2017. It is just trying to put the old laws together and make them work like a multipurpose all-weather contraption that can be found in rural areas all over India and is called *jugaad*.

The second is technical issues. The mistake in the invoicing format is only one of the major issues being rectified by GSTN. Of the 40-odd major technical issues identified, the Infosys-backed non-governmental organisation (NGO) handling the project had finished just about half by the deadline of the end of October 2017. This was only those errors that were identified early and were given to them by the GSTN council. *But, since the crucial structural issues remain unsolved, the software part would have to be redone repetitively.*

Make in India Affected

GST is essentially a consumption tax. It should be levied in a way such that consumers—and not manufacturers—bear a bigger burden. But, high GST of 28% on several key manufacturing essentials like cement or cables or 18% on steel imposed initially shows that our priority does not lie in boosting the manufacturing industry. Some of this has been now rationalised, but a lot more needs to be done for the manufacturing sector to thrive.

It is also unfortunate that we are not using this opportunity to discourage imports of non-essential goods, especially considering continuously rising trade deficit with China. While China tweaks its policy to ensure that the manufacturing industry of other nations is undermined by its own subsidised and liberally financed exports, Indian policymakers have no concern for Make in India. This despite PM Modi's goal to make Indian manufacturing prosper.

Part III

Energy

CHAPTER 5

Coal Makes a New Beginning: Production and Distribution Revives

The UPA government's reluctance to reform despite serious governance bottlenecks was slowing down the economy by the year 2012. The media tagged the UPA II government as one suffering from policy paralysis. Coal shortage and the resultant power crisis was one of the major challenges that the nation faced. By early 2012, power cuts became rampant. During August 2012, the northern grid collapsed, bringing down the interconnected eastern grid. Six hundred million Indians faced a nationwide blackout lasting nearly two days.

The centre blamed the power-starved northern states for overdrawing from the national grid. UP, Bihar and Punjab were facing acute power shortage. But, the real reason was a shortage of coal due to which states could not generate adequate electricity. Even the 24,000 megawatt (MW) of thermal power capacity added during the UPA II rule became inoperative and ineffective as it could not get local coal. The state-owned miners of Coal India Ltd (CIL) and Bharat Coking Coal Ltd (BCCL) that produced 90% of the nation's coal had not been able to ramp up production and meet the demand.

Policy paralysis meant indecision and reluctance to change what was rapidly deteriorating. In this case, it was the short supply of coal that hit the headlines. Power cuts due to coal shortage were rampant during the UPA decade. Apart from coal mining that was stagnating, railways racks were inadequate because of which there was a delay in supplying the mined output. Besides, the quality of coal supplied was below par.

The Coalgate Scam and the Clean Up

One of the first things that the Modi government did on assuming office was clean up coal auctioning procedure, the details of which have been elaborated in Chapter 2. These were long-pending reforms that were not done by the UPA government despite repeated prodding by the CAG. The opaque auctioning procedures of coalfields during the UPA rule had invoked the wrath of the CAG. The SC in 2014 ruled that the operators had obtained their licences through malpractice and cancelled the licences. One of the major problems was that the mine operators were holding on to their leased mines instead of developing them.

The mine operators had their own grouse. Corruption was rampant during the UPA regime. Getting the licences for mining through corruption was just the beginning. For developing a mine, you needed hundreds of clearances—land, environment, water, electricity, roads, transport. For each, you had to pay a price. Besides environmental clearance, a new social clearance clause had been incorporated by the UPA. This openly empowered NGOs that opposed miners tooth and nail. It gave them the opportunity to mobilise locals against miners. The clearances involved block, district, state and central-level clearances. And at each level, delays were endless and the payout was massive. Even the regimes close to the UPA faced huge roadblocks in developing the allotted mines. The total time for development of a mine after due diligence and completion of approval cycles was estimated to be 12 years.

Joining the dots gave a full picture. Coal shortage had hit the power sector. This resulted in power cuts and massive grid crash. Long hours without electricity directly affected the people. Meanwhile, acute coal shortage resulted in the rise of imports. This led to more foreign exchange outflow and affected the BOP. It, in turn, affected the CAD.

In March 2012, the Coalgate scam first came to light. The CAG draft report accused the central government of malpractices in the allocation of coal blocks. It said that between 2004 to 2009, the auction procedures were opaque, resulting in low coal output and losses. Soon the media was talking of a coal scam. During the summer of 2012, coal shortage and resultant power cuts across the nation made headlines. The media was now talking of coal shortage. On Monday 30 July, the northern grid collapsed due to overdrawing of power by energy-starved states of UP and Punjab. The power supply was restored 12 hours later but it was followed by another bigger grid collapse that saw both the northern as well as the eastern grid consumers plunged in darkness for 18 more hours. It was easy to connect policy paralysis on coal to the blackout. The media was now talking of the grid failure due to coal shortage.

The dots were all connected. The media and members of parliament made no bones about an inefficient government unable to manage coal production and the power situation. Coal and power shortfall became the talk of the town along with the talk of coal scam. There was a sense of doom and policy paralysis in the economy. A few weeks later, in August 2012, the final CAG report was placed in the parliament. It resulted in an immense uproar. The CAG estimated that losses of ₹1.86 lakh crore (₹1.86 trillion) were incurred due to malpractices in coal licensing.

Among the 25 private-sector power producers named as beneficiaries were Tata Steel, Tata Power, Jindal Steel and Power, Hindalco and Essar Steel. The report pointed to several malpractices and irregularities in tendering procedures that led to revenue loss for the exchequer. Following the scathing criticism by the CAG, the Standing Committee on Coal and Steel was set up that submitted its report to the parliament in 2013. It reported that the allocation of 193 coal blocks between 1993 to 2008 was conducted in an unauthorised manner. The SC took cognisance of the CAG report and cancelled allocation of 204 such coal licences in the year 2014.

Reducing Imports and Increasing Domestic Production

The UPA decade was one of the best for importers. Be it coal, oil or fertiliser, domestic production stagnated or declined even as imports rose. The fund flow into India was at its peak after Goldman Sachs discovered BRICS—an association of five major emerging national economies comprising Brazil, Russia, India, China and South Africa—at the turn of the century. Following the 9/11 attack on the US, many multinational enterprises also started hedging their bets and spreading their risks worldwide. The 2008 Wall Street crash further accentuated this trend and capital moved eastward. The easy flow of capital was used by India not to build domestic assets, but to pump up imports into India. This ensured lower prices but pushed up the trade deficit and hurt the BOP. The rupee increasingly came under pressure and in 2013 it finally crashed, losing 30% of its value to the US dollar in a couple of months.

The average import cost of coal in India as per data available at the Coal Controller's office was very high during the UPA II rule. At ₹6,128 per metric tonne, the five-year average was one of the highest in the world. As per International Energy Agency (IEA) data, other South Asian nations that imported coal during that period did so at 20% cheaper rates. The over-invoicing happened with the help of import agents facilitating payments into offshore accounts of *netas* and *babus*. Not many of them have been investigated.

However, a 2017 investigation by Directorate of Revenue Intelligence (DRI) reveals that Tamil Nadu Generation and Distribution Corporation, owned by the state government, was involved in an over-invoicing scam. The agency imported 24.4 million metric tonnes (MMT) of coal at a cost of ₹12,444 crore from Indonesia after 2012. The deals of five importers were channelled through middlemen in Dubai, Singapore, Hong Kong and the British Isles and invoices were inflated by 50% to 100%. Coal import deals from 2011 to 2014 were at their peak and often at inflated prices.

It was not due to corruption in licensing but the corruption in CIL and BCCL coalfields that created the shortage of coal supply during UPA II. CIL's coal production remained stagnant at 431 MMT during the fiscal year ending 2010 and 2011 and rose marginally to 436 MMT in 2012. As the pressure to supply coal mounted, the CIL let its minimum stock level dwindle and improved supplies marginally. The state-controlled miner sold around 452 MMT of coal in 2012–2013 and 462 MMT of coal in 2014–2015.

Even the cash-flushed public-sector giant NTPC Ltd (formerly known as National Thermal Power Corporation Ltd) was struggling to get sufficient and good-quality coal out of CIL and BCCL mines. NTPC Chairman and Managing Director Arup Roy Chowdhury told me when I interviewed him in May 2013, 'NTPC wants coal to be priced as per quality and that can happen only if an independent certifying authority exists that checks the various grades of coal coming out of the mines and certifies them as per calorific value.' The power producer was getting substandard quality coal from CIL that had low calorific value than specified and higher content of non-combustibles.

The big challenge was to revive domestic production and reduce imports. After the Modi government came to power, both the domestic coal supply and the power position improved. Imports jumped initially to 217.8 MMT during the year 2014–2015 to meet the initial shortfall but since then have fallen to 203 MMT in 2015–2016 and 191 MMT in the year ending March 2017.

The average procurement price of imported coal has also dropped by 25% and a 3-year average price works lower at ₹4,594 per metric tonne. As per the data available with the Coal Controller, both the import cost as well as the import volumes of coal were significantly higher during the UPA II. Figure 5.1 shows consumption and imports of coal from 2005.

Figure 5.1: Coal Production and Imports (2005–2018)

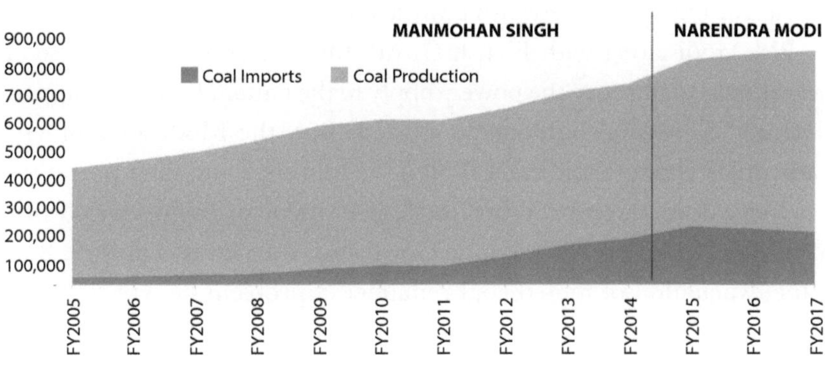

Data source: Indian School of Mines and IEA

However, risks remain as the sector is still starved of cash. With the price of imported coal rising and poor cash flow in the industry, there is little room for complacency. Coal crisis is not a thing of the past. The surplus capacity build-up that was expected in both the coal sector as well as the railways is still to happen. True, there is no problem when all things are normal. However, *in early 2018 when the price of imported coal rose sharply, plants depending on imported coal had to shut down.* Though the coal secretary confirmed that supply position was comfortable, 11 power plants operated with just seven days of coal, seven plants had four days' stock while five plants including the giant 2,000 MW Mundra power station run by the Adanis were shut down. This was against the stated objective of the government to run the plants with the recommended 21 days' stock of coal.

Reviving Coal and Power Supplies

The Modi government groped around with solutions in the beginning as it started making policy changes. The efficiency of decision-making and the speed of execution initially was questionable. However, the intent to improve domestic production and bring down coal imports was never questioned. The coal imports that began under UPA grew threefold under UPA II from 48.8 MMT in 2007–2008 to 166.8 MMT in 2013–2014. We must remember that during this period coal production in CIL stagnated and no effort was made to improve the same. Imported coal at a higher cost was brought in as an emergency measure and the power and steel sector barely survived with a week's stock in hand.

PM Modi along with Piyush Goyal, the concerned minister, took several steps to improve the power supply to the nation. It did not happen overnight as several bottlenecks existed. But, the Modi government made quick changes and even shifted the ministers and their portfolios to achieve desired results. When the first 44-member cabinet was sworn in, in May 2014, D. V. Sadananda Gowda was the railway minister. But, as the evacuation of mined coal remained a problem he was replaced by Suresh Prabhu in the November 2014 cabinet reshuffle. Prabhu had handled the power ministry during the Vajpayee rule and was the chief of the advisory board to integrate the working of the energy and the coal sector.

The coal supply from the state mines started improving once the new government took over. Piyush Goyal as a minister of state was given the independent charge of power, coal and renewable energy. The mandate was to do whatever was possible to improve the power situation. The fact that CIL Chairman and Managing Director (CMD) S. Narsing Rao quit to join the state government under Chandrababu Naidu in May 2014 made the job easier for BJP. A new chief could be appointed to rejuvenate the monolithic organisation.

However, finding a new chief was not easy. The government reportedly spent ₹1.5 crore to advertise for this supposedly powerful and lucrative post. Unfortunately, there were no takers as CIL's reputation had taken a beating due to several controversies during UPA II. It took six months before S. Bhattacharya, former CMD of Singareni Colliery—a top coal mine at Singareni, who was on superannuation, was selected for the high-profile job.

One of the first things the Modi government did when it assumed office was clean up the faulty licensing procedures. A transparent e-auction procedure was set up within a couple of months.

CIL's coal output improved in the financial year 2014–2015 to 489 MMT but missed the target of 507 MMT due to a shortage of railway tracks. Though supplies rose significantly in the next year to 538 MMT, demand constraints ensured a moderate output of 559 MMT in the financial year 2016–2017. So, though the power situation is better than before, there is no steady growth in consumption even after four years. This shows lack of experience of the politicians and the administrators to identify real problems. The issues are associated partly with inadequate demand but largely with large-scale destitution in rural India. On the one hand, 240 million rural poor across India live in darkness and, on the other, power producers find idle capacities with no buyers.

The power sector still has many legacy problems that have been carried forward from the UPA era. The distribution companies are saddled with debt and largely running hand to mouth. A third of the country has very poor quality and inadequate power supply and infrastructure. Over 50 million rural homes still remain in darkness largely due to poverty.

CHAPTER 6

Opportunity to Build Oil Infrastructure Lost: High Taxes Hurt the Consumer

The Modi government had bad luck that it inherited an economy in distress. But, it was also blessed with good luck. Oil prices that roiled the global markets during the UPA rule were subdued in 2014. It gave the new government a much-needed fiscal relief. Crude prices continued to plummet for the next 18 months and as a result, India's import bill plummeted. Importantly, the pressure on the BOP eased.

However, the Modi government did not take advantage of the situation. They did not start building the nation's oil infrastructure with the surplus. Nor did they pass on the benefits of low crude prices to the citizens. Instead, they cut the subsidy and raised taxes on oil products. As a result, the price of petroleum products dropped only marginally in India. While people around the world enjoyed the benefits of low crude prices, the Indian consumer could not benefit from *achhe din.* And with those taxes, the Modi government focused on bringing down the fiscal deficit. It also spent a lot of money on development projects outside the oil sector.

The fiscal deficit in 2014 was just 4.5%, which is not too high. Even during the later years of the UPA regime there was a conscious effort to reduce the deficit. When UPA II came back to power in 2008, the fiscal deficit was a high 7.8% and the subsidies as a percentage of GDP exceeded 2.3%. But, even as subsidies rose (Figure 6.1), there was a steady effort to raise taxes and reduce spendings by the Manmohan Singh government. All at the cost of infrastructure building.

Figure 6.1: Oil Subsidies (March 2005–March 2018) (INR billion)

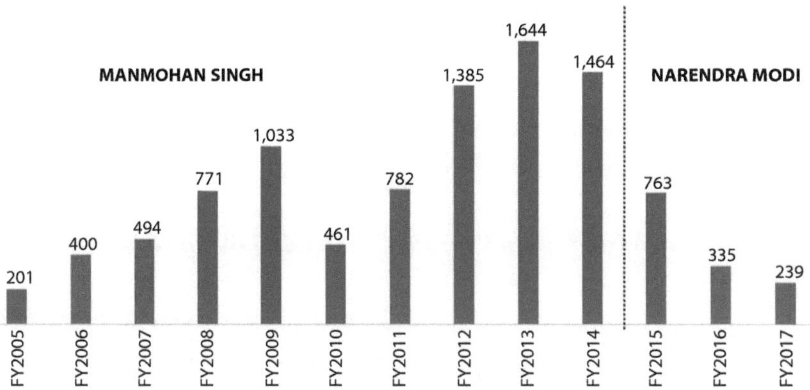

Data source: Ministry of Petroleum and Natural Gas

According to Gabriel Sterne of *Oxford Economics*, every $20-fall in oil price could increase global growth by 0.4%. Sterne, quoted in the *European Tribune* in December 2014, says, 'Producers have financial surpluses and don't tend to cut back, while lower prices redistribute to those who have a higher propensity to consume and to invest.' But, this wealth redistribution did not happen in India. Neither did the Modi government consume more and build up the much-needed oil reserves, nor did they invest heavily in infrastructure. The Indian economy could have taken off like a slingshot if the savings of crude oil during the three-year period of 2014–2017 had been invested in building up the energy sector infrastructure.

What Were the Crude Oil Savings?

The median price of global crude during the last three years of the Manmohan Singh government from April 2011 to March 2014 was $90 per barrel. The first three years of the Modi government saw the median price drop to $40 per barrel. Oil prices even nosedived to below $30 in the later part of 2015. The average saving in import price of crude was a humongous $50 per barrel. If these savings were invested judiciously, it would have brought 1% additional growth to the Indian economy in the first three years of the Modi government.

India imported a total of 545 MMT of crude in the last three years of the UPA rule with an import bill of $427 billion between 2011 to 2014.

The first three years of the Modi government saw higher total imports of 606 MMT as domestic production kept slipping. However, the import bill sharply dropped to $247 billion in the three-year period (2014 to 2017) resulting in savings of over $180 billion. Figure 6.2 gives the details of oil production and imports. This translated to humongous savings of ₹12,00,000 crore during the three-year period from 2014 to 2017.

Figure 6.2: Production and Import of Crude Oil (MMT)

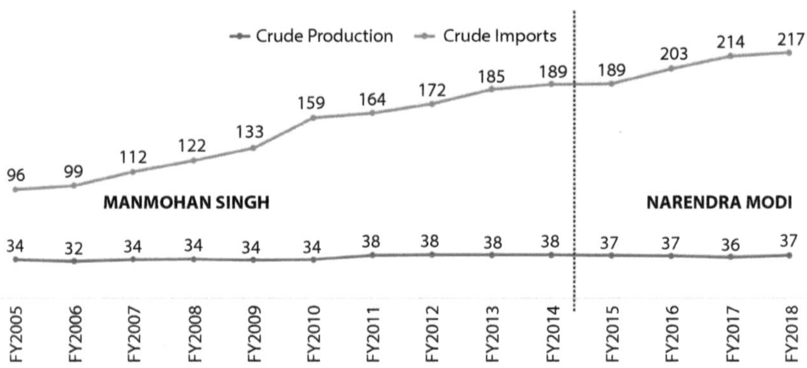

Data source: Ministry of Petroleum and Natural Gas

In the first three years of the Modi government, India saved around 2% of its GDP each year due to low oil prices. Had part of this been spent in boosting oil infrastructure and building storage capacity, it could have led to high growth. But, it was used in reducing the fiscal deficit and plugging in social projects like SBM. Some of it was frittered away due to unplanned measures such as demonetisation. As a result, India failed to make headway taking advantage of this enormous opportunity provided by low crude prices.

First Steps Towards Consolidation of Oil Majors

A year after the Modi government came to power, they mooted a proposal for consolidating the public-sector players in the oil sector. The consolidation made sense because of three reasons. Firstly, it would create integrated players with the capability of drilling, refining and marketing. Secondly, it would increase the capital base of the companies and make them world-scale players who could match global oil majors in financial muscle. Thirdly, and most importantly, it could help them counter oil volatility and manage operations better.

All over the world, major players like ExxonMobil, Shell, British Petroleum (BP), Chevron and Total have worked steadfastly towards integrating their service capabilities. Even Saudi Arabia with Aramco, Russia with Rosneft and Gazprom, and China with Sinopec have consolidated its offerings. Besides, each of these companies is many times bigger than Oil and Natural Gas Corporation Ltd (ONGC) and Indian Oil Corporation Ltd (IOC), the two largest Indian corporations. If India's oil sector had to grow and prosper, integration was the way forward.

Soon after the announcement of consolidation in the 2016–2017 budget, there was a discussion on India's oil strategy on Lok Sabha Television (Lok Sabha TV). Here I was engaged in a discussion with former petroleum secretary S. C. Tripathi who said that the proposal to consolidate the upstream and downstream companies first came up in 2005 when he was the secretary of the petroleum ministry during the UPA I. However, it was struck down by the expert committee despite obvious benefits. The 2016–2017 budget proposal was also pushed into the back-burner by the committees who looked into it. For this whole year, very little was said or done about it.

It was the fiscal deficit gap of the financial year 2017–2018 that brought about the actual consolidation in the oil sector. The decision to disinvest the 51.1% government stake in Hindustan Petroleum Corporation Ltd (HPCL) to ONGC for ₹369.15 billion (₹36,915 crore) was taken late in January 2018. With this, the government exceeded its disinvestment target by ₹20,000 crore and kept the deficit pegged at 3.5%.

ONGC Chairman Shashi Shanker, when asked if this would be followed up by the acquisition of Mangalore Refinery and Petrochemicals Ltd, said, 'That is a logical step. We see an advantage in that but cannot give a time frame.' The merger of the drilling major with the refinery and marketing arms will help create the first of the two integrated oil majors that India needs. The second should come about by the consolidation of Indian Oil Corporation (IOC) with Gail (India) Ltd (formerly Gas Authority of India Ltd), Oil India Ltd (OIL) and Bharat Petroleum

Corporation Ltd (BPCL). But, nobody knows if this will happen or when it will happen.

India Needs an Energy Security Plan that Reduces Imports

To be a $5 trillion economy by 2025, India needs to invest in energy resources massively. The trend should be towards reducing the carbon footprint as well as improving the efficiency of investment. While renewable energy is the future, it will not be enough anytime soon to give energy security that India needs for the next 10 years.

India needs a comprehensive energy security plan. It needs to not only invest in renewable energy but also reduce dependence on coal. For that to happen, it needs to make the oil supply chain more efficient. Its oil infrastructure needs to be upgraded, especially the natural gas sector that has a much lower carbon footprint and can help meet India's air pollution challenge.

India needs investment in horizontal drilling technology to improve chances of discovery in older fields. It needs to add an additional 60-days storage capacity along its ports. It needs thousands of kilometres of supply pipelines to bring the oil and gas to its cities. Pipelines are always the cheapest and the safest form of transport for oil and gas. It needs a few more natural gas terminals to ensure smooth and organised imports of gas. India's reluctance to pump money into oil infrastructure is surprising.

Creating oil and gas infrastructure not only reduces the energy cost, but it also brings in investment and generates employment. President Barack Obama laid forth an ambitious energy security plan in his first term that promised to reduce US oil imports by half in a decade. During his first term, the US cut oil imports by 3.6 million barrels a day.

According to The Environmental Protection Agency (EPA), their carbon dioxide emissions reduced by an estimated 13% and fuel economy values increased by 16% between 2007 and 2012.

By the end of his eight-year term, US oil production had grown by 88% from 5 million barrel per day to 9.4 million barrels per day. In 2008, the US crude oil net imports were 11.1 million barrels per day. At the end of President Obama's term, thanks to the investment in solar, wind and oil production, the US had reduced imports to just 4.7 million barrel of oil per day.

Gas Must Replace Coal to Reduce Atmospheric Pollution

India also needs to use more gas in its utilities and industrial plants and reduce the atmospheric carbon content. Air pollution has become a key issue for cities in northern India. Very little is being done about it though the problem is increasing each year since the last decade.

This is going to create a massive health crisis across northern India and surge of respiratory diseases. I have spoken about these in my discussions in Lok Sabha TV and Rajya Sabha TV and also in several newspapers like *The Indian Express* and *DNA*. I have also written about it in think tank publications of Centre for Science and Environment (CSE)—*Down to Earth*, The Energy and Resources Institute (TERI)—*TerraGreen*, Observer Research Foundation (ORF) and Pragati (refer Bibliography). But, very little seems to happen. The Central Pollution Control Board, the government and the courts are going after diverse solutions they are unable to control or even manage. But, they are not trying to do the obvious.

They are not trying to reduce the use of dirty fuels and step up the use of clean fuels. The World Health Organisation (WHO) report each year brings out a report on air pollution across the globe. It also identifies the most-polluted cities around the globe. During the last decade, China undergoing rapid industrialisation, found as many as 27 of its cities in the list of 50 most-polluted cities in the WHO list. India started finding itself in the top 10 most-polluted cities of the world with the arrival of Delhi and Agra in the WHO air pollution list in 2010.

China went on ignoring the inevitable as under the law, discussion was not allowed on air pollution in China before 2015. But, a few of its activists kept on working relentlessly and posting news and videos of the polluted cities. Governments of other countries started using health advisories against travel to China. As the pollution level dropped from bad to worse in 2015, the Chinese government suddenly changed its stand.

It clamped down on coal-fired boilers in industries and homes and on the use of petroleum coke (petcoke). It gave them three months' notice to change over to natural gas or shut down. This was especially difficult as China is a cold country where coal-fired boilers provided heating to Chinese homes. Also, China is the largest global producer of cement and aluminium, having over 50% of the world's production capacity. And apart from coal, these units used petcoke, which was a bottom-of-the-barrel petroleum distillate at least 13 times more damaging than coal. Both the alumina manufacturing units and the cement units used petcoke that China imported from the US.

China also opened up and permitted discussion of air pollution in public. It speedily set up small, inexpensive air pollution checking units near the smoke belching units that were dirtying the skyline. China went a step further and encouraged public participation in identifying air pollution and the result was dramatic. Within a year of China's dramatic crackdown on coal and petcoke and switchover to natural gas in 2016, most of its cities exited from the WHO list of most-polluted cities. That year Indian cities replaced them and 14 of the 15 most-polluted cities of the world in WHO 2016 list were Indian cities.

Decrease in Production and Import of Natural Gas

One of the major drawbacks of the Modi government has been its inability to push up gas production and augment its gas imports. Unlike China, use of petcoke and coal are rising in India and the use of natural gas is reducing. While Delhi chokes under smog each winter, Delhi's gas power plants—270 MW Indraprastha Power Generation Co Ltd (IPGCL) unit at Pragati Maidan and 1500 MW gas station at Bawana—lie underutilised due to lack of natural gas. As a matter of fact, the generation of these stations, set up at a cost of over ₹5,000 crore, never even exceeded 50% because agreements for buying of gas were not completed.

The Bawana gas project was set up with a lot of fanfare by the Sheila Dixit government around a decade ago. Politicians then promised to the people that with this massive investment Delhi will have clean air and will be self-sufficient. It will not have to depend on dirty coal power from NTPC in Badarpur in the heart of South Delhi to meet the power needs of the city. But, those politicians have gone and the new Aam Aadmi Party

(AAP) ministry at Delhi and the Modi government at the centre have not taken an initiative to augment gas supplies to run the Bawana utility at its full capacity.

When I talked to V. Kumar, additional general manager, Solar & Gas of the IPGCL Bawana project, he told me that domestic gas supply is insufficient and imported gas is unaffordable. Production of natural gas has fallen by nearly 40% from 52,219 Million Metric Standard Cubic Metres (MMSCM) in 2010–2011 to 31,897 MMSCM in 2016–2017. Figure 6.3 gives the details of the steady fall in production of natural gas since 2011. So, the IPGCL plants have worked far below capacity. The unavailability of local gas and the high cost of imported gas is to blame for the underutilisation of plants. The distribution companies (discoms) will not buy expensive power from imported gas. So, IPGCL has not entered into a contract to buy expensive gas, immaterial of the fact that the capital is high on health hazard.

Figure 6.3: Natural Gas Production (March 2005–March 2018)

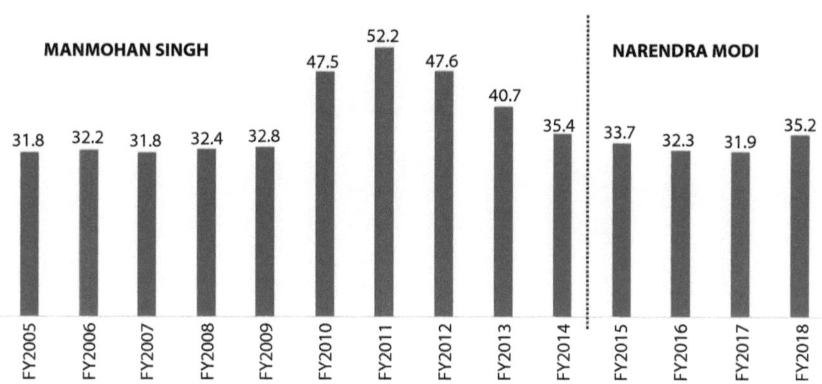

Data source: Ministry of Petroleum and Natural Gas

India needs to raise its domestic gas production. This is must, both for the public and the private sector. Krishna Godavari (KG) basin has shown increasingly poor output despite Reliance Industries Ltd having brought in global oil major BP into exploration business. ONGC has also been unable to significantly raise its gas output over the years. New players in the exploration area need to be welcomed. Besides, we need to recall that players like Equinor ASA (formerly known as Statoil) of Norway who had evinced interest were forced to withdraw from KG basin due to non-signing of agreements by the UPA government.

Also, it is important to sign cost-effective agreements for import of gas and install more liquefied natural gas (LNG) terminals. China and the US have invested hugely in gas pipelines. China is aggressively investing in gas infrastructure and planning to double its LNG terminals. State-owned Sinopec is planning to step up its LNG terminals to import 26 million tonnes of LNG. Currently 17 LNG terminals are used to import seven million tonnes of LNG at its east coast. China is going ahead with full steam to replace at least 10% of coal power plants with natural gas because it wants to reduce pollution. The Indian government should take the cue and take steps to improve its natural gas availability.

CHAPTER 7

A Remarkable Progress in Renewable Energy: Solar, Wind Cheaper Than Fossils

Few would have thought even a decade ago that renewable energy costs would drop as sharply as it did during the last five years. So, when the Modi government decided to go the whole hog and back the adoption of solar energy in India, there were sceptics. Would solar energy prices really drop and make it viable and competitive for large-scale adoption? Or would it be too early and too soon, like in the case of Spain, and leave behind a debt-ridden economy? After all, at above ₹5 per unit installation cost in 2014, it could hardly be viable, considering that existing coal-fired units were running at half the cost.

Fortune favours the brave. The Modi government took the risk soon after it assumed office. Installations of solar stations started on a massive scale. Along with the Indian government, the industry too willingly took the risk. And installation prices plummeted. India, which was hugely energy deficient at the time, had a chimera of hope that it could in the near future give all its citizens basic electricity supply at an affordable cost.

The success of solar energy was also due to the fact that China and the developed world adopted it on a large scale. That helped reduce the cost of manufacturing dramatically. Made-in-China solar panels, photovoltaic (PV) cells and components were cheaply available in the global market. But, having cheap components does not mean having a low-cost reliable energy-generating unit. There were several other challenges, including poor finances of utilities run by state governments. Additionally, lack of workforce ready to switch over to the new-age technology was missing.

The Success of Transparent Bidding

To make that happen, the Indian government adopted a robust time-tested procedure. It adopted a transparent, efficient, electronic, global tendering procedure with a reverse auction principle that was free of corruption and tampering. A reverse auction is a process in which all parties get a second chance to bid after the initial prices are disclosed. It gives a chance for the buyer to get the best prices. It effectively ensured that Indian utility companies run by state governments that carried big baggage of corruption and poor finances could also benefit from the transparent and centralised tendering procedure.

Installing a solar PV station is much less complicated and relatively faster than installing a thermal power plant. It is less of engineering and more of trained assembly technology. It is here that global solar engineering, procurement and construction (EPC) companies and Indian players competed to provide low-cost solar stations for use by discoms or electricity-distribution companies.

Apart from a few old horses like Tata Power and Vikram Solar, most of the Indian companies in solar energy were millennials. They, along with foreign players like SunEdison, Gehrlicher Solar, BELECTRIC, Suntech Power, Solairedirect infused fresh breath and capital into the ageing Indian energy industry. By creating a transparent bidding process and low-cost efficient delivering mechanism, the complexity of state electricity boards (SEBs) running and operating solar plants was dispensed with. A new generation of power producers took birth who were not saddled with the old baggage of high debt and recurring losses of the SEBs. Besides, each project by a foreign EPC contractor brought in sizeable foreign direct investment (FDI) in the sector. The results were almost instant.

Upping the Ante in PV Installations

India added 20,000 MW of solar power between 2010 and 2017 with 9.6 gigawatt (GW) installations added in 2017 alone. According to Mercom, India's solar project tracker, 18.4 GW installations were utility-level installations while 1.6 were rooftop solar installations. Telangana, Karnataka, Andhra Pradesh and Rajasthan accounted for more than 50% of the installations. The push given by the Modi government to solar power ever since it assumed office in 2014 ensured that the target of 20 GW by 2022 was achieved four years ahead of schedule. Figure 7.1 gives details of solar installations in the last decade. The revised target for renewable energy for 2022 is 100 GW, which looks achievable, considering China is adding around 60 GW solar installations every year.

Figure 7.1: Solar Installations (March 2005–March 2018) (MW)

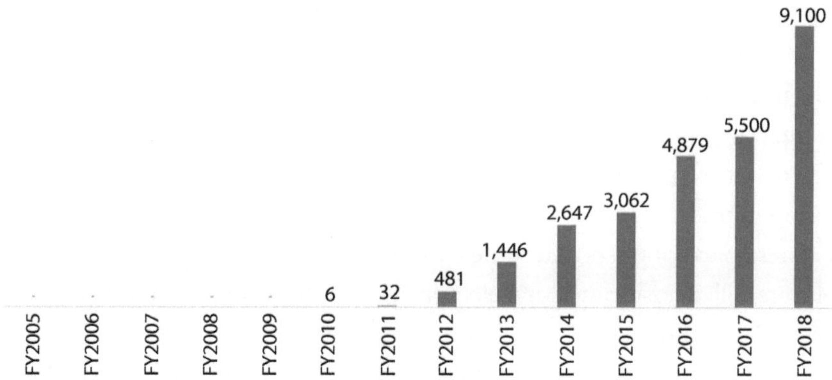

Data source: Ministry of New and Renewable Energy

The year 2017 saw the world install nearly 100 GW of solar plants. China accounted for almost around 55 GW to 60 GW, followed by the US with 10 GW and India with 9.6 GW. For the first time ever, India witnessed more solar installations than the installation of thermal plants. At the same time, the rate of solar power fell below the rate of thermal power in reverse auctions. In Bhadla, Rajasthan, the rate of solar electricity at reverse auction was as low as ₹2.44 per unit—much below the rate of power from an NTPC coal-fired station.

Falling Prices Have a Downside

It is expected that India will overtake the US next year in solar installations simply because India needs new energy plants at low cost. With the rate of solar power dipping below coal-fired plants, India has the reason to ramp up her solar installations. But, not everything is hunky-dory. The falling tariff rates are a huge issue because buyers feel that the free fall will continue. They are not buying power from the solar units that were installed when the prices were higher. This increases the risk for plant suppliers who need to be both competitive and profitable. The downside of rapidly falling prices is the disruption it causes amongst existing players. Will they remain profitable or simply go out of business? Will foreign players with much deeper pockets keep undercutting prices till local players go bankrupt? We must remember that we can add 200 GW capacity in the next five years at a low cost only if we have a strong domestic industry that manufactures nearly third of the installed capacity. Else, solar prices in India will start getting volatile and out of control like crude oil prices where our import content is around 80%.

But, Indian companies are wilting under pressure from Chinese companies who have cut PV cell prices drastically to capture the market. There are over 100 local Indian cell makers who are struggling due to the slump in prices. Most of these companies were again dependant largely on Chinese part suppliers and some consolidation was needed. Many of these players will diversify into rural electrification projects where customisation is needed that cannot be done without local engineering inputs. But, there are a lot of big names, including Jupiter Solar, Indosolar Ltd and Moser Baer India Ltd, who have set up large manufacturing capacities and are struggling to win contracts due to price undercutting by the Chinese counterparts.

States Increase Risk for Generators

In May 2018, a new risk surfaced in India's infant solar energy programme. The rates for the solar energy plummeted below coal power plants as Phelan Energy, Avaada Energy, SoftBank and Cleantech quoted rates of ₹2.63 per unit, which was 18% lower than coal tariff rates of NTPC's latest installations. Subsequently, the four-phase Bhadla plant saw even lower rates of ₹2.44 per unit being quoted.

In April 2018, Solairedirect, a French solar energy firm, had quoted ₹3.15 per unit and had won the bid for the 250 MW NTPC solar plant at Kadapa in Andhra Pradesh. That was below the rate of coal power produced by NTPC and was way below the rates for solar installations quoted in the previous year. So, everyone thought that it was a win-win deal with the state getting FDI and green power at a lower rate than conventional power.

Still, when the tariff fell by ₹0.60 in a month at the Bhadla project in Rajasthan, Andhra Pradesh turned greedy and backed off from signing the power purchase agreement because power from the Kadapa plant would be 20% more expensive than that from the Bhadla plant. Such behaviour cannot be encouraged and a no-escape clause needs to be put in place to ensure that whatever is finalised through international bidding is bought by a state.

A state should not be able to walk out when the cost of power is falling after the project has been assigned to it. The energy secretary of Andhra Pradesh Ajay Jain reportedly told the financial press, 'We do not want to buy power from Kadapa. We are surplus in power. We have given a letter to NTPC to sell power to someone else. We are yet to sign the power purchase agreement (PPA).' International agreements need to be honoured, only then will FDI flow in smoothly and seamlessly to our states. If other states start behaving as Andhra Pradesh did, the whole solar energy programme in India could crumble.

The continuously falling solar power rates in India is attributed to it being perceived as the second-largest solar market in the world where every player wants a toehold. The National Solar Mission has a target of producing 175 GW of green power by 2030, which appears easily achievable. With 300 sunny days a year, India has a potential of 750 GW of solar energy, considering six hours a day of bright sunshine. Solar power could even become disruptive in the next five years with prices crashing to below ₹1 per unit. It could lead to major changes in the energy sector and even change the way we consume energy today.

At prices lower than ₹1 per unit, energy would be truly affordable. Besides, without the carbon footprint of fossil fuels, it would be possible to consume large amount of energy without any side effects. Solar energy stored effectively in batteries could be disruptive like data stored in servers. Data costs have fallen 10,000 times in the last 50 years while data speeds and applications have increased meteorically. Energy stored in batteries will be a disruptive game changer in the coming decade with similar potential.

India's total power generation is just above 300 GW, of which just 15% is from renewable energy including hydroelectricity and 85% is from coal-fired power plants. So, the scope of adding a 100 GW of solar power in the next four years and another 75 GW by 2030 is clearly possible in India. Such an opportunity is not available in any other destination outside China. But, as China is an extremely competitive and a difficult marketplace for foreign EPC contractors, global players are making a beeline for India. These global players and FDI investors will flock to India as long as Indian buyers and state governments stick to contracts and agreements.

Wind Energy in India Has Big Players in the Fray

Though low-key, the wind energy scenario was much better than the solar energy industry before the Modi government took charge. The rates for wind energy were much lower than the rates solar producers could offer then. Many major global wind turbine makers with over 20 GW global installations had arrived in India over a decade ago. Big names like Vestas, Siemens Gamesa, Enercon and General Electric (GE), along with the homegrown global giant Suzlon, all had a manufacturing presence in India. Besides, several smaller Indian players like Inox Wind, Orient Green Power, ReGen Powertech and Indowind have come into limelight.

While solar energy capacity was just 2.34 GW in 2014, wind energy capacity was already 21 GW. With 100% FDI permitted in renewable energy projects along with various other tax incentives, the door was wide open for foreign investors. Whereas wind capacity showed a healthy growth rate in the last four years to add 13 GW of power (Figure 7.2), solar installations were one step better, adding 18 GW in this period.

Figure 7.2: Wind Installed Capacity (MW)

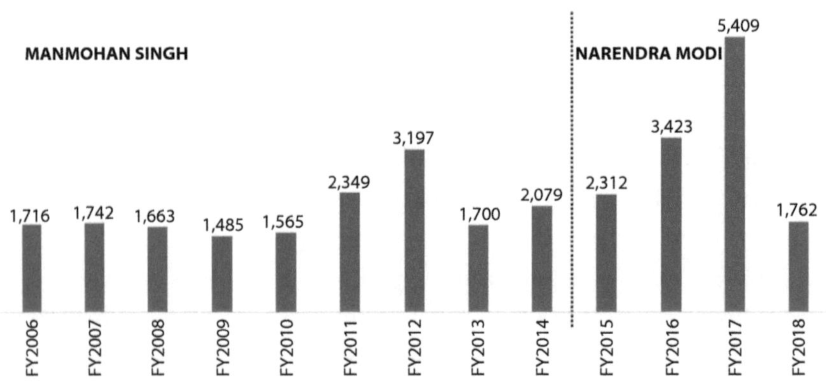

Data source: Ministry of New and Renewable Energy

However, there was a catch in the rate of power offered. The reverse auction system introduced for solar power had brought down solar energy rates to one of the lowest in the world, but wind energy rates in India remained high. While North America and Europe had seen wind energy rates dive to a level below solar energy, in India, wind power remained stubbornly at around ₹5 per unit.

Wind Energy Enters Era of Reverse Auction

In 2017, the government of India, which had set a target of 60 GW installation by 2022, decided go in for a reverse auction system. It asked Solar Energy Corporation of India (SECI) to sign a 25-year contract with the winning bidders and sell the power to electricity discoms. In doing so, it removed the risk of wind turbine makers entering into financial agreements with SEBs that were anyway in poor financial health. Besides, it also eliminated the risk of non-payment or arbitrary cancellation of contract by state governments.

To achieve the target of having 60 GW of installed wind energy capacity by 2022, the government has invited tenders for 2,000 MW of wind power projects connected to the inter-state transmission system. SECI would sign 25-year PPAs with the winning bidders and sell the power to electricity distribution utilities.

The ceiling tariff has been set at ₹2.93 per unit. A company can bid for a minimum capacity of 50 MW and a maximum capacity of 300 MW. Smaller Indian companies are unhappy with the minimum capacity because it keeps the Micro, Small and Medium Enterprises (MSME) section out of the bidding process. But, this is the only way to ramp up wind installations quickly and the government cannot be faulted on this account. Acquiring land, permissions and other infrastructure to connect upcoming wind projects to electricity grid would be a responsibility of a developer.

Power and Renewable Energy Minister R. K. Singh had announced in November 2017 the breakup of his action plan for completing 28 GW of wind auctions by financial year 2020, leaving a margin of two years to complete the projects by 2022. The present wind power installed capacity in the country is nearly 32.5 GW, comprising around 9% of total power-generation capacity.

Globally, India is at fourth position—after China, the US and Germany—in terms of wind power installed capacity. Capacity addition of wind energy had ebbed in the first half of financial year 2018. At significantly lower prices, only 421 MW was added in the period, as against the record 5.5 GW addition in 2017. However, installations are expected to improve with time.

The Ministry of New and Renewable Energy introduced the competitive bidding system for wind power procurement in February 2017, marking a shift from the feed-in tariff (FiT) regime. The reverse auction mechanism helped SECI discover an unprecedented low price of ₹2.64 per unit. Later, Gujarat recorded wind power tariffs as low as ₹2.43 per unit in December 2017, nearly half the average of ₹4.5 per unit wind tariff under FiT. It will take a few years to find out how the new policy will play out but as long as too many changes are not done it should work out fine, knowing that less than a dozen Indian states can benefit from wind power.

Off-Grid Installations

Low-cost solar and wind power will also help off-grid installations that are needed to provide connectivity to the rural hinterland in India where there is no grid power. There are many remote villages in India with a population of 500 to 1,000 people that have no electricity infrastructure. Whereas the government is trying to cover many of these villages by extending the grid infrastructure, it is not possible to do it economically by conventional methods. This is because the total electricity consumption by many of these villages is less than 100 kilowatt (KW).

The only way to give electricity to such remote isolated villages is through off-grid solar or wind power. Even isolated households where last-mile cable connectivity proves uneconomical are being fed by independent solar units. Renewable energy is one of the areas where significant strides have been taken and a lot of progress has been made. It holds out a lot of promise for the future.

India's per capita energy consumption is one of the lowest in the world and nearly a tenth of many European nations and just 7% of the US. We already have a huge pent-up demand for energy. We have also made a reasonable beginning in the installation of renewable energy plants. If our policies are right and we adopt transparent bidding procedures and good payment policies, we can meet all the energy shortfall through renewable energy in the next few years.

Fortunately, the Modi government does not have a gung-ho attitude to nuclear power as UPA had and is not hurriedly pushing through any nuclear deal. While nuclear power is a proven source of cheap and clean electricity, it is prone to risks. The hazards from nuclear plants at Chernobyl, Three Mile Island and Fukushima are too hard to ignore. India does not have disaster-management skills and technological capability to handle a major nuclear risk. As of 2018, the total installed capacity of nuclear power was 6,780 MW, which was 2% of the total generation capacity.

Not much is happening in the large hydropower sector either, though hydropower has huge potential and accounts for 13% of the total installed capacity. As of March 2018, the total installed capacity of hydropower plants was 45,403 MW as against 69,022 MW of renewable power. The reason for decline in this sector is possibly because of high-decibel protest politics that accompanies hydropower. Besides this, complex land-acquisition norms and high capital cost and gestation period of large hydropower projects are major deterrents.

Part IV

Manufacturing and Infrastructure

CHAPTER 8

Mining in the Pits:
Activism and Illegal Mining Continues

Mining in India is in a state of neglect. Things have not improved in the last few years even after the Modi government took over. The UPA rule was highly detrimental to mining in India. This was largely due to rampant corruption, illegal mining and activism. NDA has done little to reverse the trend. As a matter of fact, in some sectors, it has performed even worse. Private-sector mining that was expected to grow received several blows both from courts and state governments.

Nearly 80% of the mining done in India is in the coal sector, largely by government-owned monopolies. Some improvement has been noticed where public-sector companies are doing the mining. Similarly, there are no issues where Tatas, India's largest private-sector miner, operates mining leases. But, India owns the fourth-largest deposit of coal, the fifth-largest deposit of bauxite and the sixth-largest deposit of iron ore globally. Other than coal or iron ore mining that is largely done by the public sector, mining activities in 80 metals, non-metals and other mined products have declined. Also, operations have become more unpredictable and disjointed, leading to disruption of mining as a business activity across India.

In 2016, India found itself placed amongst the least-attractive mining destinations of the world as per Canada's Fraser Institute annual survey. The survey, which is widely regarded as authoritative by mining investors, struck India off its list in 2017. This is because India, along with a dozen other countries, failed to reply to the minimum questions needed to rate a country as an investment destination for mining. Possibly, India failed to respond because it would have had to report the closure of major mining projects and withdrawal of ArcelorMittal, Pohang Iron and Steel Company (POSCO) and Rio Tinto from India. Still, there is no major strategy being devised to stop the exit of global miners from India. Also, there is little being done to enforce mining laws strictly on those who still operate the mining leases in the country. This is a strange approach for a nation that is trying to prove itself as a business-friendly destination.

Courts Act on Environmental Violations and Politician-Miner Nexus

The mining industry in India has legacy issues from the last decade. In 2012, the SC banned mining of iron ore in Goa after several irregularities came to light. Justice M. B. Shah Commission, appointed by the SC, unearthed a scam of ₹35,000 crore that had ravaged the picturesque state, which earned its principal revenue from tourism.

The Commission's report found deep-rooted corruption and malpractices due to a nexus between politicians, bureaucrats and miners. It also found environmental abuse and degradation as miners had flouted sustainable mining norms to leave the land polluted, devastated and pock-marked. The state government failed to take any corrective action.

Following the report, erstwhile Congress chief minister, Digambar Kamat, who was also the mining minister between 2007 and 2012, has been booked, along with the principal secretary of mines Rajiv Yaduvanshi and other bureaucrats and mining contractors in several cases. But, courts and investigations in India are slow paced and there has still been no convictions. Also, adherence to mining laws did not improve much after the government at the state and the centre changed. In 2015, the SC again had to intervene and quash 88 mining leases on account of violation of environmental norms. Mining in Goa has been going on since independence, but problems have only surfaced in the last decade due to politician-miner nexus. Environment violations during this period not only ravaged the environment, but also shut down the entire industry, leading to the loss of lakhs of jobs.

In December 2017, Madhu Koda, a chief minister of Jharkhand between 2006 and 2008, along with Coal Secretary H.C. Gupta and state Chief Secretary Ashok Kumar Basu, was convicted by a CBI special court in the Coalgate scam. They were convicted of criminal conspiracy and for favours given to Jindal group in coal mine allotment at the behest of Congress member of parliament Naveen Jindal. Koda was the mining minister under Arjun Munda-led NDA government in 2005. In September 2006, Koda broke away from NDA and formed his own government supported by UPA and ruled the state till mid-2008 when Jharkhand Mukti Morcha (JMM) Chief Shibu Soren toppled his ministry.

Environmental violations by mining contractors have been rampant across India by both licensed as well as illegal miners. But, there have been several instances of responsible mining too that do not feature as highlights in media. 'Tata Steel's iron ore mine at Noamundi and National Aluminium Company's Damanjodi project are prime examples of vegetation post-mining,' points out Umesh Chandra Jena, deputy director of mines at Odisha's Directorate of Mines. As a matter of fact, the steel towns of Jamshedpur in Jharkhand, Bhilai in Madhya Pradesh and Hospet in Karnataka are prime examples of vibrant and prosperous mining towns in India.

Rio Tinto Withdraws from Bunder Diamond Deposit

India has a dozen large mining companies, most of which are in the public sector. The technological capability and financial muscle of Indian mining companies are highly limited. They mostly are active in surface mining operations that are easier but have several limitations. With open-cast mining, they often cannot retrieve high-grade ores deep below the earth, which can be retrieved by a vertical shaft or sub-surface tunnelling. Also, surface mining creates a lot of atmospheric pollution. So, in absence of foreign investors, the mining potential of India remains highly limited and grossly underutilised.

It is not that foreign investors have not been interested in India as a mining destination. Several large companies like POSCO and ArcelorMittal have evinced interest but were forced to retreat from India as anti-mining activism has been rampant and licensing is extremely time-consuming. The latest casualty was Rio Tinto that handed back the Bunder diamond deposit project to the Madhya Pradesh government after investing for 10 years in exploration. The global mining giant had discovered large deposits of diamond estimated to be around 27.4 million carats way back in 2004. If developed, it could turn Madhya Pradesh into one of the top 10 diamond-mining destinations in the world. The Indian diamond industry imports 85% of the roughs it polishes and sells mostly from Antwerp. The Bunder deposits could significantly reduce imports of roughs by the Indian diamond trade. Rio Tinto had already invested ₹1,200 crore in exploration and development of the project and had waited for more than a decade before it withdrew from the project.

The project was opposed by environmentalists as well as anti-mining activist groups. Located in the Chattarpur district of Madhya Pradesh near Panna diamond mines, the project lies in the midst of a dense forest that has limited access to road. It involved cutting down of over 5,00,000 trees that included high-quality sal and teak forests in an area of 970 hectares of reserved forest. The previous government had been dragging its feet for a decade over clearance of the project.

When the Modi government came to power, there were expectations that the project would get speedy approval. But, the three-member committee appointed to examine the case found that not only will it irreparably damage the forest cover but also disturb over a dozen wildlife species. The project was adjacent to Panna Tiger Reserve and Nauradehi Wildlife Sanctuary in a key tiger corridor. Besides tigers, the forest area was also home to leopards, sloth bear, gazelles and chowsingha.

Based on recommendation of the expert committee, the government suggested that sub-surface mining operations be conducted for raw uncut diamonds. However, the price of uncut diamonds in international market had significantly dropped with the arrival and rapid advancement of synthetic diamonds. With rising cost of underground mining, it would be a huge investment to put into the mine. Then again, the unclear Indian mining laws, political indecisiveness, bureaucratic delays, strident opposition to mining by activists and long-drawn approval procedures made the project unattractive for the global mining giant. In 2017, Rio Tinto withdrew from the project and handed back the mines to the Madhya Pradesh government.

Instability in Bauxite Mining Hits Three States

At the World Non-Ferrous Conference 2016, CRISIL (formerly Credit Rating Information Services of India Ltd), a ratings, risk and policy advisory service, presented a report titled, 'Indian Aluminium Industry: Geared for Growth'. It stated that aluminium consumption in India will grow by over 50% in the five-year period from 2016 to 2021 to 5.3 million tonnes. This was essentially based on positive demand indicators, both from the household as well as the industrial sector. Besides, export demand was also buoyant. Over the last few years, the aluminium industry has shown strong consumer demand worldwide and global aluminium prices have surged.

In the year 2015, China, which produced over half the global aluminium, cracked down on polluting smelters and forced older coal-based units to switch over to natural gas. Due to Chinese supply disruptions, global supplies were hit. Global alumina prices rose by 20% during the year 2016. As a result of better international prices, export of Indian aluminium rose by over 30% to 1.3 million tonnes from 0.97 million tonnes the previous year.

High demand of aluminium caused increase of bauxite supply but only temporarily. In the year 2015–2016, production of bauxite jumped by 24% to 28.12 million tonnes, only to drop down to 20.63 million tonnes in the next two years. One of the main reasons for the failure of the industry to ramp up bauxite mining is its inability to expand bauxite mining in the three states where its reserves are abundant. Chhattisgarh, Andhra Pradesh and Odisha have high-quality bauxite ores that are suitable for alumina production. Figure 8.1 shows India's inability to raise its output of bauxite mining despite availability of massive reserves.

Figure 8.1: Bauxite Mining (March 2005–March 2018) (MMT)

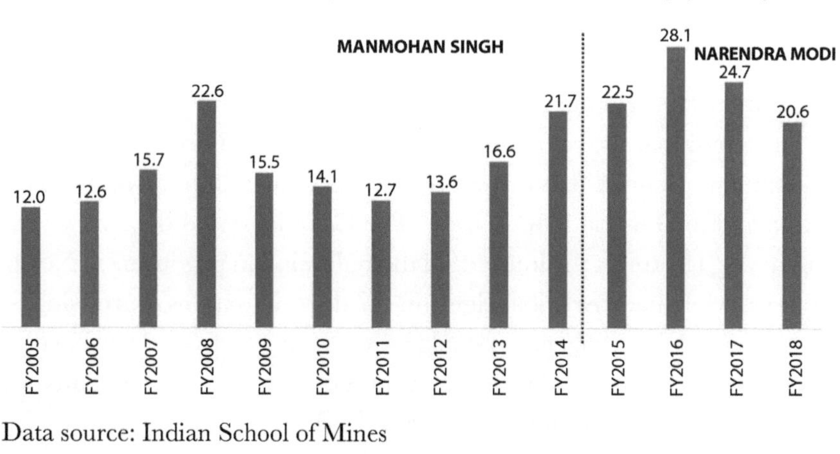

Data source: Indian School of Mines

These are three major mining states of India where over 500 coal mines and 300 iron ore mines generate a revenue of ₹8,00,000 crore annually. But, when it comes to value-added bauxite mining, these states produce less than ₹1,000 crore revenue despite having almost two-third of India's high-quality bauxite mines. The politics of bauxite mining ensures that it remains an untapped resource in the tribal belts of India despite the potential to change lives of the people by bringing prosperity to these states. Bauxite hills in Odisha, Andhra Pradesh, Chhattisgarh and along the eastern ghats are mainly just barren tracts of red soil, mostly with scarce vegetation or forest cover. The UPA government remodelled the Indian Forest Rights Act 2006 to empower the indigenous people who would now have the last say on whether there will be any mining or industrial activity on the land.

Skewed Battle for Niyamgiri

In 2007 the Odisha government, while replying to an SC query, clarified that only 1.52% of the total forest area was affected by bauxite mining in the Koraput and the Kalahandi district of Odisha. Still, violent protests were orchestrated by activists and environment groups when the proposal to mine Niyamgiri hills took shape during the UPA II rule. The reason for the protest was nothing to do with the destruction of forests or any conservation effort. The UPA government, who brought about the Forest Rights Act in 2006, unleashed 10,000-odd NGOs to work in mining belts across India so that they could actively campaign against legal mining in the guise of defending tribal rights.

A dozen tribal villages along with the NGOs, backed by Canadian International Development Agency (CIDA) and the United States Agency for International Development supported by ministers in the UPA government, claimed that the entire hill range should not be mined as it was sacred to Dongria Kondh tribe. The Canadians and the Americans were trying to protect the interests of their aluminium producers in North America while backing tribal rights in third-world nations. Surprisingly, they never indulge indigenous people in North America. So, the tribal god came out of the temples of India and usurped entire territories of bauxite-rich barren hillsides of Odisha's poorest districts.

The battle of mining in Niyamgiri in Kalahandi district was a bitterly-fought, no-holds-barred battle that ousted global mining majors from India's bauxite belt. There were many interested parties, including the Korean aluminium major POCSO, European conglomerate ArcelorMittal and London Stock Exchange (LSE)-listed Vedanta, who had evinced interest in mining projects in Odisha. Between the three, they had mining projects worth ₹1,00,000 crore (₹1 trillion) lined up in the state. One of the key projects that was in the eye of the storm was Vedanta's Lanjigarh alumina refinery project of one million tonnes per annum, set up at a cost of ₹5,000 crore (₹50 billion).

To feed bauxite to the refinery, the company along with the state-run Odisha Mining Corporation had planned to mine in nearby Niyamgiri hills. The project and the mining approval given by the UPA government saw the alumina plant being set up and the mine development start. But, in August 2010, Ministry of Environment and Forests (MOEF) rejected the forest clearance given to the mining project, sighting the 2006 Forest Rights Act. Why had they initially cleared the mining project is, however, not understood. When the state government went to court, SC, citing the 2006 Forest Rights Act, advised the state to get the consent of the *gram sabhas* or village council.

The state clarified that only 3% of the mining project would involve cutting down of trees. But, the court directed that as per the amended Forest Act, residents of the 12 villages directly affected by the project would have to be consulted before permission to mine could be granted. Meanwhile, K. C. Deo, the minister incharge of tribal welfare in UPA wrote to governors of the three states to stop bauxite mining and cancel all leases.

The UPA government not only amended the Forest Act and actively stopped bauxite mining in the three states, they also ensured that 10,000 NGOs working in the tribal belts actively opposed bauxite mining activities and organised the poor and uneducated villagers against mining and industrial development. In August 2013, it was at the behest of 1,500 villagers from 12 villages around Niyamgiri hills that the courts directed to stop mining in the region, on a land area of around 250 square km.

FDI Projects Shut Down Due to Non-Supply of Bauxite

It was farcical that a larger body of citizens in India (comprising of 1.3 billion people), who were the true owners of the mineral resources, was not consulted. Just 1,500 locals stopped bauxite mining in India. While Vedanta refused to quit and carried on its refinery gamely even after it lost the battle for Niyamgiri, ArcelorMittal dropped its steel plant proposal worth ₹50,000 crore and quit Odisha soon after mining was banned in Niyamgiri. Not only Vedanta and ArcelorMittal but even the Anrak Aluminium's United Arab Emirates (UAE)-backed FDI project shut down due to non-supply of bauxite.

Activism against bauxite mining was intense. Tribals, coached by foreign-funded NGOs, spoke a language of violence. They forcefully squatted and usurped the rights of the land and threatened to shoot down, with bows and arrows, anybody who mined. 'Wherever there are mineral deposits, locals will say that they worship according to their tradition, but it is the state government that should take the final call,' said the then Kalahandi district collector Bijay Ketan Upadhyaya. But, nobody was listening. Rampant activism in the areas influenced the tribals and made mining impossible. Tribal agitation was fomented particularly to cut the supply lines of FDI projects. And where tribal agitations did not succeed, Maoist rebels stepped in with a grenade and automatic rifles to stop all legitimate mining activity.

Such was the campaign against bauxite mining that the state-owned Andhra Pradesh Mining Development Corporation (APMDC) backed out of a contract to supply bauxite to Anrak Aluminium, a joint-sector FDI project. UAE's Ras Al Khaimah Investment Authority (RAKIA) had invested $44.71 million in this state-of-the-art alumina project, approved by Yuvajana Sramika Rythu (YSR)-led Congress government of Andhra Pradesh way back in 2007. As per the project terms, APMDC was to supply 224 million tonnes of bauxite to Anrak Aluminium per year.

The 1.5-million-tonne alumina refinery was completed in 2013 at a cost of ₹5,600 crore. The debt component was financed by a consortium of bankers led by SBI. However, no bauxite was supplied by APMDC, as a result of which the project's trial run and commissioning was held up. The Congress government refused to ensure bauxite supplies to the project during UPA II. It was expected that the logjam would be resolved after the BJP government came to power at the centre and its ally, Chandrababu Naidu took office in the state. But, the pressure of tribal politics has been too much for the Naidu government to handle.

After two years of delay and non-supply, APMDC unilaterally cancelled the bauxite supply deal. 'The deal is structured in a way that it will not benefit tribal people in any manner and is in the interests of the joint venture company,' Chief Minister Naidu said while announcing the cancellation of the contract in 2015. As a result of this decision, the foreign investor UAE's RAKIA has gone in arbitration to United Nations Conference on Trade and Development for non-supply of bauxite by India.

Bauxite mining in India is retreating and the Modi government has not been able to stop the tide. Bauxite is key to making of aluminium—the new-age lightweight metal that is vital for manufacturing. China produces half the aluminium in the world. It opens its door to value-added manufacturing. Aluminium production is key to its reduction of manufacturing costs. If India wants to be successful in manufacturing, it must build its capacities in aluminium. For that, India needs global investment in both bauxite mining and aluminium production. Unless that happens, Make in India will be an unachievable dream.

CHAPTER 9
Infrastructure: Reasonable Growth but Environmental Concerns Remain

Infrastructure development has been a strong point with all NDA governments, and with the Modi government it has been no different. Roads and airports are key focus areas but the environment and supportive infrastructure take a back seat. So, while there are some big pluses, there are some big minuses too in infrastructure development. There is a lot of sincere effort to develop infrastructure. But, while there has been reasonable growth in some areas, it is not sustainable in the long run because of certain fundamental deficiencies.

India is still at that stage of development where its planners are on a learning curve. So, while we have the capability to build aerial roads to ease city traffic, we do not have the vision to plan out the roads that become potential hotspots of congestion. A similar problem exists in our planning of the railway network. Twenty years ago, India had one of the largest rail traffic in the world. But, today it is woefully behind China and has been unable to create a proper high-speed congestion-free network for either freight or passenger traffic. We are planning bullet trains but since Rajdhani Express was introduced 50 years ago in 1969, we have not been able to increase the average speed of trains. As a matter of fact, the average speed of Rajdhani Express was reduced a decade after its introduction because supporting infrastructure was not conducive.

Similarly, our airports and sea ports have problems of infrastructure planning. While we are able to create spanking new airports and ports for air and sea traffic, we are unable to ensure that roads that lead to these airports and ports are planned well for quick entry and exit of humans and goods. A consignment takes just 12 hours to be imported or exported out of Sri Lanka and one week to four weeks to come in and go out of India by sea route.

Our cities, including our large metropolitan towns, have similar infrastructure problems. Drainage around cities is poorly designed and maintained. Even the new flagship town of Gurugram gets waterlogged and virtually submerged every monsoon due to the absence of adequate storm water drains. Smart city projects are being planned all across India in many states. They are also being planned without primary infrastructural capability, much like what is Gurugram today. These, unlike the smart cities of New York and London that have maintained and sustained leadership in infrastructure development for several 100 years, cannot grow beyond a certain limit due to lack of sub-city infrastructure.

Infrastructure Development in the Past Four Years

The progress of roads under NHAI was slow and patchy during the UPA rule. This is usually an effort jointly taken up with states and involves land acquisition. Whereas states give land to create infrastructure, NHAI takes up the work and completes the projects. Apart from the national highway projects under NHAI, there are state highway projects too that build a bulk of the infrastructure. Though the road-building effort has been streamlined in certain states, a lot more needs to be done. Replying to a parliament question, Urban Development Minister Nitin Gadkari in March 2017 said that 261 four-laning projects with a total length of 14,268 km, amounting to ₹1,83,180 crore (₹1,831.80 billion), 'are presently ongoing at different stages and are likely to be completed by May 2019'.

NHAI road-building effort has improved but is nowhere close to global benchmarks. NHAI says it will construct 10,000 km of road at a pace of 42 km per day in 2018. As per its press release, this is more than twice the 4,260 km of road built in 2014. For a nation as big as India, the effort is small and only three states—Maharashtra, UP and Rajasthan—built more than 1,000 km of highways annually.

Infrastructure development in India has been traditionally deficient. The weakness in India exists because of the failure of its planners to understand the two-layer structure that is needed for sustainable growth of any active city and commercial establishment. The infrastructure is built on weak foundations in India, but before we delve deep into the technicalities let us look at other services.

In the field of airport infrastructure, the situation is more encouraging but concerns exist. There are bright spots as well as dark spots. Let us see the dark areas first. Cabinet ministers in India, over the past 70 years, have made railway stations and airports in their constituencies despite it being unviable and with no significant traffic. Taxpayers' money has been spent without any accountability whatsoever. According to Civil Aviation Minister A. Gajapathi Raju, there are 25 ghost airports that were started in the last decade but have never been operated though regular maintenance and salary expenditure is being incurred on them. The maximum number of such ghost airports lies in Maharashtra. There is one at Gondia—which was former civil aviation minister Praful Patel's constituency, one besides Juhu, one each in Kolhapur and Sholapur, and the ones in Akola and Jalgaon have no traffic. Rajasthan and Punjab have three each, at stations such as Jaisalmer and Bhatinda. Apart from these underutilised destinations, another dark spot is infrastructure being stretched beyond capacity at airports where traffic has been growing at a rate of over 15% compound annual growth rate (CAGR). These are high-use airports where infrastructure facility has failed to keep pace. India needs quick and critical investment in high-speed roads for connecting to her top five airports.

But, there are bright spots too, especially on the demand side. Passenger traffic grew by over 18% to 265 million passengers in the year ending March 2017. Passenger traffic has been growing at 12.39% CAGR during the period 2006–2017 and freight traffic by 7.08% CAGR during the decade. Over 61% of freight traffic was international. This was possibly because India is a nation where e-commerce is just about taking roots. Three major airport projects are being planned along with two ports that are part of the government's flagship projects. But, it is clear as daylight that India's airport infrastructure will be inadequate and would lag behind the demand curve for at least one more decade.

Pollution and Environment Issues Have Often Taken a Back Seat

City infrastructure is in very bad shape across most Indian towns. This is a legacy issue and not only the fault of the current regime. Roads are clogged, housing is inadequate, garbage is spilling on the roads. Poorly and inadequately designed drainage systems cause waterlogging in streets. During monsoons, waterlogged streets develop potholes rapidly that further cause traffic snarls, accidents and disruptions. In winters, smog envelopes Indian cities. Particle matter suspended in air rises to as much as 10 times the safety limit. It causes respiratory diseases and kills thousands of young and old every year. Hospitals are inadequate and so are schools. Here too, like in everything else, demand exceeds supply hugely and services break down once too often.

In its attempt to push the development agenda, the Modi government has ignored environmental concerns in many cases and has been pulled up by NGT and the SC more than once. But, it still went ahead, speeding up clearances without necessary due diligence and without safeguarding the environment, for which a heavy price would have to be paid by this generation and the next. It is not that there were no environmental issues before. But, instead of tackling them urgently, the steps taken by the Modi government to boost infrastructure has augmented the environmental degradation, leading us to a near-crisis condition.

Three major environmental concerns affect the health of Indian citizens critically. In the coming decade, they may kill millions. The first is the rise of atmospheric pollution, followed by deteriorating quality of water and rapidly rising solid waste that remains uncollected on India's streets. It is not that the government is unaware and complacent about the issues. It is just that they are unable to find the right solutions in most cases. So, though some long-term measures have been taken to set things right, not enough short-term goals have been met to mitigate the current-day problems that we can witness right now.

India is Embracing Dirty Fuels despite Rising Air Pollution

Let us take the case of air pollution first. India has the dubious distinction of having 14 of its cities in the top 15 most-polluted cities list by WHO. It's capital Delhi, along with Agra, entered the top 10 most-polluted cities list first in 2010. Since then the number of cities from India has kept increasing and the capital city of Delhi has been severely affected by smog and particulate matter specially in the winter months of November to February every year. In May 2018, I wrote a piece in *DNA India*, titled 'Pollution Test! India Can Learn from China's Experience'. The article talked about how China improved its air quality by switching over to natural gas.

One of the prime reasons for air pollution is rise in carbon emissions. India is taking the right long-term measures and investing in renewable energy to reduce its dependence on fossil fuels. India's speed of implementation of renewable energy projects and its ability to bring prices of solar and wind power to the same level as coal-fired thermal power plants are commendable long-term measures. But, its failure to ramp up production of gas in both its public-sector as well as private-sector gas-exploration projects has diminished its ability to replace coal with gas, which is much less polluting. Most nations have opted for this solution to counter air pollution on short term, but India has been unable to do so. The details of India's inability to increase LNG consumption is already elaborated in Chapter 6 along with data given in Figure 6.3.

In fact, the use of dirty fuel namely petcoke and coal has increased since 2014 and is a cause of major environmental concern. While China cracked down on these two polluting fuels and forced millions of homes and factories to switch over to natural gas, India increased its consumption of both these fossil fuels. According to data released by petroleum ministry's Petroleum Planning & Analysis Cell (PPAC) in May 2018, gross domestic production of petcoke jumped four times to 13.9 MMT from 2013–2014 to 2017–2018 while imports of petcoke rose sixfold to 12.3 MMT. Though environmentalists have attempted to stop the imports by petitioning in the courts, their attempts have been futile. This, despite the SC-appointed Environment Pollution (Prevention & Control) Authority (EPCA) confirming that petcoke contains 17 times more sulphur than coal and 1,380 times more sulphur than diesel.

At the same time, the country's inability to run its gas power plants, in which it has invested billions, is a major cause of concern. Both production and imports of natural gas have been stagnant during the last four years, according to the data from petroleum ministry. The ministry says that the prime reason for the lack of rise in domestic production has been falling inputs from the KG basin exploration site run by Reliance Industries Ltd. On the other hand, India has not been able to negotiate reasonable prices for imports of natural gas. This has led to limited procurement and shortage in utility and fertiliser plants.

Deficiency in Water Quality and Quantity Needs Urgent Attention

Another area of deep concern is the condition of water supplies to both urban and rural India. The water availability in India has fallen to 1,400 cubic metre per person, making India a water-deficient nation. Though billions of rupees have been spent during the last decade on water infrastructure projects through MGNREGA, it has not been able to improve rural groundwater infrastructure due to lack of quality enforcement. The flagship project of UPA missed out on the chance to deliver due to poor execution. It should not be abandoned but revitalised and restructured to create high-quality aquifers and water body recharging system across India. This is a deeply technical subject that needs expertise and thorough planning and clinical execution. I wrote several articles in think tanks of CSE, TERI and ORF highlighting the problems (refer Bibliography), some of which has been elaborated in subsequent chapters on social development.

Apart from the quantity reduction, the quality of water has also deteriorated over the last two decades. In the first week of August 2018, Minister of State for Water Resources Arjun Ram Meghwal told Rajya Sabha that as many as 16 states in northern and western India had uranium presence in water well above safe limits prescribed by the WHO. These states included UP, Rajasthan, Jharkhand, Punjab, Haryana Chhattisgarh, Jammu and Kashmir, Gujarat and Maharashtra. Of these, the most severe effect was in Rajasthan where 75 out of 224 borewells dug showed uranium presence higher than that considered safe by WHO.

'No individual radioactive parameters have been specifically identified in India,' the minister added.

Similarly, in eastern India, there is a high presence of arsenic and heavy metals in groundwater. Several districts of UP, Bihar, West Bengal, Assam and Manipur are in grip of severe arsenic poisoning since the last decade. Although the central government has promised to take action, not much has been done on either preservation or updating data of aquifers and groundwater bodies by the Central Ground Water Board, the nodal authority that needs to be proactive. Periodic quality checking of aquifers and other groundwater sources is a must and the ministry needs to update the data each year on its website. The problem is that there is either no data or data that is 10 years old in most cases. So, whereas there are growing complaints of arsenic poisoning in half a dozen states from the health department, we have no clue of the number of waterbodies that need to be earmarked or isolated as unfit for drinking water purposes. The minister ended his answer by pointing out—just like other ministers have done for the last 70 years—that water is a state subject.

Solid Waste Needs Sustainable Management

The situation in managing solid waste is equally precarious. There is a lack of awareness and data on garbage and municipal solid waste (MSW), nearly a quarter of which remains uncollected and nearly three-quarters of which remain unprocessed. The data on MSW gets updated once in a decade during census—last held in 2010–2011. India has around 220 municipal towns. But, the last census provided data from only 59 towns or cities. The Central Pollution Control Board used to display this data on its website prominently a few years ago but does not do so any longer. Though the Modi government has several websites on *Swachh Bharat*, none of them display this data. As Indians are increasingly consuming more Fast-Moving Consumer Goods (FMCG) products, more plastic packaging is being used. This is accelerating garbage creation in our cities and landfills are overflowing. To cope with this situation, we need annual updating of MSW data and a clear-cut plan to tackle waste.

Apart from data, we need equipment and infrastructure to collect and manage the waste. The municipal corporations of India are dysfunctional and weakly structured to manage the services. The municipalities across India are perpetually cash starved and do not have the necessary equipment for collection and mechanised disposal of waste. Besides, there is corruption and incompetence at all levels. Apart from this, they are also faultily structured. Instead of having municipal authorities under the state government that controls land and police, municipalities come under corporations that have a separately elected body.

There is lot of chatter in India about local governments. But, the moot question—do they work?—remains. It has been observed by expert bodies that municipal body elections do not give enough autonomy or authority to the elected members. They are time and again dependant on state governments that oversee most functions. In the capital city, the AAP's state government and BJP that controls the municipalities are often seen squabbling over petty matters due to which the city suffers. It is time India takes a new approach to this outdated structure of city governance and creates a mechanism under a single political master who has control over the state.

Simply speaking, we are not doing enough to keep India clean. Previously the governments never used to acknowledge the problem. Today, they do talk a lot about it and are even investing serious resources. But, the efforts have not yielded significant results and the actions need to be revisited and new strategies need to be developed. Emphasis is needed on real-time data mapping through satellite and updating solid waste data showing collection and disposal on a real-time basis. Also, resources need to be pumped into commercialised solid waste disposal without segregation. Technologies like Polymer Injection Technology or any other alternative solutions that exist today which deals with MSW need to be adopted.

Smart Cities or Mega Cities, India Needs to Build Its Sub-City Infrastructure

One of the flagship programmes of the Modi government is smart city initiative. The attempt is to free up its urban metropolises from congestion and spread the growth of urban infrastructure and commerce to greenfield areas. Like many other programmes of the Modi government, the building of 100 smart cities is a long-term vision that will take a lot of developmental efforts to materialise. It is unlikely to deliver in the next decade. These cities may not also have investors or resources to support the needed infrastructure due to its incomplete conceptualisation. Building mega cities in itself has a huge learning curve that India has not mastered. Infrastructure planning and development is still pretty ordinary. Building smart cities is the next level to that, so it should be perhaps attempted only when level one is mastered.

India's mega cities are in very poor shape. Every year the monsoon sees massive waterlogging of roads and drains. Public transport is affected and vehicular traffic slows down to a crawl. Often, power, internet and TV transmission are disrupted. At times collapse of buildings hit newspaper headlines and at other times open drains bring misery and death. During winter, pollution and smog affects cities, including the capital city. Traffic once again comes to a standstill. Healthcare is always under pressure due to rising respiratory and water-borne diseases. Landfills overflow and waterbodies are at times choked with plastic waste. Most of India's large cities like Delhi, Mumbai, Kolkata and Bengaluru become dysfunctional during monsoon and at times during other seasons too. In the south and east of the country, cities are badly affected due to deforestation and climate change and there is severe flooding and severe drought. From cyclones to tsunami, natural disasters do not spare India. Cities like Mumbai, Chennai and seaside states like Kerala can get inundated any time just due to seasonal rains. Few lessons in protecting cities have been learnt in the past years.

Mega cities need deep-rooted support systems. India needs to develop its sub-city infrastructure in order to accommodate and support its large urban population with world-class infrastructure. That is still an unexplored avenue for India that has mostly developed its city infrastructure above ground. Developing sub-city infrastructure has some definitive advantages. It gives a city a three-dimensional support system and better access to citizens. Not only do services reach you from all corners of the city but also from within.

Many of the successful world cities have supportive sub-city infrastructure. New York and London are front runners in this technology-driven city infrastructure that they mastered and perfected for over a century. London developed its subway in 1863. It also created its underground sewerage and water recycling system that took the water and sludge away from municipal areas through a natural slant. New York, known as the city of skyscrapers, went one step ahead. In 1890 when city planners first started building skyscrapers, they visualised that the city will develop an innovative deep-dive infrastructure simultaneously to support the city life underground.

In the next 100 years, a massive sub-city had been developed 80-stories deep under New York and also beneath Hudson River that operates as a lifeline to the lively metropolis. It consists of 32 million miles of utility lines, 440 miles of underground high-speed subways, 22 underwater water-supply and sewage-disposal tunnels and three-layer underground highways for trucks to supply to the city on a 24/7 basis. Many large US cities have developed their infrastructure underground. They have built by-laws for multiple infrastructure and supply lines to coexist without conflict in the sub-cities and seamlessly serve the cities and its citizens overground. Most Japanese cities are also built with sub-cities. It is a science India needs to adopt and develop as it aspires to build its mega cities and smart cities.

CHAPTER 10

Manufacturing:
Moving Out of the Woods but Slowly

Manufacturing has never been India's strong point even though it accounts for nearly 15% of the GDP. This has been largely because of our inability to build requisite infrastructure for manufacturing. The Modi government has been vocal about Make in India. Unfortunately, not much has been done to create a manufacturing infrastructure within the country. This is not only due to lack of investment by the government but also due to lack of domestic private-sector investment. As a result, there has been no real progress in the manufacturing sector. Instead domestic producers have continued to suffer because of rampant imports and no real thrust on Make in India. Whereas we have failed to defend our own domestic markets, our exporters have also failed to prize open the economies of the US and China, two of India's largest trading partners, who are engaged in what appears to be an all-out trade war.

Silver Lining in Dark Clouds for Manufacturing

It is not that there were no success stories in Indian manufacturing. The automobile sector has done fairly well despite the trade war. Indian automobile makers Tata Motors and Mahindra exceeded expectations, both in local as well as international sales. Maruti Suzuki and Hyundai Motors kept adding capacities and were important success stories for global manufacturers setting up large manufacturing plants in India.

Importantly, the big Chinese (Goldstone) and Korean (Kia) electric bus manufacturers have set up manufacturing plants in India and could alter the thrust of the automotive sector in the coming years. The total number of vehicles—from two-wheelers to trucks—produced by the industry in the financial year ending March 2018 was 29 million against 25.3 million the previous year. The new vehicle population showed an impressive rise of 14.78% in spite of city traffic congestion. Despite a rise in fuel prices, the sale of vehicles shows no signs of slowing down. Sale of domestic passenger vehicles grew by 7.89% while that of commercial vehicles locally rose by 19%. Automobile exports also grew at a hectic pace by 16.12% during the year.

Similarly, the mobile phones industry has seen a meteoric growth and new manufacturing capacities being added. This has been largely foreign manufacturing in the first leg of indigenisation where certain parts are locally made. With the Indian government increasing duty on mobile phones and some components by 10%, the first move towards partial indigenisation was seen. Chinese phone makers like Oppo, Vivo, Xiaomi and Huawei have swamped the Indian market, some setting up assembly plants to take on market leaders Samsung and Apple. As the Chinese phone makers gained in market share, both Apple and Samsung decided to open facilities in India at a global scale. Apple's Taiwanese partner Wistron is planning to set up an assembly plant near Bengaluru. Samsung already has a decade-old manufacturing plant in Greater Noida. It went a step further by kicking off an expansion project worth ₹5,000 crore that will increase the capacity of their handset plant from 68 million units per annum to 120 million units per annum.

Make in India 2.0 programme announced by the government earmarked several champion sectors including capital goods, automobile, defence, pharmaceutical, renewable energy, biotechnology, electronics, leather, textiles, food processing, gems and jewellery, construction, shipping and railways. But, apart from automobiles and pharma, there is a lot needed to make other manufacturing sectors look like champions. Even in the normally healthy pharma sector, two years after 2014 have been strenuous largely due to slowing exports to the developed markets of the European Union (EU) and the US. In the year ending March 2018, there was some recovery as both revenues and profits grew in double digits. Similarly, whereas there has been strong growth in renewable energy projects, the Indian manufacturers are facing distress conditions due to rampant price-cutting by Chinese companies. Let us analyse why despite having a presence in all areas of manufacturing, India is unable to step up its product presence at a global stage.

Availability of Markets, Entrepreneurship, Capital and Technology

There are four elements needed to build large manufacturing capacities. To become a successful manufacturing nation, you need designated markets to supply to. You also need entrepreneurship for building products. Those entrepreneurs must have access to capital and technology needed for manufacturing goods to be sold to those designated markets. But interestingly, if you have the markets, you will find that everyone gravitates towards it. On the other hand, if you do not have a captive and domestic market, you have to work twice as hard like Japan and South Korea to survive as a nation that must export to stay prosperous.

The EU was formed on the premise of unified markets alone. As big manufacturing and exporting nations like Germany, Italy and France faced tough competition from the US, and later from Japan in the 1950s through the 1970s, they decided to expand and consolidate their domestic market in their neighbourhood. It gave them a population base of nearly half a billion people, which was more than the US population. Also, they had a remarkably higher population density. Over the last 50 years, the EU has worked hard to settle their political differences just because the unified nations provided them with a captive market.

Fortunately, India and China are not in that space and have large captive markets. The population is much higher in these nations than the US and the EU combined. So, both nations are not really dependent on export markets for growth. China, however, behaves like it is export-dependent and a lot of its current woes and prosperity is due to this insecurity. It strives hard to capture international markets and takes unusual risks, some of which pay and some do not.

India is too laid-back to make the effort China makes to capture foreign markets. That is not an issue but the bigger problem is that it does precious little to protect its own markets. As a result, both value-added as well as cheap imports flood the Indian market and Indian manufacturing takes a back seat. Despite PM Modi's call to Make in India, the import bill in India keeps rising every year. So does the trade deficit with China, which has tripled in the past decade and crossed $50 billion in the year ending March 2017.

A look at Indian markets and its imports show that other than petroleum products and electronic components, a very large number of imports that India does are non-essential. From toys to chemicals and olive oil to apples, textiles to consumer durables, there are hundreds of products in the Indian market. But, these are not Indian toys or kitchenware but cheap Chinese toys and consumer durables that are visible on online market portals and retail stores. This is just because our regulatory bodies are not in place to check rampant imports. However, we will talk here of only one area that is key to India's manufacturing prowess. Energy equipment is one area where imports need to be reduced and duties need to be introduced because domestic capacities exist in abundance. From thermal power plants to solar panels and from light-emitting diode (LED) lights to power cables, imports in this area have grown indiscriminately in the last decade.

Markets—Chinese Predatory Credits and Predatory Pricing Rule

Bharat Heavy Electricals Ltd (BHEL) has been one of India's largest original equipment manufacturers in the power sector since the 1960s. It is one of the biggest losers largely due to needless imports from China. Chinese suppliers not only undercut in price but also offer long-term credit with their supplies. The Chinese power equipment suppliers give credit on easy terms till a buyer's plant starts producing power, which may take even two or three years. BHEL started losing its market share during UPA II when the Manmohan Singh government opened its doors to Chinese power equipment companies. In 2012, BHEL clocked revenues of ₹47,000 crore and profits of ₹7,000 crore. By 2017–2018, the revenues had declined to ₹10,341 crore and the net profits were a paper-thin ₹457 crore. The Modi government has done little to reverse this decline of the engineering giant brought about by UPA's open-door equipment-import policy.

Whereas import duties can counter predatory pricing, they cannot combat long-term credit that Chinese use to sell their goods and equipment. When Americans were rebuilding Iraq after occupation, following the devastating war against Saddam Hussain, Chinese companies would work in Iraq against the United Nations and the US tenders without advance or interim stage-wise payment against completion. Payment terms, believe it or not, was not after plant commissioning but after completion of warranty period. No wonder, they swept the contracts because Iraq did not have to pay for the product for a year after use. The technique employed of providing the product for free initially disrupted international tendering procedures completely. They even got an entry when some of them did not have enough experience to meet pre-qualification requirements. Chinese not only use predatory pricing but also such predatory credit terms to win orders.

Besides, they export through subsidiary companies located outside of China to dominate. So, you can't keep out a Chinese product with punitive tariffs alone. For example, a Chinese company based in China would compete with a Chinese company from Malaysia and another Chinese company from Singapore to give three exorbitantly low bids to grab the major share of any market. A buyer in such cases believes that the local producers have not been price-competitive and tends to ignore their claim to supply.

The above trends can be seen also in the solar equipment industry where panel and cell supplies have been dominated by the Chinese. The import of solar cells has jumped sixfold in India from 1,275 MW in 2014–2015 to 9,790 MW in 2017–2018. The use of Indian solar cells has stagnated as a result and presently stands at 842 MW. This is less than a tenth of the total cells used in projects during the year 2017–2018. This has affected Indian producers and half a dozen manufacturers, like Websol Energy, Mundra Solar, Indosolar, Jupiter Solar and Helios Photo Voltaic, who have asked for safeguard duty on imports. But, very little regulatory action has been taken.

India does not have a Make in India policy that protects Indian manufacturers and defends domestic markets against rampant imports. This is unlike China or the US. Instead of raising duties on imported LED bulbs, the 2017 budget imposed import duties on printed circuit boards (PCB) that are used in making LED lights. This in turn makes domestic producers much less competitive.

LED lights is an area where Chinese offers 20–30% margin in addition to liberal credit to Indian retail traders and skew the plot. Credit terms for the trade offered by the Chinese are often undisclosed and are extremely liberal. Traders' associations within India represent to the government to keep import duties low. Politicians and bureaucracy are simply not interested in protecting domestic manufacturing, be it the NDA or the UPA government. Their excuse is that under World Trade Organisation (WTO), they simply cannot do much.

After much prodding, the Modi government introduced and raised customs duties on toys and a few electronic items in 2017 but the duties levied were both delayed and inadequate. Protection of domestic markets is a fine art that the Chinese do with extreme skill and professionalism. WTO rules apply to China as much as they do to India. But it does not stop China from closing doors to unnecessary imports. More needs to be done to protect the domestic market, without which India cannot ever become a manufacturing nation. It needs to be done cleverly and imaginatively with quality checks, standardisation, adherence to Indian standards and other roadblocks, so that WTO stipulations do not apply.

Entrepreneurship—The Fever Catches On

One of the positive features of the Modi government is its multi-pronged approach to solve any problem. So, if a defence of domestic markets has been a policy failure, the boost to entrepreneurship has been a policy success. Ease of business has been truly attempted in right earnest and though bottlenecks remain, floodgates to doing business quickly and simply have been opened. This has been made possible largely by simplification of laws and adopting the digitisation process. That itself is no mean feat, given the reluctance of the traditional political class and bureaucracy in India.

We must remember that India is largely a federal republic in which various states have the final decision-making authority on the allocation of land, electricity, water and infrastructure facilities needed to do business. So, the credit of boosting entrepreneurship goes as much to states as it does to the central government. Surely, having 20 state governments under the BJP rule helped. But, even state governments ruled by opposition leaders critical of the PM, like West Bengal Chief Minister Mamata Banerjee and Andhra Pradesh Chief Minister Chandrababu Naidu, also did very well to push the development agenda and boost entrepreneurship.

India has improved its position in the country ratings for entrepreneurship, overall attitude and potential in the Global Entrepreneurship Index (GEI). From seventy-sixth position in 2014, India got to sixty-eighth position in 2018. Global Entrepreneurship Development Institute, a Washington-based policy think tank rates 137 nations on various parameters, and the US is the top-ranked nation in entrepreneurship. Among BRIC nations, India has a GEI index of 284 and is placed behind China, which has an overall ranking of 43 and a GEI index 411. Russia is third at seventy-sixth position with GEI index of 252 and Brazil is last at ninety-eighth position with a GEI index of 203.

But, it was not only the rating score that improved. Number of entrepreneurs in the country grew by leaps and bounds. This was to some extent helped by initiatives like Start-Up India but was largely due to easier availability of finance. Also, though bank finance to large corporates dropped due to rising NPAs, loans given by banks and micro-financing companies to women entrepreneurs increased. Several new schemes like MUDRA loans for entrepreneurs up to a sum of ₹10 lakh, the Small Industries Development Bank of India (SIDBI)-refinanced Credit Guarantee Scheme (CGS) up to a sum of ₹100 lakh and the increase in the Start-Up India scheme for scheduled castes, scheduled tribes and women entrepreneurs from ₹10 lakh to ₹1 crore helped small entrepreneurs find capital without offering collaterals.

One of the success stories of Indian entrepreneurship was the acquisition of Flipkart by Walmart for an astounding sum of $16 billion in May 2018. Two entrepreneurs, Sachin and Binnie Bansal, who had started a business from their IIT dorm barely a decade ago had created India's biggest online business. It had for years held the top position in the Indian e-commerce marketplace, having 31.9% of market share against that of 31.1% by Amazon. If that was not enough, the Indian e-commerce market is having a double-digit growth, clocking $21 billion in sales. When Walmart, with a revenue of $500 billion, decided to opt for majority stakes in Flipkart, it was a clear message that entrepreneurship in India has arrived and that Indian entrepreneurs have succeeded in building a high-value enterprise.

Another reason why entrepreneurship grew quickly during the past few years was ease of business. Aadhaar card made applying for land, electricity connection, water supply easier. Digitisation of forms helped speed up things. In the World Bank report on ease of doing business, India jumped 30 places in 2018 to be placed at the hundredth spot among 190 nations. This was the biggest jump amongst all the nations and was due to eight reforms done by India as cited in the report. Among the reforms were faster construction permits, reduction in time for employee provident fund (EPF) and employee state insurance corporation (ESIC) resolution, establishment of debt-recovery tribunals and many others. India used to be last amongst BRIC nations till 2016 but by 2018 Brazil slipped to the bottom of the table.

Capital Flows from Investors but Only Intermittently

The UPA government was caught in a bind as CAD had ballooned to $87.8 billion or 5.1% of the GDP by 2013. The external debt had grown by 350% to $390 billion and short-time external debt had spiralled to 33.1% of forex reserves. Policy paralysis had gripped the nation and investor confidence in India was at an all-time low. Capital flight from India was high and FDI inflows from investors during the year 2013–2014 declined from $18.28 billion to $16.05 billion in the year 2012–2013. The above figures do not include NRI remittances but only foreign investor equity inflows.

By the time the Modi government came to power, UPA had put into place several strong measures and controlled the rupee downslide. The most important move was to bring in Raghuram Rajan, a global financial expert as the RBI governor. Rajan was already an advisor to PM Manmohan Singh during the rupee crash and quickly moved in and took several measures to stop flight of capital and speculation on rupee. Though the flight of capital was nearly halted, the trend of receding foreign-investment growth could not be reversed by the Manmohan Singh government.

As the Modi government came to power on promises of good governance, FDI inflows jumped by 54% to $24.75 billion. But, the execution of the development agenda was slower than expected. Also, the inability of BJP to push through multiple reforms in Rajya Sabha stemmed initial euphoria. Though FDI rose by nearly 46% to $36.07 billion in the year 2015–2016 (Figure 10.1), it stagnated at $36.32 billion in the financial year ending March 2017, as per an RBI annual report issued in August. The first two years were pretty difficult for the Modi government despite the thumping majority it received in Lok Sabha. This slowed down FDI equity flows during its third year in office after the initial burst of confidence the Modi government received from foreign investors.

Figure 10.1: FDI Equity Inflows (USD billion)

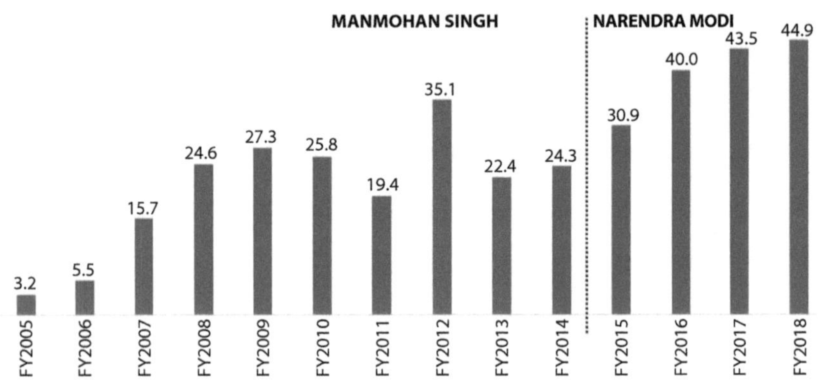

Data source: Department of Industrial Policy and Promotion

However, sustained efforts by the government have brought results and change in fortunes. While demonetisation and GST, in their original avatars, added to economic woes, the work done in the energy and the agriculture sector, and the banking sector reforms turned the tide and the perception of investors towards the government's intent and capability. Though several social issues like air pollution and safety of women and minorities remain a global concern, the introduction of several laws and quick execution of development projects made investors look again at India despite Trump's trade-war disruptions.

The manufacturing sector FDIs have looked up recently after four tortuous years. In 2012–2013, FDI equity to the manufacturing sector was $6.53 billion. It has gone through a seesaw ride over the last four years and was at last looking up at $11.97 billion in the year ending March 2017. However, unless there is sustained growth for a couple of years, we will not know whether the policies being put in place ever so slowly are effective.

In the first nine months of the financial year 2017–2018, total FDI equity inflows rose by nearly 25% to $35.94 billion as per as a quarterly fact sheet released by RBI. After a year of stagnation, it again raised expectations of a revival of growth in FDI equity inflows. But, even though the numbers improved, it is not a rosy picture. This is because despite the revised treaty with Mauritius and other tax havens that were supposed to remove undue concessions, FDI equity from Mauritius surged in 2016–2017.

As per RBI data, Mauritius displaced Singapore as the most-favoured offshore haven in the year ending March 2017. A whopping $13.38 billion in India was invested through the Mauritius route. That was more than a third of the total FDI equity investment of $36.3 billion made in 2016–2017. This is farcical, considering that the nominal GDP of Mauritius in the year 2014 was just $13.24 billion. It is obvious that FDI is coming to India through shell companies in Mauritius. These shell companies are in tax havens that permit investors to do business under a pseudo name. So not only do they pay a minimum tax but also are able to hide their identity from tax authorities of any nation.

Capital—90% of Investment into India Routed through Shell Companies!

India gets over 90% of its FDI equity flows routed from shell companies located in tax havens like Mauritius, Cyprus and Singapore. The tax treaties with these tax havens have been such since 2005 that it has been more profitable for an investor to invest through these destinations than directly from their home country. During the last decade, India has been known to give incentives to those who route their money through tax havens than those who invest directly in India.

Mauritius alone accounted for a third of foreign investment routed to India. Why did this happen? It happened due to what is called 'treaty shopping', explains Centre of Budget and Governance Accountability (CBGA). Multinationals willing to invest in India have been pushed to open accounts in tax havens and invest through these offshore destination for a better tax deal. CBGA explains it thus—suppose a British investor has to invest in India. They can invest as per combined tax laws of India, Britain and Double Tax Avoidance Agreement (DTAA) signed between India and Britain. They, however, opt to open a shell company—a subsidiary based in Mauritius—and invest through the Mauritius route because tax treaty between India and Mauritius helps them pay lesser tax.

CBGA report shows that over 48% of UK investments, 26% of investments from the US, 34% of investments from Switzerland and 83% of investments from Netherlands during the decade 2004–2014 have been routed flows. Three nations—Mauritius, Singapore and Cyprus—accounted for 90% of the routed capital. In short, over 97% of the capital invested from Mauritius, 94% from Cyprus and 90% from Singapore were routed money invested by other nations through shell companies.

After the demonetisation drive of November 2016, the Modi government started cracking down on corporates that were operating outside the purview of law. It brought in the Benami Properties Act to identify fictitious account holders. It struck off 226,000 companies off its list for not filing tax returns for two years. It also signed a treaty with Organisation for Economic Cooperation and Development (OECD) members that seeks to deter the practice of corporates who use low-tax offshore destinations to reduce taxes artificially.

The Modi government asserted that it will create a level-playing field as well as remove shell companies that indulge in money laundering. It revised skewed tax treaties with these nations whose effect will be felt in the next two to five years, after the existing agreements expire. However, unless the new treaties come into force, we will not be sure whether the revised agreements bring about transparency or just ensures business as usual. Manufacturing businesses are serious investments and bringing transparency to FDI will help big-ticket investors avoid shell companies when they invest in India.

Adoption of Technology Slow in India's Manufacturing Sector

After markets, enterprise and capital, technology is the fourth pillar around which successful manufacturing nations have been built. Like capital flow, technology flow into India along with technology adoption has been patchy and intermittent. In many cases agreements for technology transfer are not in place. In some other cases, though the transfer of technology documentation is there, the actual transfer has not taken place.

In some cases, Indian companies have gone in for old and obsolete technology. In other cases, inefficient technology has been adopted due to certain constraints. *There is a huge gap in knowledge between Indians employed locally and Indians employed by multinational firms globally.* All these things need to be rectified and processes need to be streamlined. In World Bank's report on the ease of doing business, India fared very low in technological adoption criteria and this is a huge cause for concern.

One of the biggest failures of India to adopt the right technology was witnessed in the steel sector that has seen the largest plant closures in the past decade. India has many integrated steel plants that have been running efficiently since the 1950s and the 1960s. Still, turn of the century witnessed India adopting sponge iron route to counter the shortage of iron ore and coking coal. At that time, there were 20-odd plants, mostly large units, producing 7 MMT of sponge iron. During the next decade, shortage of iron ore as well as coking coal saw a proliferation of sponge iron plants. By 2014, there were 450-odd sponge iron plants, mostly small and medium units, producing 42 MMT of sponge iron each year. A large number of them had also turned sick and closed down simply because they were uncompetitive.

The lack of iron ore and coking coal had forced faulty technology adoption and created industry sickness of unprecedented scale and nature in the steel industry. Simply put, steel-making route through sponge iron is profitable only when steel prices are high, like they were prior to Beijing Olympics. Also, if an artificial shortage of iron ore and coking coal is there due to the closure of domestic mines and expensive imports, making of steel through sponge iron becomes profitable.

However, steel produced through sponge iron or via electric furnace can never compete with steel produced in integrated steel plants that have an advantage of scale. Besides, sponge iron plants being in the MSME sector cause massive pollution. They do not take adequate pollution-control measures. Open storing of sponge iron, lack of pollution-control equipment, cramming of plants close to cities and discharge of non-treated effluents and ash have created chaos and distress amongst local residents.

The world is taking an important leap in futuristic machine learning, robotics and artificial intelligence (AI) while Indian industry is struggling at a basic level. For this, it is not only the government but the private sector too that is to be blamed. Lack of interest of domestic industry to come up with large manufacturing plants has slowed down the growth of the country. Whereas Indians became the largest ethnic group to invest in Dubai in 2018, it is very disappointing to see domestic investment, especially in the manufacturing sector, facing a slow decline. This will need some soul-searching both by the government and by India Incorporated. Unless domestic private-sector investment in the manufacturing sector improves, Make in India will remain just an unfulfilled dream.

Part V

Food and Agriculture

CHAPTER 11

Volatility in Food Prices: Can It Be Controlled?

The Indian kitchen has been under siege since the year 2011. Fruit and vegetable prices in India were reasonable till 2010. A kilogram (kg) of potato would cost less than ₹5 in winters and less than ₹10 in summers in retail markets of the capital city. But since 2011, vegetable prices have been volatile. Also, the price of pulses and spices galloped during the last decade. There are various reasons why this happened.

Nearly a decade ago, agricultural commodities, horticulture products and livestock markets started getting organised. Futures markets of National Commodity and Derivatives Exchange Ltd (NCDEX) brought into play investors. Here investors could speculate and invest in future market prices of agriculture commodities. For example, a trader or a farmer could estimate that the supply of pulses could exceed demand in the coming season while there could be a shortage of turmeric. This could be due to a variety of reasons including water shortage, excess rainfall, pest attacks, shortage or excess of global production or any other. Accordingly, he would expect that prices of pulses will fall and prices of turmeric could rise. So, if he wanted, he could invest ₹8,000 on turmeric and ₹2,000 on pulses and take a position in dictating the future prices of the next season. The NCDEX gives opportunities for such online trading to all investors in agriculture commodities just like the share market gives for listed companies.

These investors could take large positions in the forward market and even stock up agriculture commodities in NCDEX-approved warehouses. At around that time, Pune-Nashik-Mumbai belt traders also saw consolidation into politically aligned camps. Nationalist Congress Party (NCP), the party of the Agriculture Minister Sharad Pawar of UPA, had already moved into this space early on. But soon, Congress and BJP had its own farmer-trader lobbies. Along with futures market traders, they started betting on and even manipulating agriculture commodities, vegetable trade and later fruit markets of India. And food prices became volatile.

There was another trend that was creating a demographic shift across India. The more educated Hindus and Sikhs were moving out of farming as a profession into city jobs that were less arduous and far more remunerative. The rural vacuum saw the poor Muslim community almost completely dominate the farm sector by default. It was back-breaking work with uncertain returns for them. A poor farming community pitted against politically powerful, tech-savvy, cash-rich commodity traders.

Mandi Politics and Monopoly

Once upon a time, mandis—vegetable markets—of India were thriving local marketplaces. They were nearby destinations where a farmer could sell his produce at a good price. But slowly, these *mandi* committees saw an influx of politicians who started creating coteries and monopolising the mandis. Most farmers outside the coterie had to wait for days to get their chance to sell in the *mandis* unless they paid a commission to mandi-authorised commission agents or *dalals*. Then there were huge price manipulation, weight manipulation and delayed payments. Agricultural Produce Market Committee Act (APMC) was first proposed in 2003. Laws of APMC were drafted by each state separately and never favoured free trade. They made *mandi* committees all powerful and put farmers at the mercy of committees and commission agents.

The Act not only mandated farmers to sell exclusively at the *mandi*, but it also created a series of brokers and commission agents who would act as negotiators between farmers and traders. As a result, a farmer who could not negotiate cleverly and had less financial capacity to hold stocks got less than half the price of the commodities resold by traders to other centres. As farmers remained poor, commission agents and big traders became richer and politically influential.

The nexus of big farmer traders with political parties and moneybags of NCDEX futures market also contributed to the rise of trading cartels. Nashik and Lasalgaon *mandis* have traditionally been the centre of India's onion and tomato trade. Farmer-traders understood the political power of onion, whose price has been volatile before elections since the 1980s. Less than a dozen traders reportedly control over 50% of the onion trade in India. APMC *mandi* committee system, where farmers are forced to sell their products only through *mandis*, is believed to have created such monopolies.

Since onions and tomatoes are integral to the Indian curry, a rise in the price of any of the two vegetables upsets kitchen budget. The political class that controlled the *mandis* in Maharashtra started using this leverage in politics. Elections soon became synonymous with volatility in the price of onions. Onion price volatility was extended to tomato price during the last decade, though tomato production is spread over much larger geography.

Potatoes, Grown in Agra, Stocked in Pune

In the winter of 2011, there was an excess production of potato in Punjab. Farmers in Jalandhar started throwing potato on the streets because prices had dipped below ₹100 per quintal (₹1 per kg) and did not cover even the transport costs to the *mandi*. Agriculture Minister Sharad Pawar stepped in and got traders of the prosperous Mumbai-Pune belt to pick up excess stocks.

Potatoes grown in Punjab and in the Indo-Gangetic belt were transported over 1,000 miles to be stored in cold storages of Maharashtra and Karnataka. Soon this trend was witnessed across the potato-growing belt. *Mandi* arrivals at UP, Bihar and West Bengal, which produced and consumed most potatoes, fell while that of Maharashtra and Karnataka rose. Potato, onion and tomato—namely the POT—were the three vegetables that accounted for 40% of all the vegetables consumed in India. Together with onions and tomatoes grown in Maharashtra, the potato trade shifted to Maharashtra traders in the Mumbai-Pune belt, who had deep pockets and created a trading cartel. They started manipulating prices of potato, onion and tomatoes, making kitchens sizzle. Vegetable prices rose fourfold in the next five years. They not only rose steeply but they also became volatile. Traders ensured that prices dipped during procurement season so that they could buy cheaply. This caused acute farmer distress. They also ensured that prices peaked mid-season so that they could maximise profits. So, while farmers got hurt by the price volatility so did the consumer, as traders ruled the roost.

I wrote two articles, one in *Women's Era* titled 'Kitchen Under Siege' and another in *The Hindu Business Line* titled 'Potato Farming: India Makes a Hash of it', giving the details of meagre potato arrivals in Agra, Patna and Kolkata *mandis* in the year 2013. Nearly three-quarters of India's potatoes are grown in the Indo-Gangetic belt. But since 2011, the potatoes are stored in godowns at Maharashtra and Karnataka by the POT trading cartel.

The effect of this hoarding at away centres can be seen in Figure 11.1—a graph plotted with data from National Horticulture Board in 2013. Though 73% of the potatoes were grown in the Indo-Gangetic belt in the three populous states of UP, Bihar and West Bengal, that year just 6% of the potatoes found their way to the large mandis at Agra, Lucknow, Patna and Kolkata. On the other hand, two states of Maharashtra and Karnataka where just 3% of the potato crop was produced saw 52% of the potato arrivals in the mandis. It was not that the mandi arrivals were at the consumer centres. The three large states of UP, Bihar and Bengal have a population touching 40 crore (400 million) which accounts for nearly a third of India's potato consumers. Maharashtra and Karnataka have a population of 17 crore (170 million) by comparison. The data shows that the humble potato had to travel needlessly to distant godowns more than 1,000 miles away from major production and consumption centres, just because investors chose to stock it at away centres. Potato prices shot up unnecessarily as the consumer paid the cost of moving the potato stock to and fro that was incidentally more than what the farmer received for his produce.

Figure 11.1: Potato Hoarding at Away Centres

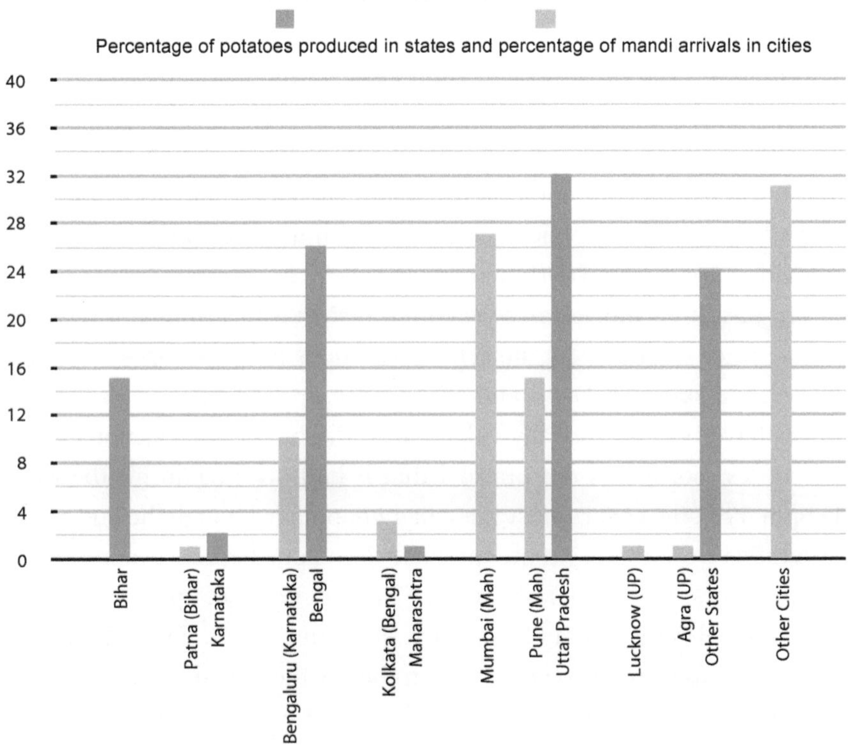

Data source: National Horticulture Board (2012–2013)

This trend of hoarding at away centres accelerated in the last decade with the POT trade largely under control of the traders of the Mumbai-Pune-Nashik belt. It is reported that in the case of high-value pulses and spices, some of the produce is exported and the stocking is done in the Middle East. The price stability of the kitchen was completely lost during the period 2011–2015, but we will come to that later. The price rise was accompanied by wild seasonal swings, particularly during election seasons. It plagued the UPA government and is now plaguing the NDA regime. It is not that political parties and successive governments have not done anything to keep the prices under control. It is only that they have not done enough. They created the volatility and are now being bitten by a genie, totally out of control.

Like UPA, the Modi government has also been troubled by volatile food prices. They made several efforts to tame the volatile markets. It started on a very strong promise in 2014 when it introduced the price-stabilisation fund (PSF) worth ₹500 crore in its first budget. PSF was set up under the agriculture ministry within six months of the new government coming to office. Its aim was to curb volatility in agricultural and horticultural commodities like onions, potatoes, tomatoes and later on pulses. However, typical to most government schemes in India, it remained pretty much dysfunctional for more than a year.

In July 2015, more than a year after the Modi government was sworn in, the price of onions hit the ceiling. Elections in a few states including the crucial states of Delhi and Bihar were around the corner. Onion prices have been historically volatile in India before the elections, since the 1980s. So, it was not unusual that it had once again hit the roof. Despite PSF, the government was caught napping. Though the budgetary provisions were there, no procurement of onions had been done. Even modus operandi of imports using PSF had not been set up.

National Agricultural Cooperative Marketing Federation of India Ltd (NAFED) was directed to import onions but by the time the onions arrived in India, it was late September. The imported onions hit the markets in October 2015, just before the November crop arrived. This depressed prices and hurt the farmers just because of the belated action and wrong timing of imports. As a result, housewives were angry and farmers were distressed.

Volatility took firm roots as the Modi government was repeatedly outwitted by the traders' cartel. In 2017, just before the Gujarat elections, the price of onions and tomatoes in retail markets touched ₹70 per kg. The government conducted raids on seven big traders of Nashik *mandi* and seized stocks of onions. But, the onion cartel hit back with a strike in Nashik *mandi* and got supplies diverted to nearby *mandis*, maintaining the pressure of high prices. The prices of onion and tomatoes remained firm despite the income tax raids and only dropped a week after the Gujarat elections were over.

Meat and Fish Trade Gets Disrupted

Apart from POT, prices of fruits and other vegetable have seen a sharp rise due to various reasons. Domestic production stagnated and grew at a rate of less than 3% YOY. Imports of fruits and vegetables rose from ₹40 billion in 2010–2011 to ₹120 billion in 2015–2016. Prices of fruits have grown fourfold in retail markets of metro cities since 2010. As affordability of the upper middle class rose, wholesalers and retailers pushed up the prices, seizing the opportunity to capitalise on a high-profit market. The middle class and the poor were left high and dry because local cartels did not permit cheaper products to be sold in residential areas.

Meat and fish product prices were also seeing a steady increase due to rising demand for protein foods. Per capita intake of proteins in India is one of the lowest in the world. Part of it is due to lifestyle reasons and part of it is due to prices and convenience. Consumption of protein is not only low but falling across India, says IMRB International, the market research bureau. It conducted a survey of 1,260 respondents between the age of 30 to 55 years in seven cities in the year 2015. The only protein that was universally popular across India was pulses, which was consumed by vegetarian as well as non-vegetarian population across towns and villages.

In 2017, after BJP swept to power in UP, Yogi Adityanath's government cracked down on illegal slaughterhouses across the state. The chief minister was himself a vegetarian and a supporter of the Gau Raksha movement, so some action was expected. But, the initial crackdown on meat and fish shops across the state was unprecedented and unnecessary and broke the back of the supply chain. Some viewed it as a push against a particular community while others said it was an attempt to bring the industry under regulation and quality control. During Samajwadi Party's rule in UP before 2017, many unauthorised meat and fish shops started functioning even from homes in residential colonies that had become a health hazard for communities. So, some regulation was needed. But, after a year of disruption, many of the shops have returned and are operating in an unauthorised manner once again due to local police station-level corruption. Only bribes being given to district administration and police have become fatter.

Commodity Traders Cartelise the Trading of Pulses

Pulses have always been a low-cost vegetarian protein diet of the Indian household. The price rise of onions was accompanied by the unprecedented spike in prices of pulses in 2015, before the Delhi assembly elections. In January 2015, prices of pulses jumped by 20–30% as supply exceeded demand. The initial spurt was due to firming of prices of moong dal, reportedly due to deficient monsoon. Pulse production in 2014–2015 was estimated to fall to 18.43 MMT from 19.78 MMT in the previous year. The 7% drop was considered manageable and caused no jitters amongst the planners.

But, stock levels of all four dals kept falling due to sustained buying by a cartel during the next six months. By June 2015, just before onion prices made headlines, retail prices of pulses had jumped by 60%. *Urad* dal that was sold at around ₹70 per kg in Delhi's retail market a year before was now priced at ₹120 per kg. *Tur*, moong, *masoor* all showed increased demand and reduced supplies and a consequently sharp rise in prices.

The government went into a tizzy as this was an election year for several key states. By the time the government started the imports process, the festival season was around the corner when natural demand is usually at its peak. Before Diwali, prices of dal had crossed ₹200-per-kg mark in metro cities. The government belatedly ordered income tax raids across the country to stop hoarding of stocks. The income tax department seized 75,000 metric tonnes of pulses over the next two months in over 6,000 raids across the country. They also found incriminating documents that showed the collusion of a nationwide cartel of traders with international commodity traders led by none other than the Anglo-Swiss commodity giant Glencore.

The 2,000-page income tax report titled, 'Appraisal Report in the Case of Pulse Importers and Traders Group' submitted to the Ministry of Finance showed the presence of a three-tier cartel. They reportedly indulged in monopolistic buying and hoarding stocks of pulses in both Indian and overseas markets. It also alleged hoarding of physical stocks by sustained buying, manipulation of futures markets, delaying imports and profiteering as prices peaked. There was also evidence of suppressing profits by false-invoicing and under-invoicing besides money laundering. Further, there was evidence of dumping of stocks when crops arrived to force farmers into distressed selling.

The three-tier cartel was allegedly led by the multinational commodity trader Glencore, which controls large chunks of Canadian and Australian supply markets. Glencore is a low-profile, $200 billion commodity conglomerate known for its sharp practices. *The Paradise Papers* unveiled by International Consortium of Investigative Journalists (ICIJ) gives a detailed account of some of its operations as it was a client of Appleby, one of the largest providers of offshore legal services. In 2017, the ICIJ exposed one of the biggest clandestine operations of money laundering when it laid bare thousands of documents of Appleby and its clients who reportedly siphoned of money to tax havens. Glencore trades in mining, metals, energy, food products and commodities and allegedly controls several farm products including the pulse trade in India.

It expanded its operations in India in 2010 and is now being investigated by the income tax department for money laundering and under-invoicing, thereby understating its revenues and profits ever since. Among the others involved were Export Trading Group (ETG), a much smaller commodity trader with interests in Africa and Myanmar and one which is being partly acquired by Glencore. Edelweiss, a Mumbai-based financial brokerage company with little commodity-trading background, was also involved. It was possibly brought into the circuit allegedly as an entry operator who would facilitate the laundering of money.

While tier-one companies worked as importers and financiers, tier-two companies were in the thick of operations. Tier-two operators included traditional wholesalers of grain and pulses who worked on a profit-sharing arrangement, right to tier-three that was the retailer end. This 10,000-plus network was allegedly spearheaded by Jindal Agro of Dalip and Pradip Jindal, Superior Group of Vikas Gupta and SV Agri Trade and Sharp Mint Group of Manoj Agarwal. The third tier reportedly consisted of importer and exporter networks that were also involved in money laundering and included Riddhi Siddhi Impex, Parth International, Gayatri Maa, Gunn Enterprises, Charles India and several other proprietorship companies who traded on the NCDEX commodity exchange. The cartel still operates to create price volatility that hurts both farmers and the housewives and benefits the traders.

Indian Spices Become Volatile as Traders Increase Stranglehold

Along with a rise in the prices of meat, pulses, vegetable and fruits, the price of spices has also risen sharply. India has traditionally been the largest consumer as well as a major producer of spices. Among the most commonly used spices are *jeera* or cumin seeds, *dhaniya* or coriander seeds, *haldi* or turmeric, *lal mirch* or red chili, *sarson* or mustard seeds and *garam masala* consisting of cardamom, cloves, black pepper, bay leaf and cinnamon. Most of these spices are traded in NCDEX futures market and have seen firm prices with strong export demands. Export of spices has been India's ancient trade.

Exports of spices have been buoyant during the past five years as more people around the world are adopting spiced-up Indian food. Uncertainties in Iraq, Syria, Turkey and Iran have led to intermittent supplies. Traders from the futures market have capitalised on the same and pushed up the prices. At the same time, traders have time and again restricted the supply of cumin and coriander into the 600-odd NCDEX-authorised godowns on quality issues, to restrict supplies and maintain a high demand, justifying high prices. Here again is another example of traders manipulating prices of commodities by keeping farmers out of the discussion.

Control of trading cartels is expanding in India. They are loosely networked but work in unison to distort prices. From onions, it expanded to POT. Thereafter, it has snared the pulse and the spice market as well. But, all those have been seasonal volatility in prices. In garlic trade, for the first-time, the trader lobby was able to manipulate prices at the same time in two markets. While farm prices crashed in Rajasthan, retail prices remained firm in neighbouring Delhi and traders profited hugely at the expense of farmers and the housewives.

Garlic and ginger are key ingredients in an Indian kitchen. In early 2018, farmers in Madhya Pradesh and Rajasthan, which accounts for more than half the production of garlic, saw prices plummet. In early June, farm-gate prices in Neemuch dipped to ₹800 per quintal (₹8 per kg), a third of the prices just six weeks ago, despite support from the Madhya Pradesh government. By mid-June, garlic prices dropped to

₹100 per quintal (₹1 per kg) in Kota-Jhalawar belt and the Rajasthan government promised to buy 15 lakh quintals at a reserve price of ₹3,200 per quintal (₹32 per kg). However, buying has been slow and distress has been widespread amongst farming community.

Retail prices of garlic, however, did not dip in city centres of Mumbai and Delhi. Retail prices in Delhi, barely 500 miles away, were ranging from ₹8,000 to ₹16,000 per quintal (₹80–₹160 per kg). Azadpur *mandi* did not see prices dipping below ₹5,000 per quintal (₹50 per kg) during the entire summer season.

So far, traders had ensured the seasonal price volatility of food and horticulture products. But, here traders were able to put both farmers and housewives simultaneously under pressure and corner the profits entirely for the trade. This is going to be the key challenge of the 2019 elections for the Narendra Modi government. If they are able to keep the price of food products low and ensure fair prices to farmers, voters will vote for them. If not, they could be routed. The silver lining in this cartelisation is the coming of online retailers like Amazon, Bigbasket and Grofers and the acquisition of Flipkart by the world's biggest grocer Walmart. If they enter the marketplace in a big way, they can disrupt the cartels and keep food prices at ground zero. They can also create a responsible supply chain that benefits the producers—the farm community—without creating undue market volatility.

CHAPTER 12
Indian Agriculture at Crossroads: New Direction Needed

Problems in Indian agriculture don't seem to go away. Apart from price volatility and marketing that has been discussed in the previous chapter, there are many other problems that need solutions if farmers' income has to be increased. Three years ago, PM Modi had announced that he would work towards doubling the income of farmers. This, when the farming community was facing one of the worst existential crises of high-input costs and low-crop realisations, of high debt and low income. Three years down the line, the Modi government has made a lot of effort but is far from succeeding. The production of food grain is rising (as shown in Figure 12.1) YOY to meet the consumer demand, but the farming community is not getting its share, because of several faulty policies and practices since independence.

There are several issues that need to be sorted out in the farm sector in order of priority. They are all structural issues and will take a decade or two to yield results. So, political promises of magical solutions in quick time are unlikely to succeed. As a matter of fact, some of these solutions have been tried over the last few decades but have been counterproductive. So, even before we seriously start discussing the problems and their solutions, we must understand that the farming community in India is not one homogenous block, unlike in the US. As a tropical country, the variety of produce is unlimited. We must start appreciating the difference between a rich farmer and a poor farmer. We also need to look at some of the

Figure 12.1: Agricultural Production in India (March 2005–March 2018) (MMT)

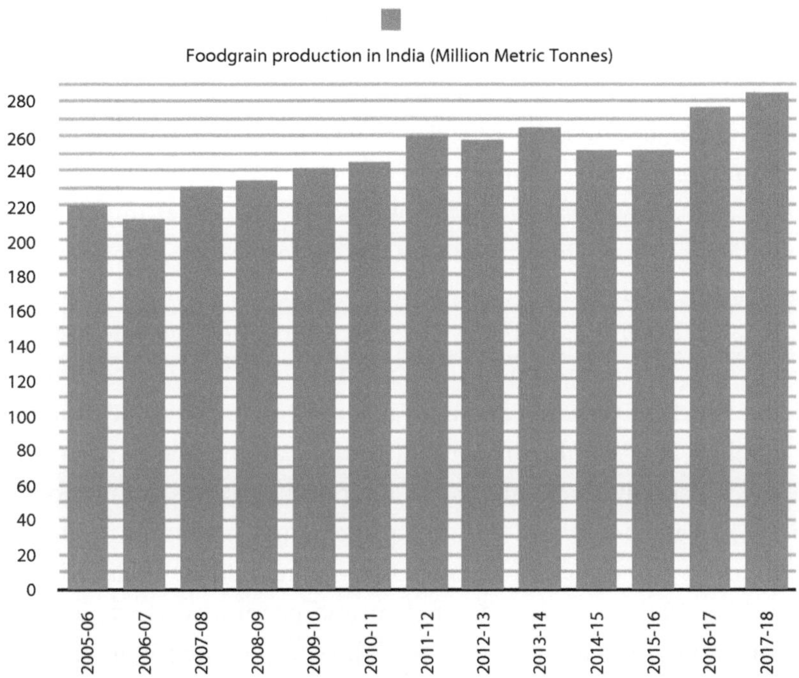

Data source: Ministry of Agriculture

myths and understand policy mistakes made since the independence. These are creating a bigger disparity between the two segments and adding to India's agricultural crisis.

Three Myths of the Indian Farmland that Need to Be Dispelled

The first and foremost myth is that Indian farmers are poor because they do not have large holdings. That because they do not have large tracts of land, they cannot practise mechanised farming like agriculturists of North America, and hence, are poor. And that in absence of mechanised farming, agricultural output in India is low. That India has limited arable land and that is the prime reason why our agricultural produce is stagnating. These are wrong notions—nothing could be further from the truth, because many nations with lesser per capita arable land have much higher output.

The second myth is that irrigation canals help agricultural productivity and farming community. This is largely untrue because irrigation canals in the country have consumed disproportionate resources and have helped less than 10% of the farming community. As a matter of fact, irrigation canals have over the years increased the disparity between rich and poor farmers. It has incentivised wasteful use of water. That in turn has caused acute water crisis across India.

The third myth is that MSP offered by the government helps farmers in distress. This is again a false notion. MSP only helps the richest farmers. This is because farmers who can offer good-quality grains in high volume to Food Corporation of India get their stocks lifted by Food Corporation of India at MSP. The procurement issues with the Food Corporation are many and reforms are overdue. But, the key inability is to sell the procured quantity into the marketplace and manage the supply chain effectively. Besides the organisation is poorly structured with politicians and not professional managers in charge of the day-to-day operations. Apart from being poorly managed, it is allegedly staffed with many inefficient and corrupt workers, leading to wastage and mammoth losses, subsidised by the taxpayer. In May 2012, I had written an op-ed piece for *The Economic Times* titled 'Stop This Waste'. Very little has changed in the past five years despite the change of government. This includes the procurement policy which is heavily skewed in favour of three states. So, MSP, whether it is at an old rate or at a revised rate, only assists the rich farmers largely of north India who produce the best quality of grains. They are politically powerful farmers and unfortunately the hike in MSPs do not actually help farmers in distress.

China's Farms Are Small, Efficient and Productive

India has the second-highest acreage of arable agriculture land next to the US. India's agricultural land is blessed with both sunshine and rainfall. Indian farms, except in parts of Jammu and Kashmir, do not suffer from extreme climatic conditions. They have the ability to grow two or more than two crops every year. Some areas are even fortunate to have three to four crops a year. Risks to Indian farmers is lower with multiple crops.

Still yield is low and crop output per acre is stagnant when compared to many other Asian nations.

Though China's landmass is three times bigger, India's arable land is marginally higher than China's. Besides, two times more people are engaged in farming in China. Despite this, China produces 40% more wheat and rice than India and almost three times the amount of fruits. China is not only a manufacturing power but an agricultural power despite its small farm sizes. It not only produces enough to feed its own people but produces 50% more than it consumes. It has hence positioned itself as the largest food producer and the biggest exporter of processed foods worldwide.

Forty years ago, India and China had similar yields in farmlands. China had almost 40% more people to feed than India. India had small landholdings but China had even smaller. India's Land Ceiling Act—a state legislation—was loosely enforced till amendments to the Act were incorporated in 1971 by Indira Gandhi's government and then adopted by states. As per the census of 1970–1971, average landholding in India was 2.28 hectares. Forty years later, it halved to 1.15 hectares in the census of 2010–2011. China has an average landholding of 0.6 hectares per farm.

Now let us see how China improved its farm productivity despite its low farm size. In 2004, China had 28 million hectares under paddy cultivation while India had 42 million hectares. That year, China produced 186 MMT of rice against 124 MMT produced by India. By 2014, China had produced 207 MMT of rice. As per International Rice Research Institute (IRRI), China has a dozen collaborations with it that started in the 1970s and has helped China develop 49 varieties of high-yielding hybrid rice. This has helped its yield grow to 6.5 tonnes per hectare—almost three times the yield of India's farms.

The Modi government has taken the cue from China. IRRI is setting up a regional research centre at Varanasi to develop new varieties of rice conducive to Indian climatic conditions. It is an effort that should have been made at least a decade ago. It is not that high-yield varieties of crops have not been tried before. India has produced, with its own effort, several high-yielding varieties of wheat and rice. But now, there is a realisation of getting the best international advice as yields that had slipped to below 2.2 tonnes per hectare need to be improved quickly.

Similarly, in pulses, oil seeds and cereals, China has the highest yield despite growing non-genetically modified (GM) variety of them in small farms like India does. It is time that India also focuses on improving yields of these crops that are low and stagnant. In the case of pulses and oil seeds, India needs to alter its policy on nutrients. Disproportionate subsidies on nitrogen fertilisers like urea have made it a cheap and all-purpose fertiliser in India. As a result, Indian soil is no longer rich in sulphur and hence not conducive to the production of oil seeds and pulses that need high sulphur content to have better yields. Twenty years ago, the single super phosphate was a key low-cost nutrient widely produced in India. The UPA emphasis on importing di-ammonium phosphate (DAP) fertiliser broke the back of the single super phosphate (SSP) industry. It is time to bring SSP back centre stage if we want to increase the yield of oil seeds and pulses.

As a matter of fact, India needs a crop, land and nutrient-based agricultural advisory to educate its farmers on how to manage farmlands. Indian governments, both at states and the centre, have been always doing its bit to disseminate the right information through television. But now, in the age of the mobile phones, the message has to be passed on through various web-based and app-based programmes. Besides, India needs to promote organic farming that is practised today by small and marginal farmers who cannot afford chemical fertilisers. Only 2.59% of farmland is under organic farming despite the inherent demand for organic foods in European markets. It is also necessary that India develops small farm equipment like China. This is something that India lacks, though it has several farm equipment manufacturing companies like Escorts, Sonalika, John Deere, Mahindra and Tractors and Farm Equipment Ltd (TAFE) in the farm equipment segment.

Also, we need to have user-friendly ways to lease them out on an hourly basis. EM3 Agri Services is a Venture Capital (VC) funded start-up operating in central India. It is attempting to do that through its call centres and an app. But because most farmers are not yet on smartphones and internet connectivity is poor in rural India, spreading information is a challenge. Others like Gold Farm and Trringo, a Mahindra enterprise, has also set up shop recently for small equipment. Once services of farm equipment-on-hire and information on farm products start reaching rural India, it will start making a difference to India's farm productivity.

Are Irrigation Canals Productive in a Land of Water Shortage?

In 2017 budget, Finance Minister Arun Jaitley announced a massive financial package of ₹0.865 trillion (₹86,500 crore) for funding 99 canal-irrigation projects in dry districts of India. This effort will further accentuate the water shortage that India faces today and will benefit only a handful of farmers. Successive governments in India have pumped in vast sums of money into open water canal-irrigation projects. These are inherently wasteful and divert scarce resources to a few politically connected farmer-politician constituencies. Despite this, less than 10% of India's farms have canal water irrigation while nearly 30% are located in river plains. Remaining 60% of farms are dependent on rain.

Though the Economic Survey of India (ESI) tabled ahead of 2018 budget stated that 53% of India is not under irrigation, World Bank data claims that 65% of Indian agriculture is rain-fed. The ESI data also reveals that of the 60 million hectares of irrigated land, only 9,13,000 (9.13 lakh) hectares is irrigated by canals. Canal irrigation in India was started by the British initially in the eighteenth century to ramp up poppy production in Malwa and Oudh region of central India.

The British converted cotton and paddy fields of India into poppy-growing estates. The poppy produced opium, which it smuggled into China where it was banned. It was done to penetrate the Chinese market which, unlike India, refused to buy British products. But, since the demand for Chinese tea and silks was high in England, the British used fishing boats to smuggle in opium to the Chinese mainland in lieu of Chinese products. This led to two opium wars of 1839 and 1856 that the British won and forced the Chinese to a 100-year lease of Hong Kong. The British also altered the catchment area of Kallanai dam built by a Chola king and now it irrigates about one million acres through the open-irrigation-canal system. It is possibly a reason why there is no water in Cauvery to provide drinking water to the downstream state of Tamil Nadu.

After India's independence, powerful farmer constituencies of Punjab and Haryana ensured that they receive the largesse of canal water irrigation. More than a third of India's canal-irrigation projects are located in these two states catering to rich and politically powerful farmer-politician constituencies. Punjab, which was the land of five rivers, did not need this support. It resulted in wasteful consumption because with free water and free electric supply came powerful pumps that guzzled a costly resource mindlessly. A resource that would soon become a scarce commodity because water-surplus states like Punjab, Haryana and Karnataka use it lavishly, leaving little for downstream states in India's vast hinterland.

But, not all canal-irrigation projects have been counterproductive. A few canal-irrigation projects have had long-term benefits for overall agricultural development of the nation. The Rajasthan Canal Project—a 360-km canal-irrigation project—was devised in the 1970s to bring water from Sutlej-Beas confluence in Punjab to nine parched districts of Rajasthan. It helped in creating a green revolution in the Thar desert and brought prosperity to the barren land.

Also, it is not only irrigation canals that are wasteful. Farm-water supply in India has been wasteful also because electricity provided to farmers is either free or subsidised. Also, modern methods of sustainable farming through drip irrigation or water harvesting have not been introduced in most parts of India. Though some effort is now being made, both in the government and private sector to educate farmers on water conservation, a lot more needs to be done. A major water crisis hit India recently due to indiscriminate use of water in a traditionally water-deficient area of the nation.

Water Crisis—Why Is Water Use in the Agriculture Sector so Unregulated?

Water crisis across India is a man-made creation and is solvable. It happened in Latur in 2016 and in Shimla in 2018 and could happen in more cities in times to come. In 2015 and 2016, cultivation of sugar cane and soya beans in Marathwada region caused an acute and unprecedented water crisis. The region is dry and traditionally farmers used to plant crops like millet which consumed little water. But, farmers were misled to believe that they could earn more by planting cash crops that fetched better rates. So, despite water shortage, they dug borewells and drew water from sub-surface to feed the water-guzzling cash crops. This resulted in the water table receding and a shortage of drinking water in the town of Latur. In May 2018, I discussed the lessons from the Latur water crisis in the think tank, ORF, in an article titled, 'If 80% of Water Is for Agriculture, Why Is it so Unregulated and Inefficient?'

More borewells were dug by the local administration to supply water to Latur city dwellers but they too ran dry. Soon water was supplied by tankers through contractors who dug even deeper borewells, accentuating the crisis. On 19 April 2016, railways had to step in and supply 4,00,000 litres of water by Jaldoot Express. The ferrying of water over a distance of 340 km from Miraj to Latur continued for weeks as the government had to send several trainloads of water to meet the water crisis at Latur. In an article for *Woman's Era* in 2016, titled 'India's *Panghats* Running Dry', I highlighted the plight of women when they face water shortage. Indian homemakers face this water crisis almost single-handedly, only because getting water has been traditionally a woman's duty as she manages kitchen, children and elderly. Indian films have always very graphically depicted this aspect of Indian society, cutting across regions. The politics in a Shekhar Kapur film *Paani* is not easily forgotten.

A year later, nearly four million hectares of agricultural land faced a water crisis in 2017. This resulted in a reduction of land area for cultivation of water-intensive large farm crops like paddy, sugar cane, pulses, coarse serials and oil seeds. While the government is taking several measures to help farmers, including augmentation of water supply, it would be prudent to take measures to reduce water consumption in India's farmlands. Not much authentic data is available on the subject and there is little being done to research and authentically report on sector-wise water consumption across India.

A decade-old Central Water Commission (CWC) report states that 85.3% of India's water was consumed by the agriculture sector in the year 2000. The consumption was expected to marginally reduce to 83.3% by the year 2025. According to CWC, water consumption in other areas like industries and utility sector was less than 5% each. Unfortunately, most of India's water-conservation efforts are done by the industry and utility sector, where the scope to reduce consumption is low. The agriculture sector consuming the most water sees wasteful and unregulated water consumption and no conservation effort. Not much has been done since the independence to reduce water consumption in this sector. As a result, India today faces a needless and unprecedented water crisis.

On basis of 2010–2011 census, India became known as a water-deficient economy after per capita availability of water fell to 1,545 cubic metres per person. It was 15% lower than the previous census and well below the benchmark of 1,700 cubic metres per person, below which nations are considered water deficient. Water availability by 2019 would probably dip further to 1,400 cubic metre per person and various cities like Shimla and Latur have already witnessed acute water crisis. India not only has inadequate data to find out the reasons for this water crisis but lacks the urgency to manage this unprecedented crisis.

We need to quickly introduce conservation measures in agriculture and reduce consumption, if we have to get out of this water crisis. Fields of Punjab, Haryana, Uttarakhand and Western UP are needlessly consuming excessive water for irrigation, in turn starving downstream areas. Similarly, usage of water from rivers south of Vindhyas, namely Krishna, Cauvery and Godavari, is creating deep distress to farmlands downstream. Dispute of Cauvery waters between Karnataka and Tamil Nadu would not have existed if conservation measures had been adopted in farmlands of north Karnataka.

Solution to India's water crisis is available if we look around the globe. A tiny desert state of Israel is one nation that turned from a water-deficient to a water-surplus nation in just one decade. It not only changed over to drip irrigation to manage farms but recycled city storm and waste water—water which is slightly less pure than drinking water and hence reduces the cost of recycling—into agriculture water. It used technology in sowing, planting and cropping to make each operation efficient and sustainable. The Modi government has begun working with conservationists and agriculturists from Israel to bring the learnings to our farmlands.

Does MSP Help Reduce Farm Distress?

It is widely believed that raising MSP periodically is good enough to alleviate the woes of the farming community. Nothing could be farther from the truth. MSP is merely a price point agreed between the government buyers—the state and the central procurement agencies—and farmers or the *mandi* committee commission agents. Though MSP does influence market prices to some extent, it does nothing to ensure a fair price to a majority of farmers. As a matter of fact, MSP helps prosperous farmers in rich agricultural states and does little for poor and marginal farmers across the nation.

In July 2018, the government announced a rise in MSP prices of 20 farm products and linked it to A2+FL (actual paid out cost plus imputed value of family labour) or 1.5 times of cost price on basis of actual paid-out cost plus an imputed value of agriculture labour. It gave a political scoring point to the government but did nothing to alleviate farmers' woes. This is because, apart from wheat and rice, procurement in other crops on which MSP has been raised like sunflower, soya bean, ragi and *jowar* saw little or no procurement by central agencies in 2016–2017. With Food Corporation of India godowns overflowing and lacking the space to stock and state corporations lacking cash muscle, it is highly unlikely that even by the end of financial year 2018–2019 end meaningful procurement will take place. Wheat and rice procurement only helps rich farmers.

A look at the procurement pattern of Food Corporation of India or state corporations shows how biased the system is towards small landholders. Food Corporation lifts 40–50% of rice and wheat stock every year while state corporations do balance procurement. Both in wheat and rice, Food Corporation of India procures 30% of its stocks from Punjab alone and mostly from the biggest farmers of the state.

The bias towards big farms of Punjab and Haryana was even more in the past. Corporation officers say that it is because the quality of wheat and rice is the best. Smaller the farms, lower the quality making it unfit for procurement. Hence, chance of small and marginal farmers benefiting from Food Corporation of India buying stocks or MSP prices being increased is low. Besides, most of the procurement Food Corporation of India does is from north India. As a matter of fact, Tamil Nadu and Kerala, both rice-growing states, are surprisingly given complete short shrift by central procurement agencies.

Under any circumstance, a rise in MSP is no guarantee for removal of farm distress. It is merely a myth and successive governments have gained political mileage by announcing MSP hikes. As a matter of fact, contract farming provides a better all-round realisation. But, state governments are yet to reframe and do away with restrictive policies under the APMC Act that makes it mandatory for farmers to sell through APMC *mandi*. Recently, the central government initiated Model Agriculture Produce and Livestock Marketing Act that permits farmers to sell to anyone they want to—be it food processors, wholesalers, grocery merchants or even internet e-commerce sellers. However, unless states free farmers from APMC Act and give them the freedom to market their products, it would be difficult for agriculture to prosper in India.

Part VI

Social Sector

CHAPTER 13

MGNREGA: Need Wage Distribution and Rural Asset Building

Despite high-decibel slugfest between the ruling party and the opposition during the last four years, there are signs of a healthy and maturing democracy developing in India. Almost every development programme started by or before UPA has been restructured, at times renamed and often improved and implemented by NDA. Nothing has been abandoned. They have merely been renamed, refined, repackaged and executed in a better way. Similarly, states ruled by opposition parties have in many cases implemented central government's schemes with improved modifications, more fervour and due diligence than the BJP-ruled states.

Though schemes may have changed names in opposition-ruled states, budget allocation has been put to good use and development agenda pursued with equal or more vigour. This was observed in the states of West Bengal, Tamil Nadu, Andhra Pradesh and Telangana. This is a very healthy trend because it shows respect for institutions and social programmes, irrespective of political party or leader who may have initiated the narrative.

MGNREGA scheme was a flagship programme of critical social importance that saw a lot of change under the Modi government. True, it did not see the same gusto and energy that Aadhaar or rural electrification programme saw but it did see some very critical restructuring that was needed for the longevity of such country-wide rural employment programmes. UPA, in all its wisdom, designed the MGNREGA scheme as a social welfare scheme for poor across rural India. Its primary focus was the distribution of 100 days of wages each year to unemployed manual labour. The wages were to be paid for manual labour doing designated work under MGNREGA. The designated work would be primarily beneficial to villages that were part of the scheme and their long-term development. The vision of the programme was to uplift the status of the rural poor in 600 poorest districts of the country and simultaneously benefit the village infrastructure and economy. It was a bold and pragmatic vision of generating employment for the poorest of the poor and the UPA supremo Sonia Gandhi deserves full credit for it.

Ever since its start in 2005, each year, around ₹40,000 crore (₹400 billion) were being spent on MGNREGA rural wage programme. It was one of the largest poverty-alleviation programmes in the world. Since the primary focus of UPA was poverty alleviation and not building rural assets, it had little checks and balances to ensure rigour and productivity of work. The scheme was hence both lauded as well as derided by sociologists and economists around the globe—lauded for mitigation of acute poverty and distress across rural India; derided for corruption and also wastage and inefficient use of taxpayers' money to fund assets that were not productive and permanent.

Importantly, MGNREGA has improved the livelihood of small and marginal farmers who have used the scheme to augment falling agriculture incomes. It has helped increase rural wages. Its effect has been positive and that has been substantiated by National Sample Survey Office (NSSO) data on landless labourers. At the same time, it has created tightness in job markets, which again is an indicator of higher rural wages and prosperity across rural India. But, it has also created a lot of corruption and wasted funds that could have been easily used for rural development.

Revamping MGNREGA

MGNREGA, like Aadhaar, was another laudable scheme that was poorly structured and poorly executed by UPA. According to the scheme's website, 53% of the expenditure done during 2011–2012 and 58% expenses incurred during 2012–2013 were spent on water conservation projects in over 620 poorest districts of the country. This was a sorely-needed initiative because in 2010, India entered the league of water-deficient nations. That is when per capita availability of water dropped to less than 1,700 cubic metres per person. In 2018, it is estimated to have fallen to around 1,400 cubic metres per person. Also, as per a World Bank report, nearly 29% of waterbodies across the nation were in a critical or semi-critical condition that year. The numbers would have grown in the past decade.

Poverty alleviation and asset building to ensure adequate water resources to villages was a heady mix of good politics and good economics that UPA initiated but missed out on. Had UPA ensured and insisted on creating durable assets and a mechanism to ensure recharging and monitoring of waterbodies and aquifers in MGNREGA, they could have taken the programme to the next level. Unfortunately, UPA has faced several challenges in the implementation of the flagship programme since its initiation.

Scheme for how the work is to be done under MGNREGA was not structured and laid out properly. Detailed work specifications were either missing or incomplete. So, auditing of programme done initially by CAG highlighted systemic deficiencies and suggested changes to make the programme more robust and effective. But, not much action was taken because of vested interests that profited from lack of auditing and accountability. Whereas there was widespread criticism of corruption and wastage in the execution of MGNREGA, the Congress party both at the centre and at states failed to respond and rectify the shortcomings. MGNREGA was not a free wages scheme. It was a right-to-work scheme. Under the scheme 620 poorest districts of the country were identified. In every district, the unemployed would be entitled to 100 days of work as specified in the act within 5 km from home. However, on scrutiny it was found that while wages were distributed, little or no work was done. Under pressure from audit agencies and the parliament, the UPA even went on to assert that MGNREGA was a rural wage scheme and not an asset-building exercise. This, however, did not get them expected votes.

Harvesters Replace Humans as Rural Migration Slows

MGNREGA had both a positive and a negative effect on the rural economy. MGNREGA curbed growing rural migration. Since some sort of employment was locally available for 100 days a year, rural poor and landless peasants from UP and Bihar stopped migrating to Punjab and Haryana in search of jobs. As a result of this approach, farm labour became very expensive in north India. Daily wages, especially of agriculture labour, in Punjab and Haryana nearly doubled in the first three years of implementation of MGNREGA, leading to use of more farm equipment.

Combined harvesters found their way to golden fields of Punjab and Haryana along with a lot of small farm equipment that eventually replaced humans. They also improved productivity immensely. But, human job losses became permanent. In 2012–2013, sensing high demand, global conglomerates like Germany's Claas and America's Deere and Company set up operations in the two states. Till then, half a dozen local harvester makers had operated in the space. Use of harvesters grew meteorically not only in Punjab and Haryana but in neighbouring states of UP, Rajasthan, Madhya Pradesh, Maharashtra and Gujarat.

So, the scheme to give jobs to poor across rural India actually made them dispensable and redundant. Farm labour from UP and Bihar had built a reputation for decades as a dependable low-cost migrant workforce in prosperous rural farmlands of northern India. Some of them had worked in Punjab for generations and spoke fluent Punjabi and resided in temporary or permanent homes in villages there. It was a thriving ecosystem of hundreds and thousands of migrants supporting India's largest agricultural community. With the arrival of MGNREGA, that market took a beating as the labour did not often return to work at the farms. As a result, the cost of farm labour in north India doubled. So, farm-input costs in Punjab rose significantly. Also, the market for immigrant farm labour collapsed with the arrival of MGNREGA.

But, there is strong evidence suggesting that MGNREGA did not actually hurt farm labour in local markets. In short, it did curb migration but it did not take away farmers from agriculture work. Rather farm labour from UP and Bihar did not migrate but used MGNREGA wages to supplement their local income from agriculture. This, because average employment under MGNREGA was at least 54 days each year, if not 100, under the scheme. MGNREGA did not make them prosperous but did help them raise their incomes. So, landless labourers had a choice of employment without going to distant markets for work.

Whereas the scheme as such had high potential to create rural assets, the persistent reluctance to create transparent benchmarks made the scheme wasteful and open to corrupt practices. It was obvious that the scheme would be restructured and revamped once the new government came to power. But, when the Modi government at the centre proposed social audits of the scheme and new benchmarks to evaluate the performance of the programme, there was a lot of resistance from states. It was only after the centre agreed to pay for audits and the salaries of officers involved in the process, that states agreed to the audit process.

Centre Funds Social Audits of MGNREGA for Three Years

The Modi government finally initiated the social audit process in 2015. Social audit ensured the proper implementation of the project. Despite its provision in the Act, states had earlier showed an unwillingness to conduct social audits citing lack of funds, say officials under the Ministry of Rural Development. Now that the central government has decided to take care of expenses incurred during audits for the first three years, states do not have room to refuse it. Regular social audits have started in most states and compliance has improved.

After the audit process was set, restructuring the world's largest rural employment programme began. This again is complicated and will be time-consuming. Powerful vested interests, who have profited from badly-run government programmes, still block reforms at every level. So, objections will be raised by departments of both central and state governments and also activists and NGOs who profited from the system. A back-of-the-envelope calculation shows that expenditure on MGNREGA should have created rural assets worth ₹3 trillion (₹3 lakh crore) during the last decade. But, neither were any permanent assets—like water reservoirs, ponds, aquifers, roads—created, nor were there any reasonable assessments of this inventory.

Vested interests also include patwaris and local district administrators who sanction the payments. Most of them want to maintain the status quo. They do not want current ways of evaluation and verification of work mechanisms at MGNREGA to change. They repeatedly speak of delayed payments despite the fact that during the UPA regime, payments were often delayed by as much as six to nine months. This backlog of wages under MGNREGA is a legacy issue of redistribution of wealth from centre to states and stays high in as many as 20 states. This, however, does not mean that MGNREGA payments to beneficiaries are delayed in most states by six months.

NDA, to its credit, has used Aadhaar and created a mechanism for direct payment of wages into bank accounts of people who worked and benefitted from the scheme. This has improved and hastened the payment process. It also bypassed a heady mix of politicians and officers at block and panchayat level, social workers, state and central government officers and senior politicians who were enjoying unauthorised benefits from the redistribution of wealth. These people, irrespective of political leanings, want to stop reforms at the department as well as the political level. A false campaign saying that NDA was trying to stop MGNREGA was created. The fact that some major states ruled by the BJP, like Goa, Gujarat and UP, slowed down projects under MGNREGA gave credence to rumour mills.

Meanwhile, the NDA government steadily continued to strengthen the social audit system instead of changing it with an external audit mechanism. Besides, some opposition-ruled states did take advantage of MGNREGA payouts and delivered to people as well as created permanent assets to improve local waterbodies. West Bengal was one state that had a tradition of nurturing ponds and waterbodies, both in rural areas as well as in cities. Over the last 30 years, depleting groundwater levels and growth of the building industry has converted a large number of ponds into brick kilns. This has helped grow development and infrastructure at the cost of environmental damage.

The state took upon itself to recharge its waterbodies with the help of MGNREGA. Replying to All India Trinamool Congress (TMC) member of parliament Manas Bhuiyan in Rajya Sabha, Minister of State for Rural Development Ram Kripal Yadav stated that West Bengal generated more than 28.21 crore work days under the scheme so far in 2017–2018 and spent more than ₹7,335.31 crore for it. Tamil Nadu, another state with a history of conserving waterbodies, and Andhra Pradesh spent over ₹5,000 crore each under the scheme, showing that MGNREGA was perfectly working for state governments willing to use it for development.

MGNREGA Reforms Start with Emphasis on Durable Assets

After a slow and hesitant start, the much-needed reforms to the scheme did start to happen in 2017. The Modi government incorporated the much-needed change in MGNREGA by inserting the following clause—'Only those components of admissible works that lead to the creation of durable assets may be taken up under MGNREGA. Items of expenditure that are recurring in nature and/or do not lead to the creation of durable assets, are not permitted under MGNREGA'.

This was an understated but essential reform to ensure accountability of India's flagship rural employment programme. MGNREGA has the potential to be a game changer for the rural economy and ensure water security for rural India. But, the clause mandating the creation of durable assets was only the beginning of reforms. There were several other structural changes made to the Act that changed the capability of the programme to build durable assets.

All these were notified in the master circular—a programme implementation guide—issued each year. This included a change of wages to material ratio and permission to use machines in unavoidable circumstances in building activity. Use of machines was not permitted before, possibly because MGNREGA was essentially conceived as a rural employment programme. UPA, which conceived the programme, did not want machine construction to take over fund flow and relegate humans in distress. This is an important objective but cannot be the sole criteria for any development work. Especially because the benefit of speedy and sustainable development benefits people at large.

Quality benchmarks and timely delivery of social projects are very important, especially in the rural sector where development work has been languishing for decades. Water crisis across the country makes timely completion of water-conservation projects even more important. Whereas it is important to give rural employment, it is equally important to bring correct and productive solutions. Digging a hole in ground serves no purpose. Water-conservation projects need scientific and technological inputs to ensure they are functional and beneficial. This eventually will lead to revisions of specifications depending on location, terrain, water table and other geographical features to maintain waterbodies and recharge aquifers. It will also ensure that the waterbodies built are monitored from time to time, contain clean and adequate water and are sustainable.

The government has already permitted Member of Parliament Local Area Development Scheme (MPLADS) funds to be used for MGNREGA projects. This means that members of parliament who are given ₹50 million (₹5 crore) to spend in their constituency each year can spend those funds for MGNREGA. Afforestation, tree plantation and horticultural activities have been permitted under the scheme. Also, activities can be taken up in forest and common as well as private lands, under 2018–2019 master circular issued by the Ministry of Rural Development. There is also a move to use MGNREGA labour for agriculture and plantation and several other government projects. Purists will always say that making agriculture or government rural development projects a part of MGNREGA would dilute its objective. But, it is more important to expand work base and scope for such long-term projects under the scheme instead of sticking to a rigid and small definition.

One of the criteria for giving jobs under MGNREGA is that it should be within 5 km from a beneficiary's home, so that he/she does not have to travel long distances for work. This means the work comes to the person and not vice versa as the case in most other jobs. As the work under MGNREGA has to be manual, productive and durable as well as location specific, it is good that it becomes part of a greater ecosystem that thrives and caters to the larger goal of rural and village development.

MGNREGA is important because it supports rural poor, most of whom are skilled to do only manual labour. It is also critical to the rural and the national economy as it spends more than half its resources in water-conservation efforts. If these two important goals are focused on and a productive output generated, it will indeed be extremely beneficial for the rural economy. In this context, efforts of National Institution for Transforming India (NITI Aayog)—the rejigged and renamed Planning

Commission—to create benchmarks for states in water-conservation projects is commendable.

Real development work will happen not because political leadership thinks of a bright idea and talks about its implementation, it will only happen if state and central government institutions work together and make it happen. That is the most important part of the reform process and can be a win-win solution for all if implemented properly. It is too early to say if that will happen with MGNREGA but there are early indications that reforms will give the flagship project of UPA better accountability and a chance to prosper. That would help mitigate woes of rural agriculture labour, especially those, including women and the elderly, who do not have skill sets beyond manual field work. A component of work commensurate with a disability needs to be worked into the reforms.

CHAPTER 14

Swachh Bharat Mission: Is Rural India Using the Toilets Build?

Like MGNREGA, SBM is a social cause that will have a far-reaching impact on millions of poor Indian households that do not have access to basic sanitation facilities. Like MGNREGA, it is a flagship programme taken up by the government on an unprecedented scale. The only difference is that the MGNREGA programme was a rural employment programme brought in by UPA. SBM is a health and sanitation programme brought in by the NDA government under PM Narendra Modi.

Considering that it was a programme conceived by the PM himself, SBM went ahead full steam from 2015, a year after the Modi government took office. States were directed to take up the work under SBM and report the same through an online mechanism with data of all beneficiaries made public online.

It was not that toilets had not been built previously with assistance from the government. Rural sanitation programme was first started in 1986 under Central Rural Sanitation Programme (CRSP). A United Nations Development Programme (UNDP) health report of 1982 and the Human Development Report 1998 of UNDP had identified open defecation as a key reason for poor health and widespread diseases across rural India. In 1999, the Indian government introduced the Total Sanitation Campaign (TSC) throughout the nation. It was scaled up and made operational in 572 districts. But in 2013, a six-country study commissioned by a Washington-based Water and Sanitation Program revealed that 72.63% people in rural

India practised open defecation. The reason was primarily reluctance of people to change their traditional habits. For years the government of India carried on with toilet-building projects with fund support from UNDP without any accountability. A World Bank data quoting WHO/United Nations International Children's Emergency Fund Joint Monitoring Programme for Water Supply and Sanitation shows that the percentage of the population practising open defecation in India was 66% in the year 2000 and though it has receded, it is still high at 40% in the year 2015. UPA II rechristened TSC programme to Nirmal Bharat in 2008–2009. It built around 10 million toilets a year for around three years, after which the drive tapered off. Most of those toilets were dysfunctional and not in use and the UPA government had maintained no data on the website of the concerned ministry. This was unlike the current government, which has tried to put all data on the SBM website and has made an all-out effort to reboot the cleanliness drive, though again without much success.

PM Modi's initiative was a powerful drive from the highest level, prioritising Clean India drive with SBM-Urban (SBM-U) and SBM-Grameen (SBM-G) programmes and a promise of delivery. Everybody expected it would succeed and that results would be noticeable soon. The NDA government under PM Modi had delivered on Aadhaar—a scheme started by UPA but one that it could not complete. NDA had also delivered on GST after UPA could not get it legislated during its decade-long rule. NDA had also delivered on coal and spectrum auctions within one year—something that UPA failed to do despite frequent admonishing by the SC and the CAG. So, everybody expected that SBM would be a grand success.

How Many Toilets Were Built and Used?

SBM programme got off to a flying start with targets set at five million for the year 2014–2015 and 12 million for the year 2015–2016. States reported good progress of work with 5.85 million toilets built in the first year and 12.75 million in the next. However, in 2016–2017, the Ministry of Drinking Water and Sanitation claimed that 21.9 million toilets were built under SBM against a target of 15 million. The data was as sent by the states and compiled by the central government. But, the sudden spike in toilet-building activity in the year ending March 2017 created doubts about its veracity. That is when the data started coming under media scrutiny and number crunching began. This was because of two reasons.

First, toilets were to be built against budgetary allocation of ₹7,200 per household from central government and ₹4,800 per household from state governments. During 2014–2015, only ₹2,850 crore was allocated to SBM-G and during the next year, ₹6,524 crore was allocated under the scheme, both of which were insufficient to meet the assigned annual targets. With no additional provisioning from central government, only 10 million toilets could have been built in the first two years against a target of 17 million. Also, the funds allocated by the centre in the first three years could fund only 22 million toilets against the target given of 32 million toilets to be built. How could the results have exceeded the target with 40 million toilets being built when funds were allocated only for half of that?

Second, ground reports from states did not suggest a major shift in toilet habits. A major challenge, as before, was not only constructing toilets but about ease of use and actual usage of toilets. True, the Modi government has made efforts to change the design of toilets in SBM-G. Design improvements included the adoption of eco-friendly toilets. A twin leach pit design helped in creating more sustainable toilets than single leach pit or sceptic tank toilets. There are several other innovative toilet designs that have been introduced in the last few years including bio-digester toilets introduced by Defence Research and Development Organisation (DRDO), bamboo toilets developed by Nagaland Bamboo Development Agency, Nano Membrane toilet and unmanned solar-powered e-toilets. But, the use of toilets by rural households has been unusually slow and uncertain.

The government has proactively started to look into low use of toilets. Expert teams appointed by the ministry confirmed that only a third of the toilets constructed are sustainable and safe in the long run. The reason is primarily lack of information about the toilets before installation. Also, lack of interest and ownership of households that created the infrastructure on government directive and money. This was identified as the key reason why the money was not well spent in SBM-G programme. Some schemes were introduced by local bodies in Vellore and Tiruchi in Tamil Nadu to incentivise the use of toilets by monetising through micro-composting. But, these efforts are at an early stage and will take time to yield results.

There is no doubt that the central government has been spending money on television advertisement about Clean India and spreading awareness. But still, a major gap in communication between the government and the rural citizens exists on the use of toilets and a lot more has to be done to educate the masses. Unless rural folk genuinely understand its importance and use, it is extremely difficult for any government to impose toilets on half a billion citizens. So, an incentive to build toilets will work only when awareness about why a toilet should be installed and regularly used is created repeatedly. That is a huge challenge but one that needs to be seized by the horn if health and sanitation of the nation have to improve.

Parliamentary Committee Report

Since *Swachh Bharat* has been conceived and implemented with an initiative from the PM himself, its design, layout and execution were expected to be smooth and trouble-free. Unfortunately, it was not. The programme has witnessed teething problems. The biggest problem is the mindset of rural people and religious believes that have been deeply ingrained in their ethos. To get over those prejudices, people need to be educated about sanitation and health. People must be coaxed and cajoled to get out of deep-rooted caste and religious prejudices. They need to be trained to develop a civic sense and collective responsibility to keep India clean. That itself is a complex task and may take a decade to be achieved.

We must understand that the sanitation challenge under SBM is largely a rural challenge. As per government data released in the end of 2017, rural household toilets constructed were 53.8 million against 3.3 million urban toilets. Urban users want those toilets and use them. Over one million toilet applications are awaiting approval under SBM-U scheme. On the other hand, rural users avoid using them due to deep-rooted social prejudices. The still-entrenched caste-based system that relegates toilet cleaners—the community of Dalits—to the position of untouchables, makes the toilet an unholy place. That is the biggest challenge for SBM-G. Perhaps a village-to-village demonstration of scientific conversion of faecal matter into money-spinning manure in sunny India will bring results. It will also help the same untouchable community get gainful employment through science and technology.

Many Indians in rural India believe that the toilet is an unclean and unholy place and hence cannot be part of the house. They believe that it is impure, and so every time you go there, you have to take a bath to be able to go to the bedroom or the prayer room. So, the problems are fundamental—it is resistance to the use of toilets due to social prejudices. Cleaning of toilets and disposal of waste are taboo. It is this near-hostile approach of rural consumers to the use of toilet that needs to be overcome. Unless that barrier is crossed, all other efforts will fail. People need to be told that they use the fields where they defecate to grow food. The faecal matter turns into manure. Converted faecal matter is equally sustainable.

To overcome that barrier, more expenditure has to be done on educating the people. SBM has a provision for expenditure on information, education and communication (IEC). Normally, a private-sector company would be spending around 10% of its expenses on communication and marketing in case they would be challenged with a conceptually difficult product like the toilet to rural India. However, the data on the amount spent on IEC available on SBM-G website by different state governments is revealing. Only north-eastern states of Sikkim, Arunachal Pradesh, Meghalaya and Nagaland along with Haryana spent 3–4% of their budget on education and communication, the rest spent around 1% or less. This is also because literacy and awareness of personal hygiene are high in these north-eastern states.

As a matter of fact, it appears that even the governments of UP and Bihar were not convinced about the criticality of SBM. A recent inspection by the parliamentary standing committee on rural development revealed reluctance and apathy of some of India's largest states to take up SBM. Usage of toilets is minimal by households of UP and Bihar and so has been the use of funds in the building of toilets. The parliamentary committee inspecting the state of open defecation-free (ODF) India stated, 'Even a village with 100% household toilets cannot be declared ODF till all inhabitants start using them.' Unfortunately, most of the toilets constructed under the scheme have not been used due to a variety of reasons.

The parliament committee report states, 'Sanitation coverage figures seemed to be more on "paper" but actual progress at ground level is very lethargic... The visible reality through the experiences reveal(s) that much more is needed to be done so as to obtain the "behavioural change" in the rural populace to attain the real motive behind the programme.' Non-functional toilets, non-availability of water and non-completion of downstream sewerage are the key reasons for their non-use. Also, the use has been minimal because rural awareness about the scheme is not high. Not enough has been done to educate the users who have traditionally been used to open defecation.

But, this is not the only reason why SBM is not in the pink of health. The government informed Rajya Sabha that over ₹14,000 crore of SBM-G funds were returned as unutilised in the year 2017–2018. UP, Bihar, Madhya Pradesh, Assam and Odisha accounted for the largest unused funds. Now, if such large amounts of funds are unutilised, then SBM is surely not on track. The figures confirmed by the states that show targets have been exceeded cannot happen if funds have not been utilised. Getting the right data is a responsibility of the government and the government must ensure compliance from all sources that send data to adhere to global best practices or any other acceptable benchmark.

It is high time that the government does some introspection on how to get the people to use the toilets and importantly, how to get SBM back on track. Thousands of crores of taxpayers' money has been spent on toilet-building projects in rural India but the usage of toilets is minimal. There are five things to get right in SBM without which SBM-G will not succeed.

Five Things to Get Right in SBM-G

Understanding the psychology of rural people is key to the issue. Beliefs, both religious and social, are deep-rooted. It is widely believed that 90% of rural Indians feel that toilets are unclean and impure and that they should be far away from homes. But, there is no authentic and comprehensive survey done by the government to understand the psychology of the rural Indians and the deep apathy towards toilets that they today own. Are we living in denial? Should not each state government conduct multiple surveys and find out the reasons for the low usage of toilets? Why is an urban user keen to use those same toilets that a rural user refuses to?

For over a decade, the attempt to get rural Indians to stop open air defecation and use toilets has evinced poor response. But, nobody bothered to ensure that things be set right. The current high-profile push by PM Modi can get the toilets built but cannot ensure their usage. So, is it right to keep spending taxpayers' money on building toilets that no one uses? This is possibly a time to introspect on our traditional habits. We need to question ourselves. Is tradition coming in the way of health and hygiene of our nation? Why is the nation not responding despite this monumental initiative by the government? Though the degree may differ, there is apathy against toilet use in most Indian states. The reasons would possibly differ and so would the level of indifference but we need to find out why it is happening and find a way to set it right.

It is important to reach out to each state, language, ethnic group, caste, community and religion to find out their individual prejudices and responses to building toilets in their homes. In many cases, it could be a religious belief of not touching the impure but there would be other reasons also that could range from lack of user-friendliness, bad toilet design, inadequate water supply or any other. This may include lack of basic housing itself. Reaching out and interacting with each group in the society is needed because their responses would not be similar. Since India is not a homogenous group, one survey or solution would not fit all. A nationwide survey conducted by all states should take an in-depth look into it. It should be without politics, considering religious beliefs, regional biases, topography and terrain. Such surveys should be conducted by state governments in their native language, with an objective to find solutions. If necessary, expert psychologists should be employed to gauge this mass mentality that has a mind block in going to a well-built modern toilet at home but has no problems with defecating in the open.

Once the results of the surveys are analysed, measures should be taken to ensure better response as per the data received from each state. This could mean investment in education or counselling by religious and social leaders. It could also mean investment in more films and audio visuals on social causes. Some films have succeeded on such social causes. Maybe more should be made to give a continuous push. Celebrity endorsement and advertisement do help and should be pursued. Importantly, school children who are not too rigid about social and religious taboos should be educated about the health benefits of using toilets. One Akshay Kumar film is just not enough.

The second-most-important issue is to ensure data integrity of the toilets built. The right numbers built under SBM-G scheme each year should be accurately represented. Clearly, the number of toilets build under SBM-G as per the data given by the states far exceeds the funds allocated. How did this happen? Especially since some states including UP and Bihar have not utilised full funds allocated under SBM-G. If 5% of the toilets are built against allocation from other funds like MGNREGA, they should be clearly demarcated. Also, fraudulent fudging of numbers need to be stopped.

If need be, counting of numbers must be done under the supervision of a regulatory body so that the numbers provided are genuine. This is, after all, about the veracity of the accounting process of a national fund run with taxpayers' money. Audit and account bodies of each state assisted by CAG can help in the exercise of getting the numbers right. For years, government funds have been spent but are not being properly utilised despite the absence of corruption. This is a sad state of affairs and points a finger to the indifference we citizens have to '*sarkari* projects'. Bureaucracy is not bothered about it and politicians are not informed about it. Media that should report on these omissions is conspicuously absent. So, year after year, governments, irrespective of their political party, spend taxpayers' money without ensuring that its benefits reach the people.

The Modi government, over the last four years, has been taking corrective measures where its decision-making had gone wrong. We have seen it in GST that was repeatedly modified. Now it is time to revisit SBM-G programme and restructure it. The emphasis should now be on the quality and usability of the toilets built and not on counting numbers. Each state must also revisit the functionality of the toilets built. Early reports suggest that nearly a fifth of the toilets built are dysfunctional and need to be scrapped and nearly a third need upgradation to double leach pit system. This will make the toilets functional and sustainable, to be used safely over a long period of time.

The third important initiative is to ensure a water supply to all toilets. This is easier said than done as rural piped water project is awaiting to be completely functional. Pipes have been laid in some places but pumps are not yet in place in pump houses. In some cases, there are no overhead tanks so the basic 24/7 connectivity to a water source is not there. A functional toilet is something that would need a continuous water supply and that is itself a challenge in distant rural areas of the country. The departments of water supply and the departments of sanitation are different in most state governments and coordination between the two is not there in many areas.

The parliamentary standing committee on rural development chaired by Dr P. Venugopal has stated, 'Construction of toilets without adequate availability of water will be an impediment to achieving 100% sanitation coverage in rural areas.' The committee has recommended that provision of water availability should be prioritised without going into the numbers. It has opined that where no water is available along with construction of toilets, it is not possible to attain ODF status. Many villages would fall under this classification and it would be necessary to segregate them and make them water-enabled.

The fourth important feature is verifying and removing biases. Is the complaint against rural SBM-G toilets emanating foul smell true? This would mean checking for smell and pollution effect of working toilets in rural households. No such problem is usually reported in urban toilets. But in cities, our toilets are big, spacious and well aerated. They are not confined in a two-by-two cubicle. Also, they are often equipped with room fresheners, exhaust fans or air purifiers. Poor slums and underprivileged housing in our cities too do not complain. Villages have more space and are easier to aerate but they still face more complaints after toilets have been built.

Also, flushing water in the toilets is just one part of the story. The traditional belief of being impure after use of toilet makes Indians wash their backsides with water instead of wiping it clean. Anyway, production of toilet paper for one billion plus will be a huge environmental challenge. In India, the practice is to use water after ablutions instead of toilet paper. So, more use of water happens in India in our toilets. Also, after ablutions, there is washing of hands with soap and hence again more use of water. Most Indian toilets must have three source points of water to have a functional toilet. One for flushing, one for ablutions and one for hand washing. All these usages need to be integrated at liquid-solid waste management interface at the grassroots level.

Also, this would depend on the functioning of toilets after repeated use. Are they equipped with a robust cleaning and evacuation system? Are the flushing systems working and effective? Is water supply continuous? If there is a mechanical failure, are spares available to repair the same? How good is the system under continuous use and if it is not, what are the remedies? Maybe SBM-G supplier should have a service team in place to ensure maintenance.

The fifth, and one of the most important points, is connectivity of waste and sludge removal to a sewerage disposal system. Over some time, this needs to be developed and put to use especially for larger villages or semi-urban clusters. The needs of a small village and a large village differ. Then there are a wide range of hydrological conditions applicable depending on locations, terrain and geography. One solution is never possible to meet every condition.

There are toilets that can be attached to biogas plants while others where sewerage leads to treatment and recycling plants. Here again, layouts, elevations, slants, natural drainage flows and quantity of sewerage can widely differ from place to place. So, there is no single solution but multiple of ways of how sewerage and disposal systems can be designed and managed. The success of the SBM-G lies in solving a complex number of issues. It starts with removing the bias of rural folks against the use of toilets and ends with optimum designing, manufacturing and installing technologically feasible, easy-to-use, sustainable and low-cost solutions that consumers accept.

Part VII

Employment

CHAPTER 15
Jobs Are Growing, but so Are Educated Unemployed

In the age of disruptive technologies, many jobs will vanish. Large corporations will start becoming defunct as new businesses replace them. The life span of companies will become shorter as mighty Kodaks and General Motors file for bankruptcy. Those who will survive will be lean and mean. Brookings Institution reports that Foxconn, the company that manufactures Apple products, plans to automate 60,000 jobs, while Walmart, the retailer, will use AI to replace 7,000 workers in 2018.

Our low-end NRI workforce of the tech world will possibly be the first to be replaced. Many coding jobs will be lost in the first rush. Then, electric car technologies may soon make our fossil-fuel driven automobile industry obsolete. These new-generation Chinese electric vehicles produced by automated plants take a third of the manpower needed to produce a traditional diesel or petrol car. It prompted Elon Musk to joke about bankruptcy, sending Tesla shares into a nosedive in August 2018. Several manufacturing industries will soon witness an introduction of robots. This is because 'Made in China' AI products are much cheaper than Japanese or American counterparts of first-generation products.

In the next two to five years, you could see drone-assisted paddy farming driving farm labour out of business, AI-driven teaching modules making many teachers redundant, copy editors being fully replaced by AI and field reporters sacrificed by the lesser media at the altar of aggregated news. You could find completely human-less transport fleets driving millions out of business. You could possibly be watching robotic cinema where visually enhanced and digitally sculpted humans replace Tiger Shroffs and Disha Patanis in an action movie. Job security will go out of the window. Try as we may, we cannot resist this. But, what we need is alternative employment to replace jobs. We need to encourage transparent contract jobs instead of shunning them. And we need data on a real-time basis to see where corrections are needed.

It Is Not That All Jobs Are Vanishing

However, it is not that jobs are not being created. In fact, they are growing. But, so is the number of educated unemployed. As more and more young people are getting educated, the pressure on the job markets of India is relentless. Though jobs are growing both in the organised and unorganised sector, it cannot match the pace of graduates being churned out in colleges across India. Hence, the disenchantment among both rural and urban youth. Receipts of Employee Provident Fund Organisation (EPFO) show the numbers being employed. When there are seven million new accounts created in EPFO database and payments have been made by employees and employers, then surely those jobs have been created. True, some experts have challenged the numbers. But, that is only because data entry about their names were not all correct. That again has a typically bureaucratic explanation. As government departments are not permitted to hire data entry operators due to a strange rule, the data entry work is left to contract employees, hence it could be of substandard quality. Contract work incentivises quick deliveries and quality of entries could have suffered as a result. The opposition however claims that the high numbers are due to better updation of existing data and is not due to new jobs created.

Again, though the manufacturing sector is down, the service sector is buoyant with air traffic, healthcare services and travel generating jobs. Besides, data from states like West Bengal, Kerala, Andhra Pradesh and Tamil Nadu show the creation of a large number of jobs. Programmes under MGNREGA, MUDRA loan scheme, rural electrification programme and rural piped drinking water scheme, Digital India and Clean India must have created millions of jobs. But, in absence of data, there is no authentic method to certify the numbers.

Job Losses in IT Sector

Job data is one of the most important data in the US and in most maturing democracies. But, it has been missing—no longer available on the labour ministry website in India—for almost a decade. The data first went missing in 2009 when the number of jobs fell after huge job losses were reported in the US and in India's export-dependent IT sector. It was not uploaded after that. India had to do with a badly prepared annual survey of the labour bureau—which was again disbanded in 2017. This time again, it was possibly due to sudden job losses in the IT sector. Once again it was due to the events in the US markets. But, since then, India has lost the little indicator it had on the way the job markets were going.

For decades, Indian IT companies had been using contract labour from India to supplement its nimble US-based workforce. The modus operandi was simple. Contract staff from its India offices would work from India and occasionally out of the US to finish US projects. It was an accepted cost-cutting exercise that no one objected to. But, then came Trump. And with him started the investigations of malpractices by foreign companies affecting domestic US jobs.

Indian IT companies reorganised themselves quickly before being booked. They hired Americans to do the work in the US. The contract labour practice that had been in vogue for donkey's years went out of the window. All that meant additional costs. It also meant that the staff which was being contracted out of India suddenly was redundant.

Extensive interviews and surveys by business daily *Mint* revealed that retrenchment had already started by March 2017. Tech Mahindra and Wipro had respectively fired 1,000 and 600 employees already and the top seven IT companies of India were planning to shed whopping 56,000 jobs. Some other organised sectors in the private sector also showed a dismal picture.

The Needless Controversy around Payroll Reporting

To get the right employment data, labour bureau has been conducting a quarterly employment survey in a bid to access sector-wise employment situation in India. But, there are various limitations in the system that need to be addressed to give a clear picture.

On 15 January 2018, Professor Pulak Ghosh of IIM Bangalore and Dr Soumya Kanti Ghosh, chief economist at SBI, published an academic paper highlighting the limitations of the current survey and instead recommended a payroll report for India on the same lines as the US. The objective of the Ghosh and Ghosh survey as per the report was to establish that 'surveys to measure employment in India are mostly misleading'. The conclusion of the report was, 'Ideally, we must move gradually to a monthly payroll (system) like in US.' But, whereas that can perhaps be a long-term goal, it is easier said than done. The reason is the poor state of current databases of three organisations—EPFO that manages employee provident fund, National Small Industries Corporation (NSIC) that looks after state employee insurance and National Pension System (NPS) trust that handles the national pension system and all other state-run databases that government offices maintain as well as the data available with the private sector.

These databases were initially maintained manually for decades but somewhere between 2010 and 2012, these records were computerised. At that time, the work was done shoddily without proper supervision. As a result, names and details of all the beneficiaries are not correctly mentioned. There is a lot of duplication and a lot of incomplete records. Only 20% of the records have PAN. Nonetheless, payments in the aforementioned accounts keep coming in both from contributors as well as the government.

However, once the academic paper 'Towards Payroll Reporting in India' by Ghosh and Ghosh was presented to the PMO and released in the public domain, it became a needless controversy. The government advised caution on giving out the existing data. Opposition parties put the blame on the current government for not creating jobs and on hiding unemployment data. Also, allegations were made that the government was trying to pass on wrong data on jobs.

The annual labour bureau survey of 2015–2016 had already displayed that the unemployment rate had inched up to 5.1% in rural areas and 4.9% in urban areas two years ago. The survey also contradicted itself as it also reported that three out of four households in the nation had no salaried wage earner. This meant that either joblessness was higher or that self-employed accounted for more than two-third of India's workforce. But, there was once again no authentic data on the self-employed workforce.

NITI Aayog to Build New Job Data

These contradictions in job data had been there for decades but had now come under intense political scrutiny that is too hard to ignore. The government was already under attack from the opposition for low job growth. Now, with the dismal news pouring in from the IT sector, the government decided to discontinue the annual labour bureau survey and take a fresh look.

A few weeks later at a Rajya Sabha TV debate on joblessness that I attended, I learnt that the NITI Aayog had been given the task to create a new database for jobs and it was a work in progress. But, there was no official press release on this move, neither any explanation on why the labour bureau annual survey had been discontinued suddenly.

At the India Today Conclave in March 2018, Minister of State for Civil Aviation Jayant Sinha, on being quizzed about why the government was unable to create jobs, said, 'It's not about jobs, it's about data. Though NITI Aayog is doing a good job on job data, the fact is we are not picking all the jobs happening in the country.' Later, in a *Times of India* op-ed piece, he confirmed that the job data prepared by NITI Aayog would be released somewhere around September 2018.

Why Job Data Must Be Authentic

In June 2018, I wrote in an op-ed piece for *Hindustan Times,* 'To avoid a political slugfest, the transparency of employment data is crucial.' The point I made was about an ongoing and needless politicisation of data when economists, analysts and associated industry should be working with the government to create a credible database. That could be done by adopting a transparent and credible process to create a job database where the government is just an enabler and not the creator of data.

To clarify further, it is important to create a robust system for data collection and a procedure that stands scrutiny. In India, this has not been created for decades and hence the concern. Though there are ways to address the same, there are huge challenges largely due to legacy issues. The biggest challenge is the state of existing data—wherever available. Using a database that gives details of incoming payments made to EPF accounts each year, one can create an authentic record of annual gains per year.

Just around a quarter of Indians work for the organised sector. Data of some form is maintained for the organised sector. So, it is normally assumed that the data available for the sector would be robust and authentic. But it is not. And that is possibly the reason why the entire discussion around job data is being politicised and its authenticity questioned.

There are two reasons for unauthentic data in the organised sector. First, India does not have any established survey of businesses and commercial establishments as the US has. Second, a record of around 20 million Indians working in central government, state governments, quasi-government bodies like municipal corporations, joint sectors and public-sector undertakings are poorly maintained. Even EPFO, ESIC and pension funds that collect money for employee benefits do not have proper data.

It is a legacy issue of keeping records of millions of people and involving billions of rupees, which no one has bothered to address and set right before. Now that the government is trying to investigate and sanitise that data and extract the correct numbers for use, a war of words has begun. With elections of the national parliament due in 2019, the shrill debate over jobs and job data is bound to reach a crescendo. The NITI Aayog was expected to rollout quarterly job data from September 2018 as per its vice chairman. The same is yet to be released while the debate over jobs continues. It is still not clear whether this avoidable politicisation of job data will lead to better results or worse.

Four Things Need to be Done to Create Jobs

The first thing that is needed is a creation of a robust and sustainable Make in India policy. US President Trump is taking steps to protect the domestic industry in the US and so should India. Duties imposed by the US has negatively affected steel exports of India by $198.6 million and aluminium exports by $42.4 million as per government data. The government of India, in retaliation, has raised some tariff barriers on 30 items. For the next two years, tariff barriers must be raised periodically in anticipation because the US policy and the retaliatory action can have far-reaching effects.

India's imports have been rising each year. Especially the imports from China. As a result, the trade deficit with China is rising and so are our CADs. The reason for CAD is not only the rise of crude oil prices. The imports are directly hurting Indian manufacturing. Even food products like edible oil and pulses, fresh fruits, sugar and spices have seen higher imports in the current year. It is also important to check imports of manufacturing goods like thermal plant, capital machinery and electronic products. These are hurting the labour-intensive industry, the agriculture sector and the job market.

The second thing that India needs is to focus on the MSME sector. They need to create liquidity for the MSME sector. The MSME sector is given loans essentially against collaterals. They are also exposed to high credit rates. India needs to have a much lower rate for loans against collaterals. This is because the risk to a banker is much lower in case of collaterals.

Besides, India needs to promote the concept of product hubs or manufacturing clusters for MSMEs. This is because the cluster concept is easier for the supply chain to function seamlessly within a close working distance of each other. It is not that India does not have it. Pune and Gurugram have clusters in the automotive sector but many more are needed. India has to restructure its industrial estates and push the concept of manufacturing hubs like China, Japan or Korea.

The third thing that needs to be done is to exploit the opportunity created by US President Trump's trade war. Trade wars cause several exports to become uncompetitive for existing suppliers and cause old supply lines to be disrupted. This brings new suppliers into contention. The big opportunity today could be the Chinese market because of the retaliatory tariffs slapped on the US. China has particularly targeted the American farm and livestock exports, including soy, fresh and dry fruits and pork and chicken products. These are areas where Indian agriculture products could enter and create job opportunities for India.

Similarly, India needs to create a software alliance, like the solar alliance where we help create supporting software for the telecom industry.

Today in the US-China trade war, America is targeting Chinese mobile makers because they have a monopoly in software. Whether it is iOS—Apple's operating system—or Android or Microsoft, the mobile software technology is all American. That needs to change if jobs have to come to India. China has wrested hardware initiative only because they control the rare earths industry. But, they still do not have control of software. If India has to become a manufacturing hub of smartphones alongside Korea and China, then it must think of a software platform for mobile players a few years ahead.

The fourth and last thing that needs to be done is to create an acceptable process of collecting data for jobs. We know that the organised private sector can easily furnish the data each quarter or each year. So can the government sector. But, we do not still have a clear idea of how data from the unorganised sector will be collected.

We need to figure out which is the agency that will ultimately maintain the database on jobs—in what format, with what frequency, who will verify it. We also do not know how the data will be collated and used to show growth—both for the unorganised sector and the organised sector. Both areas are important as only about a quarter of the total jobs are created in the country in the organised sector. So, the first thing that needs to be done is an apolitical deliberation between academics, major industry associations and the government to create a policy on the creation of job data.

CHAPTER 16

Entrepreneurship:

Start-Ups Flourish, Unicorns Prosper

India has always been the most suitable place for start-ups to do business. There are two reasons for this. A large and growing domestic market gave incentive for entrepreneurship to thrive. Lack of a healthy job market forced the unemployed to engage into entrepreneurship. But, low capital availability and high interest rates made bootstrapping a reality for most businesses. Poor access to technology added to the woes and made *jugaad* and innovation a necessity—not a virtue. Markets, Entrepreneurship, Capital and Technology (MECT) are four things that are needed to create the start-up ecosystem.

Though the first two—markets and entrepreneurship—have been present since the 1970s, both capital and technology were missing. Nonetheless, the first rush of entrepreneurship in the early 1980s was in the IT sector. It saw giants like Infosys and HCL emerge. These companies grew due to inherent demand for technology and customers willing to pay upfront. They were not funded by VC, but had grown organically with their own export-led businesses. That gave them access to funds needed for growth. But, though both companies flourished and became iconic, little happened thereafter on the start-up front. Companies like Satyam that flourished during the dot-com boom fell away thereafter. Travel company MakeMyTrip survived the dot-com bust, thanks to funding by angel investors and VCs, but grew slowly.

India's Unicorn Start-Ups Shine

The funding of Indian tech start-ups started looking up only after the Wall Street crash of 2008. That was when investors started exploring businesses outside the US to spread their risks. Flipkart received its first round of funding of $1 million from Accel Partners in 2009. Tiger Global, which had followed Accel to invest heavily in Facebook and come out a winner, followed suit. They invested $10 million in 2009 and again $20 million in 2011. Flipkart became India's first unicorn start-up with a valuation exceeding $1 billion when it received a funding of $150 million from South African investor Naspers in 2012.

With funding came the need to restructure. E-commerce ventures needed deep pockets but India's investment laws did not permit FDI beyond 51% for multi-brand retailers. So, e-commerce start-ups that wanted to get funding beyond 51% had just two options. Either sell their stakes to a local investor who had the cash to invest or take the company abroad and operate from overseas.

Flipkart adopted a third way that was tried previously by travel start-up MakeMyTrip. It split itself into two parts. One part, which was capital and technology-intensive, was acquired by Flipkart Holdings Singapore that was set up in 2011. The second part was manpower-intensive, which was brought under Indian operation arm Flipkart Logistics in 2010. This was eventually sold to WS Retail, an Indian entity that manages its supply chain. The two co-existed in peace with India's tax laws. Here, the capital and technology-intensive part was based in Singapore and outside the purview of FDI. It provided services to bulky operations arm that was a fully Indian entity and employed people and managed the supply chain in India.

This model was followed by most other unicorns founded in 2010 like Snapdeal, Paytm and Ola Cabs. While Snapdeal received funding from Ratan Tata, SoftBank and Intel early on, both Paytm and Ola Cabs had to wait for a couple of years before investors put in sizeable sums of money after 2014. Paytm also had to diversify its business model and found major success with investors only after its digital wallet business took off vertically. Today there are a dozen diverse Indian unicorns, including Renew Power Ventures—a clean energy power company funded by Goldman Sachs, Asian Development Bank and Abu Dhabi investments amongst others.

Hike, a mobile messaging company backed by Tencent and Foxconn from China; ShopClues, another e-commerce start-up with backing from Nexus and Tiger Global; Zomato, a restaurant search website backed by Sequoia Capital and Info Edge; and advertising platforms InMobi and Quikr have made it to the MensXP list of unicorns in 2017.

Will Flipkart Lead Walmart's Online Strategy?

While becoming a unicorn is a state of adolescence for a start-up, selling out to a larger business is an ultimate sign of adulthood. In May 2018, Walmart—the $500 billion US retail giant—bought 77% holdings in Flipkart for $16 billion, a higher than the expected valuation of $21 billion. It put a final stamp on a decade-long journey that had been arduous and uncertain as valuations swung up and down over the years. Despite a bruising and battling competition with the world leader in e-commerce, Amazon, and other funded Indian e-retailers, Flipkart maintained market leadership. Before its acquisition, it led the market with a 31.9% share, with Amazon breathing down its neck, half a percentage point behind. After its acquisition, Flipkart will have an even bigger role to play.

To know why, let us look at why Walmart bought Flipkart. Walmart started investing in India nearly a decade ago but its expansion of bricks-and-mortar stores has been slow in India despite the fragmented market and inherent demand. It is way behind its biggest competitor Amazon, which doubled its marketplace sales in 2017 and earned ₹3,183 crore as commissions. Amazon also plans to go bricks and mortar in India. India's e-commerce market has been one of the fastest growing in the world and with $21 billion in sales, it is the tenth largest globally as per data from digital market research firm eMarketer.

India is the second-largest emerging economy, behind China. Walmart has not been able to make much headway in China despite its decade-long presence there. Its online presence is negligible in China. Walmart's global online sale is just $14 billion or less than 3% of its gross revenues. If Walmart has to compete with Amazon, it needs to compete online. But in North America, Amazon is way ahead with 44% of market share. Buying Flipkart in India gives Walmart a chance to battle Amazon on equal terms. After all,

India has a population of 1.2 billion—only second to China—and the highest CAGR in online retail. It also gives a bigger opportunity and responsibility to Flipkart. If Flipkart can maintain leadership in India's e-commerce market, then it would have delivered real value to the acquisition.

Funded Tech Start-Ups Grow

Though there is no data on the number of start-ups India produces, it is estimated to be well over a million a year. The primary reason for this is lack of jobs. Here again, there is no authentic job data. A start-up is a beginner starting a small business. It could be driving an auto, selling milk, or operating a tech start-up or a non-tech start-up. Only a handful of businesses in India would be tech start-ups, which can scale up quickly with the help of IT or IT-related services. Only those businesses that are IT-enabled qualify for investor funding. They could be in the energy sector, the transport sector, the banking sector or retail businesses—but they need to be IT- enabled to qualify as tech start-ups.

A small percentage of start-ups usually get funded first by their friends and families and then by angel investors in today's world. Back in olden days, this second-level support was missing. Entrepreneurs had to manage with their own savings and whatever family or friends could spare. After that they had to generate hard-earned profits to survive. Most start-ups in India still operate like the olden days. Thousands of start-ups begin their journey without angel investors or VC funding across the nation every day. Only a small percentage of them are tech start-ups. Only a small percentage of all start-ups can get funded.

Though tech start-ups by virtue of being high-risk, high-gain investments do not qualify for bank loans, PM Modi announced a $1.5 billion fund for start-ups with the name Fund For Start-Ups (FFS) scheme in January 2016. By June 2016, the cabinet had approved the bill and designated SIDBI as disbursement authority. By October 2017, the status report by Department of Industrial Policy and Promotion on Start-Up India website stated that 75 start-ups have received a total funding of $92 million from 17 alternate investment funds during the year. Thus, government banks that usually refrained from funding IT companies started to provide financial assistance to start-ups under the scheme.

A National Association of Software and Services Companies (NASSCOM) report of 2017 says that there were as many as 1,000 tech start-ups registered that year, making the total count of registered start-ups 5,200. India remains the third-largest start-up destination in the world, after China and the US. 'India is one of the fastest-growing start-up landscapes in the world and every major accelerator, investor, angel group is participating in becoming a part of this growth journey,' said NASSCOM Chairman Raman Roy at ninth product conclave of NASSCOM in November 2017.

The start-up world had more to cheer besides the big acquisition of Flipkart by Walmart. Flipkart itself acquired two of its biggest competitors Jabong and Myntra in 2016 and missed acquiring Snapdeal in 2017 after lengthy negotiations. But, the start-up ecosystem has been thriving in India even outside e-commerce. Almost 117 acquisitions were made in 2015, 155 in 2016 and 123 in 2017. These were essentially acquisitions that happened after the start-ups performed for a few years with initial funding from angel investors or VCs. The size of these acquisitions was moderate, from $30 million to $150 million, but nonetheless it was a start.

Second-stage acquisition of tech start-ups by VC firms or bigger investor groups will give confidence to first-round investors to buy more companies. Also, it is very interesting to find that as much as 10% of the start-ups are acquired by bigger businesses. That itself is a huge number. It indicates that once funded, a large number of businesses are delivering and reaching the next stage. It is giving early-fund managers more confidence to invest. The year 2017 created a record of sorts, with venture funds reportedly investing $13.7 billion in early stage deals—funding as many as 820 start-ups. The biggest investor was Accel Partners with 65 deals, followed by LetsVenture with 37 deals and Venture Catalysts with 33 deals.

However, compared to the US and China, the number of tech start-ups in India are few and capital invested is very small. Chinese start-up market is 50 times bigger and the US 30 times. They attract over $300 billion to $400 billion in investments each year. In 2017, e-commerce sales alone touched $1,115 billion in China and $455 billion in the US as against $21 billion in India. As a matter of fact, Accel and Tiger Global are only two of the top 10 VC firms that regularly do business in India. For India, this is just the beginning. Most VC firms are yet to come.

The Vibrant World Outside Tech Start-ups

Tech start-ups are just a small fraction of small businesses that spring up each year. The start-up ecosystem in India outside the tech world is even more interesting as it is diverse and complex. The reasons are many. One reason is a lack of jobs and a disorganised labour market. Another reason is rural migration to urban areas. Yet another is a large number of women entrepreneurs. Early retirement or loss of jobs by experienced industry hands also leads to this. Finally, the lack of social security in a nation of billion plus people. All these along with many more reasons forces India to produce more small businesses and entrepreneurs than any other nation across the world—possibly even more than China where things are much more organised.

Job growth in India is, to say the least, unorganised. This is not a thing which happened overnight. It has been increasingly happening since the first wave of liberalisation in the 1990s. Before the 1990s, the job market was organised and structured but opportunities were few and far between. Industries and businesses had to register themselves and file all details of operations, including how many people they employed, to the labour office. You were told to enrol at an employment exchange and wait endlessly for a job.

With the first wave of liberalisation came easing of regulations. Businesses sprung up in hundreds and thousands and the only registrations and bookkeeping that happened were related to tax or government-provided services like provident fund or employee state insurance. All other data remained only on paper and many companies even stopped filing employment data. Employment exchanges, which used to witness long queues till the 1980s, suddenly lost relevance. It is not that jobs shrunk after the 1990s; rather, they grew and have been growing every year at a rate of around 4% to 5% per annum. But, there is no data to support the numbers other than the fact that the economy is growing and with that job opportunities too.

But, there are definitive indicators that entrepreneurship is flourishing. This is because the demand of diverse industries is springing up as the GDP is growing and so are the services to meet them. Twenty years ago, you had to go abroad for many services that were not available in India.

That is not needed any more. Not only services but also most goods are available locally. They could be imported but they are already locally present. Despite contradictions and occasional shortages, the economy is chugging on smoothly. A lot of this is due to the supply chain improving vastly after the arrival of e-commerce. There is connectivity across India that was not present earlier. Part of the reason is the existence of mobile phones and television but also e-commerce, road, rail and air connectivity. Most importantly, entrepreneurship adds to these efforts.

Outsourcing Boom Creates Entrepreneurs

What is not growing are long-term permanent jobs. They have all been replaced with short-term contractual assignments that have grown in leaps and bounds. Back in the old days, there used to be typists and stenographers in government offices. With the induction of computers, there had been no recruitment of computer operators or data entry personnels. That entire sector is outsourced to private contractors or entrepreneurs who operate in manpower consultancy space. So, every government and even private enterprises have contractors and contract labour. Outsourcing as an industry took deep roots in India post-liberalisation and kept growing at a breakneck speed. It led to reduced prices, albeit at the cost of quality.

The outsourcing industry grew big and skilled, IT-literate entrepreneurs turned it into business process outsourcing (BPO) businesses. But, there was a huge and thriving industry—smaller service providers who sold their services through direct selling and yellow pages. The meteoric rise of the service sector is a pointer to the growth of start-ups and entrepreneurship in this sector. From 1991 to 2015, the service sector's share as a percentage of the GDP grew by over 10% from 42.6% to 53.4%. And most of this growth was supported by contractual labour or outsourcing. The share of agriculture as a percentage of the GDP fell from 29.5% to 15.5%, losing out to both the services and the manufacturing sector. While it was not possible for the manufacturing sector to absorb large-scale outsourcing due to skill set acquisition issues, the service sector dependent on soft skills could easily do so.

Large organised sectors like the telecom sector took outsourcing to a new level. Market leader Bharti Airtel took the lead in complete outsourcing. They only retained key marketing functions in-house and outsourced entire operations. Ericsson, Nokia and Huawei supplied all the telecom gear while Alcatel-Lucent—with 24% Airtel equity—managed its optic fibre and broadband business and Indus Towers—with 42% Airtel equity—managed its tower operations. Even its outsourcing strategy, which was outsourced to International Business Machines Corporation (IBM), has been renewed to carry on its decade-long 'total outsourcing strategy'.

Today, most large companies in India, both in the public and the private sector, have resorted to outsourcing in a very big way leading to a phenomenal rise of business-to-business (B2B) entrepreneurs. These entrepreneurs do not need VC to sustain themselves and grow on industry business, which is both organic and sustainable. Besides that, Modi's drive for digital India has boosted entrepreneurship both in the telecom and the banking sector. New applications, new features, new software, new devices are all in demand and entrepreneurs are buzzing with new ideas and new ventures to meet the demand.

Entrepreneurship Due to Rural Migration Spiral

Over the last 25 years, income from agriculture fell substantially, leading to rural migration in search of jobs. The Economic Survey 2017 states that between 2011 and 2016, an average of nine million people migrated within India in search for jobs. The major sources of migration were Bihar, Madhya Pradesh, Rajasthan, UP—tagged popularly as the *bimaru* states—West Bengal, Uttarakhand and Punjab. Destination states were Tamil Nadu, Maharashtra, Gujarat—known as manufacturing states—Andhra Pradesh and Kerala. Most of the migration also took place from rural areas to cities.

World Bank data says that India has over 140 million citizen migrants who have moved the base from one state to another in search of employment or business opportunities. A typical look at the demographic pattern will tell you that while people from Bihar are employed as rickshaw pullers and coolies, those from Madhya Pradesh and Rajasthan are usually in the building construction business. People from UP are auto drivers, milk suppliers or machine operators in factories, while those from Punjab dominate the food and catering trade. Gujarat and Bengal provide skilled artisans for jewellery trade while people from Odisha dominate plumbing works.

The rural workforce who came to the cities had little or no formal education or soft skills. A very large number, therefore, became entrepreneurs trying to survive with their high energy and willingness to deliver more than their skill set. Like immigrants across the world, this migrant population within India have spread the seeds of entrepreneurship—doing all available work that the growing urban markets in India offer. They have also prospered unbelievably when compared to the local population in the cities, leading to agitations in Mumbai for protection of the local population and ouster of migrants. Though there are reports that rural-urban immigration is slowing in India, there is no authentic data to prove the same. Instead, what you can see on roads is that some professions like driving and artisanry are dominated by migrant labourers. Competitor for Indian migrant labour is only migrant labour from neighbouring countries. The one-way traffic has been steady for the last 70–80 years.

Women Entrepreneurs Grow Due to Easy Finance

Women entrepreneurship has come a long way during the last few decades and has flourished especially during the past few years. This has been due to several reasons. Many more women are preferring to become suppliers than workers at factories because it gives them the flexibility to manage home and work. Women stay at home and produce goods that are sold by businesses and exporters to consumers. This is widely prevalent in the handicraft, hand-stitched clothing, jewellery businesses and some export houses also have pickup and delivery service at residences of the women who do such jobs for them on a contract basis regularly.

Once upon a time, finance used to be a bottleneck for women entrepreneurs. It is no longer so. As a matter of fact, MUDRA loans and several other micro-financing schemes are specifically targeted towards women in business. This has happened largely because Grameen Bank experiment in Bangladesh showed that the default of loans was negligible in the case of women borrowers and very high in case of male borrowers. It is reported that the biggest beneficiaries of MUDRA loan in the small borrower category below ₹50,000 called *Shishu* were women and minorities. The *Shishu* loans were collateral-free and hence attracted millions of applicants. There are three categories of loans in MUDRA. Apart from *Shishu*, there is the ₹50,000 to ₹5 lakh category called *Kishor* and ₹5 lakh to ₹10 lakh category called *Tarun*. Another collateral-free loan for women is being offered by Oriental Bank of Commerce to borrow up to ₹10 lakh.

Besides this, several women-centric loan schemes were launched by banks. Among this was Stree Shakti Package for women entrepreneurs by SBI, Bharatiya Mahila Bank's business loans for small and medium enterprises (SME) and micro loans, *Dena Shakti* scheme of Dena Bank, *Udyogini* scheme of PSB and *Annapurna* scheme (launched by State Bank of Mysore) financing women entrepreneurs to set up food catering businesses. The finances being offered to women has led to a lot of women becoming entrepreneurs. The government says that ₹4.6 trillion (₹4.6 lakh crore) has been disbursed under the scheme to 104 million (10.4 crore) people till March 2018. It also aims to disburse ₹3 trillion additionally in the financial year 2018–2019. Attempting to create 100 million entrepreneurs in a two-year span is no mean feat. Even if 20% of them are able to sustain themselves in the long run, it will make India one of the most happening start-up destinations in the years to come.

Experienced and Retired Entrants Create Value Propositions

With increasing prosperity and passion has come the trend of seasoned professionals quitting their careers and getting into entrepreneurship at a later stage in life. Some of them enter the phase late also because they have lost their jobs at a later stage in their career. With experience and more capital at their command, they are able to scale up their organisations faster. Besides being better networked professionally, they are able to leverage their professional contacts in their business ventures. Middle-aged professionals are another segment of entrants who have made their mark in entrepreneurship today in India.

Normally, these entrepreneurs choose the same field they were previously working in, though there are those who look for a second career elsewhere. For those who choose the same industry, it is particularly easier to survive because normally they have all four components of MECT available to them. They know the market well and usually have developed contacts with clients, which help them secure their first orders easily. Besides, their professional credentials are well established and that helps their credibility in the market. That—along with their entrepreneurship vigour—helps them get an early entry into the markets. Also, they come with greater financial stability than freshers starting out as entrepreneurs. Hence, they usually have a lasting power to cope up with ups and downs of entrepreneurship. Finally, they know where to get the technology from. The learning curve period of the work to be done is usually not applicable to them. So, experienced people with a better control of MECT are more successful in building value-added corporations and that is increasingly being seen across India today.

Job losses are also causing experienced people to enter entrepreneurship late in life. The Short Service Commission that gives army personnels just 10 years to serve has been a great source of security for personnel and administration officials across India Incorporated. Besides, there are many other areas like electrical, plumbing and mechanical skill-based jobs where many experienced professionals are making their mark. If we understand the Indian ecosystem, only a quarter of all jobs are produced in the organised sector. In rest of the job market, which is huge, it is the entrepreneur who rules. Hence, entrepreneurship is thriving across India and it brings some of the best opportunities for India to emerge.

Part VIII

Digital India

CHAPTER 17

Telecom: A Growth Story Despite Call Drops

The telecom industry in India has been through ups and downs since the last two decades. It is the brightest spot in the Indian economy especially from consumption and demand point of view. It is also the one sector that is generating jobs by the millions. Quantity growth has been steady, though quality issues like rampant call drops are posing a huge challenge. It is one sector where Make in India is happening and foreign investment is flowing in. The growth has been explosive but not easy. It has been marred with legacy issues of corruption and controversy and left behind a lot of bruised corporations, bureaucrats and politicians.

Mobile phones came to India in 1995 during Narasimha Rao's first wave of liberalisation. Rao's telecom minister, Sukh Ram, who had become popular due to a rapid spread of Public Call Offices (PCO) across India in the pre-mobile era, made the first mobile phone call to West Bengal Chief Minister Jyoti Basu. In 1996, CBI in simultaneous raids seized cash of ₹2.45 crore and ₹1.16 crore from Sukh Ram's homes in Safdarjung Enclave at New Delhi and in Mandi at Himachal respectively. CBI charged him with bribery for which he has been convicted in three separate cases in 2002, 2009 and 2011.

Indian telecom industry went through a heady growth phase for more than a decade after the Sukh Ram incident. Airtel and Vodafone were early entrants in the field. At that time, a duopoly of European phone makers Nokia and Ericsson dominated the mobile phone market with Global System for Mobile Communications (GSM) technology. Mobile phones were a new gadget and were pricey. In 2002, Reliance

Industries entered the telecom market partnering with Korean phone makers Samsung and LG Electronics. Samsung and LG were known as reliable, white goods manufacturers but not particularly hotshots in the mobile business. Reliance, then headed by Dhirubhai Ambani, brought in planeloads of mobile phones from Korean makers using Code Division Multiple Access (CDMA) technology. Prices of mobile phones crashed and the handset moved into many more homes. In September 2004, a decade after it was introduced, the number of mobile handsets exceeded fixed-line connections.

Telecom Spectrum E-Auctions Do Away with Scams

Mobile phones became a runaway hit and Apple introduced smartphones to the world in June 2007. By that time, Nokia had established itself as the market leader both in India and the world and Samsung was at number two. At that time, another scandal hit the telecom sector in India. DMK's A. Raja—telecom minister in the UPA government—was accused of issuing telecom licences in 2G bandwidth in an unconstitutional manner between 2007 and 2009. CAG pegged the notional losses at ₹1.76 lakh crore (₹1.76 trillion) in the 2G scam and the SC in 2012 cancelled licences of 122 telecom operators against a PIL on account of alleged corruption. Though jailed for over a year, both Raja and Telecom Secretary Siddharth Behura are yet to be convicted by courts.

Nonetheless, the telecom scam shook the industry in three different ways. First, it dealt a body blow to several foreign players like Telenor and Sistema who wanted to enter the Indian market but had to retreat with severe losses. Second, it hurt local players who wanted an entry into this sector. Third, it created a spectrum shortage. The acute policy paralysis that gripped UPA due to multiple scams investigated by CAG hurt its functioning and morale. As a result, it could not create a robust and transparent auction procedure for spectrum distribution. An auction held in 2012 failed to attract bidders and Congress party claimed that CAG had created unrealistic expectations by estimating notional losses of ₹1.76 trillion. So, there were no attempt to streamline telecom auctions and the telecom industry had to do with spectrum shortage till UPA was voted out of power in 2014.

One of the first things that the Modi government achieved after it came to office was setting up a transparent e-auction system for spectrum sales. The e-auction conducted was an acclaimed success where four top players of the industry engaged in a fierce bidding war lasting 19 days for 800 megahertz (MHz), 900 MHz, 1,800 MHz and 1,900 MHz bandwidths. Of 470.75 MHz offered, 89% or 418 MHz were picked up at well above reserved prices. Market leader Airtel spent ₹30,000 crore while Vodafone and Idea spent ₹28,000 crore each. The fourth player was a new entrant, Reliance Industries, spending ₹10,000 crore. Net accruals of ₹1.1 lakh crore came after a spectrum sale of ₹61,000 crore in February 2014, showing that CAG estimates of notional losses could not have been faulted. After those initial rounds, there have been several more auctions and spectrum shortage no longer troubles the industry.

The telecom industry faced several challenges after 2009 including diminishing profits and severe cash flow. The competition was intense. Still more entrants were being allowed to enter the business. To get over the problems, major players in the telecom industry hit upon an innovative method to reduce their capex costs. Already the industry had outsourced its telecom gear business. Now they decided to reduce investment in the telecom tower business. This, because they had to spend substantial amounts to buy spectrum and retain market share. Sharing fixed infrastructure gave them an opportunity to ensure higher efficiency by having one tower company for the business with joint holding. It also led to relinquishing responsibility of last-mile connectivity by the service provider that started causing frequent call drops. Nonetheless, it was a truly unique experiment to share telephone infrastructure by the three biggest players in the fray, namely Airtel, Vodafone and Idea.

Spectrum licence fees, marketing costs, telecom infrastructure costs including telecom gear and tower business are four major cost centres of the industry. In 2009, Indus Towers, the largest telecom tower company, saw the three biggest players acquire major stakes. The move was expected to save over $3 billion in shared tower costs. It was an experiment which had no parallel worldwide at that time. Three competitors came on board to own passive infrastructure and reduce costs.

Call Drops Arrive to Haunt the Industry

This unique experiment had an immediate effect on the quality of calls. Soon after the telecom companies transferred their tower businesses to third-party operators, the phenomenon of call drops reared its ugly head. In some areas the connectivity was so poor that one out of three calls materialised. Consumers found that connectivity became an issue especially when the call was between two subscribers belonging to two different mobile operators. This has been denied by telecom companies and refuted by Cellular Operators Association India (COAI) that has consistently claimed that call drop is a minor problem and is well under control.

In 2015, a year after the Modi government came to power, the then IT and communications minister Ravi Shankar Prasad raised the issue of call drops in parliament. This caught all, including the industry, by surprise. In India most ministers want to brush problems under the carpet. Rarely had we seen a minister discussing problems of his own department in the parliament. He also ordered an audit of Telecom Regulatory Authority of India (TRAI) on call drops that showed call drop rates of various telcos at 3.8%, 5.19% and 5.76% as against TRAI's guidelines of 3% at that time.

Though the minister had changed the traditional approach and looked at consumer interest, the industry failed to see the truth. The telecom industry refuted the charges and the contention that consumers were losing billions of rupees due to frequent call drops. But, calls less than 30 seconds became a regular feature of mobile telephony. Mobile operators like Airtel or Bharat Sanchar Nigam Ltd (BSNL), however, faced no call drop complaints from their consumers in fixed lines.

Telecom operators claimed that call drops were within limits and were due to a shortage of towers and the difficulty of getting licences and land for new tower installations. As per the director general of Towers and Infrastructure Providers' Association, there were just 4,25,000 telecom towers in the country and the shortfall of two lakh towers resulted in poor connectivity. But, independent analysts said that tower shortage did not exceed 80,000 towers in 2015.

Most analysts believed that tower shortage was not the only reason for call drops. As a matter of fact, an AT Kearney survey on global telecom tower industry reported in 2011 that there was actually an oversupply of towers in India when the phenomenon of call drops first surfaced. The number of mobile subscribers, which was showing double-digit YOY growth till 2010, started slowing down after 2010.

Even as more spectrum has been released increasingly over the years and more investment done in telecom towers, the phenomenon of call drop has continued to haunt consumers. TRAI conducts regular audits and has started fining telecom operators. The government asked the Department of Telecommunication to set up its own monitoring and as a result the Telecom Enforcement Resource and Monitoring wing was set up to check call quality and call drops. In August 2017, TRAI announced new benchmarks and higher penalties. Effective 17 October 2017, TRAI imposed graded penalty system for call drops with the maximum penalty of ₹10 lakh per quarter. But telcos, who have been fighting the regulator in courts and won a reprieve from the SC in 2016, are not willing to go by TRAI rulings.

TRAI had told the court, 'A cartel of 4–5 telecom firms having a billion subscribers are making ₹250 crore a day but not making investments on their network to improve the services to check call drops.' Telcos refuted these claims of TRAI and claimed that they had installed over 2 lakh telecom towers in the past 15 months. In a 2017 judgement, the SC ruled in favour of the telecom operators and overturned the ruling of Delhi High Court (HC).

Delhi HC on 16 October 2015 had upheld the decision of TRAI, making it mandatory for cellular operators to pay consumers ₹1 per call drop experienced on their networks, subject to a cap of ₹3 a day. So, it is not only the problem of increasing call drops but the fact that telcos are in denial and are not willing to accept the fact that call drops are a major issue—surprisingly our SC stops the regulator. This is an attitude problem of the industry that stops it from being world-class and improving the quality of calls, not the number of subscribers.

The Economic Times, in an article titled 'Why the Problem of Call Drops Cannot Be Solved in the Near Future', rightly analysed the issue as one of broken relations. There is no trust left between telecom majors and the regulator and nobody is ready to sit around a table and look for a solution. The resolution and improvement of the state of affairs are difficult in such circumstances, largely because of rigid positions taken by respective parties. As a result, consumers suffer and call drops keep happening despite the rules. This is the scene in most areas in India today. Nobody likes regulators and laws that make them change their way of functioning.

The citizen as well as India Incorporated is resisting change. People don't like *Swachh Bharat* because they have been traditionally defecating in the open and don't want the government to tell them how to live. People don't like to stop littering or stop using plastic bags, for littering and plastic bags is something they find convenient. Businesses don't want GST because they have been traditionally accounting with *kacchi parchi* and think that the system helps them save taxes and grow their business quickly. The telecom operators are going to court against TRAI instead of attending to the call drop issues that haunt consumers. Many corporates are resisting Securities and Exchange Board of India (SEBI) and film-makers are resisting censor board because they want freedom. Banks are resisting RBI, which is trying to impose stressed asset resolution norms tightly. Borrowers are resisting banks' move to increase compliance that will expose the scale and the nature of default. Politicians and activists don't like Aadhaar because they do not want an identification number to track them and link all their assets and transactions. They agitate against UIDAI, but are fine however with telecom service providers or social media encroaching privacy. The list is endless.

Data Consumers Relegate Voice Users as Second-Class Citizens in Voice over Internet Protocol (VoIP)

In December 2017, India became the largest consumer of digital data. The government of India was aggressively promoting digital India and pushing for a country-wide rollout for data services. Telcos were selling competitively priced data packs and smartphone users mostly in India's metros were lapping it up. YouTube, Facebook and WhatsApp showed a surge on Indian smartphone users as data consumption spiralled. NITI Aayog Chief Amitabh Kant tweeted, 'Amazing! With 150 crore gigabytes (GB) per month of mobile data consumption, India is now the world's number one mobile data consuming country. Its mobile data consumption is higher than the US-China's mobile data consumption put together.'

But, all that data consumption took a toll on India. Speed in India rarely exceeds 10 Megabits per second (Mbps) as against 100 Mbps to 1,000 Mbps in most developed nations. Videos take longer to download and networks are clogged with people sharing and seeing photos and videos. I wrote an op-ed piece for *The Times of India* titled, 'Torrent of Call Drops Makes Digital India Sound Like a Joke. One Answer: Segregate Voice from Data'. The basic intent of the article was to highlight the fact that India needs to take steps to give importance to *voice only* customers who are actually far more in number than data users. Though technically you cannot separate data from voice in VOIP technology, you can always try and use a particular bandwidth for telephony alone. It was necessary because promise of Digital India was one made by PM to the common man and not only to the smartphone-wielding elite in metros.

Call drops are a growing problem. They need a dedicated solution. The Department of Telecommunications (DoT) and TRAI need to solve the issue because telecom companies are in denial. This can perhaps be done if 2G or any other network is nurtured only for voice customers. The 2G network is anyway not preferred by smartphone users because of its inability to carry much data. This bandwidth could be perhaps used for only voice customers and upgraded for landline and mobile connectivity. More investment needs to be done in the planning and usage of networks. It is high time TRAI or DoT explores the technical feasibility of providing a dedicated network for voice consumers.

Four out of five customers use mobile phones only for talking. They have no use of data and do not download videos for entertainment, largely because they don't own smartphones. For them, the only reason they own mobile phones is to make phone calls. But, when call drops happen frequently and largely because data users are clogging up the mobile networks, it hurts four out of five mobile phone users. Since VoIP networks have voice over internet protocol, the voice and data consumer travel together. So, to make Digital India truly happen, there is a need to separate the two and provide services for 80% of India's people who do not use smartphones.

DoT in June 2018 permitted mobile carriers to allot a single mobile number for both internet and cellular telephony services, so that telcos could offer voice over Wi-Fi. This would help reduce congestion and call drops, especially in city centres and office areas where mobile networks are highly congested. Vodafone has said that it offered such services in the UK and Australia, and India is ready for the same. TRAI and DoT also need to explore whether reserving the low-frequency 2G band exclusively for voice customers is possible and worthwhile. While the emphasis on rolling out optic fibre lines across India is a commendable objective and a positive move to counter call drops, it alone is not enough. Some more urgent and innovative measures need to be taken to resolve the quality and call drop issues that have been haunting Indian consumers. This because frequent call drops are making mobile telephony undependable and also expensive for the consumer.

Investment and Jobs Grow in Telecom Sector

Call drops apart, the telecom industry has functioned extremely well during the past four years due to the competitive environment and a high consumer demand. The competition to invest and secure dominance increased as Reliance Jio entered the market and grew its market share despite roadblocks by the consortium of older GSM players. By June 2018, the top four service providers had 100 million telephone subscribers and 87% market share while 9% of the market share was held by government-owned BSNL. The industry, as of June 2018, has seen Airtel maintain its position as the market leader with nearly a third of the market share. Vodafone, Idea and newbie Reliance Jio are the next three in the market share. All are jostling for the second place with a market share between 20% to 23%. With the merger of Vodafone and Idea expected to be completed soon, there will be just three dominant players in the Indian telecom marketplace.

The three major players have bought most of the spectrum in 2014 and 2015 auctions for over ₹1,70,000 crore (₹ 1.7 trillion), which means that they have made an initial investment of ₹50,000 crore on spectrum till date. They are also investing hugely in laying of fibre network and telecom towers. Then there have been substantial investments by mobile phone manufacturers. The total investment in this sector in the last four years could exceed ₹2 lakh crore (₹2 trillion). COAI claims that the mobile operators' industry is already burdened with a debt of ₹4.5 lakh crore (₹4.5 trillion) that is leading to consolidation.

Chinese phone makers Xiaomi, Oppo, Huawei, Gionee, OnePlus have all arrived in India to set up assembly plants to sell their mobile phones.

Nearly 100 mobile manufacturing units have set up shop in India. Xiaomi with 19% market share in the year 2017–2018 has set up three small manufacturing units—including a PCB unit—in Andhra Pradesh, Tamil Nadu and Noida in UP. Some details of their manufacturing activity has been already shared in Chapter 10 on manufacturing. The units employ 10,000 people and produce two phones per second, claims its India Managing Director Manu Jain. Oppo, another Chinese phone maker, started manufacturing smartphones in India at Foxconn Sri City facility in November 2015. It, along with Foxconn, is setting up a new plant in Noida with an investment of ₹100 crore.

Telecom gear-maker Huawei set up its global service centre at Bengaluru with an investment of $20 million. The service centre will cater to customers from Asia, Middle East and Africa. OnePlus partnered with Foxconn to invest in a plant that will manufacture devices that will be primarily sold in India. OnePlus phones and Oppo phones are currently made by other vendors but Modi government has raised duties on imported smartphones by 10–20%, forcing a rethink by Chinese phone makers. One-third of OnePlus $1.4 billion sales worldwide comes from India. The company with 25% market share is only next to Apple in the premium segment and ahead of Samsung that holds 17.6% of the market.

The India Cellular and Electronics Association (ICAE) in a report released in August 2018 says, 'In 2017–2018, over 225 million handsets were assembled/manufactured in India, which was roughly 80% of the total market requirement.' It stated that while Completely Built Units (CBU) have come down drastically, imports of sub-assemblies and components have gone up significantly. This shows that the units have moved past the first stage of indigenisation and are now being assembled within the country. The net foreign exchange savings, according to ICAE, has been around ₹60,000 crore. Besides, it said that 120 new mobile phone manufacturing units have sprung up across states and employing around 4.5 lakh people.

Samsung Opens World's Largest Mobile Phone Unit in Noida

Meanwhile, Korean phone maker Samsung in a major move has planned to double its India footprint. With an investment of close to ₹5,000 crore, it has inaugurated its expansion project to produce one crore (10 million) mobile phones in its Noida plant every month. The details of the same have been given in Chapter 10. South Korea's smartphone maker plans to take on the Chinese rivals with whom it refused to enter a price war in the Indian market by strengthening its manufacturing base. Chinese brands own around 48% of the global market and over 45% of the Indian market. Their entry into the Indian market with manufacturing and assembly units dented Samsung's undisputed lead in the world's fastest-growing mobile phone markets.

The Korean company, which arrived in India over two decades ago, made white goods and CDMA phones initially. It grabbed the pole position in smartphone business both in India and globally after the Indian market leader Nokia tied up with Microsoft Windows and failed to deliver almost a decade ago. It has been holding its position as the market leader in India ever since but had lost its position to Xiaomi briefly. It recovered strongly in 2017 and leads with 23.8% market share, with a whole host of Chinese phone makers hot on its tails with more features and lower prices.

In July 2018, Samsung opened a new state-of-the-art factory in Noida that will double its current capacity of manufacturing smartphones to 120 million units per annum. Inaugurated by PM Modi and President Moon Jae-in of South Korea, Samsung will invest $716.57 million over the next three years in expanding the Noida unit. It will be the largest phone factory in the world, claims Samsung, and has plans to make India operations also work as one of its global export hubs.

The world's largest phone maker has a significant manufacturing presence in Noida since 1996, making televisions, air conditioners, refrigerators and other white goods for the Indian market. It employs 70,000 people, supplies to 1.5 lakh retailers and is an established brand across India. Its ₹5,000 crore expansion project in mobile manufacturing will help it cement its position as a market leader despite stiff competition from Chinese entrants who are trying to build their brand presence here.

Making Spectrum Sales Competitive but Not Destructive

Telecom is a modern-day answer to many of the world's problems. It is not only a tool for communication but an industry that meets the needs and expectations of its consumer and is the ultimate pipeline that could control markets. There are two challenges here. One is to make the pipeline robust and penetrative to reach most, if not all, consumers across the nation. This is the infrastructure part. The second is to enable a smooth flow of products into the pipeline—without the pipeline companies trying to monopolise it. This is the convergence part. Here, the government's role is extremely important as an enabler and the current government is doing a great job in playing this part professionally. Both ministers Ravi Shankar Prasad and Manoj Sinha have approached the complexities with caution and due diligence and delivered.

The telecom industry has come out of the stunted growth phase post-2010, due to several measures including easing of spectrum and increasing of towers. The move towards fibre networks has also helped immensely. The new plans towards digitalisation of the economy will improve the life of a consumer and also help tax collection. All that is positive. But, there are some huge concerns too. The industry today is hyper-competitive. Prices are plummeting and have become unsustainable for some large players. So, margins have disappeared. Losses have started to occur for all the players.

There is now a need to create healthy competition and stop the hyper-competition among too many players for the spectrum. If this does not happen, the entire industry will bleed and will get destroyed and India's telecom growth will abruptly stop. For this, two things are necessary. First is to encourage loss-making companies to consolidate. Second is to create a new spectrum auction system amongst survivors so that existing players will have limited resources to bid for the spectrums, like in the Indian Premier League (IPL) bidding devised by Board of Control for Cricket in India (BCCI).

As of March 2018, there were 1,035 million mobile subscribers. There were around 10 service providers in the mobile industry, of which the top five held 99.16% market share. Airtel was a market leader with 294.1 million subscribers but it reported its first quarterly loss in 15 years in March quarter of 2018. Vodafone, the second-largest player, has been making losses for several years and Idea, the third largest, reported losses for the fifth straight quarter. Reliance Jio is yet to make profits despite surging market share and public-sector BSNL, which holds 9.9% of the market, has been in the red for nearly a decade.

So, some consolidation is overdue and some is happening. Market leader Airtel recently acquired Telenor India operations. Aircel, Reliance Communication, Tata Teleservices, Tata Docomo, Mahanagar Telephone Nigam Ltd (MTNL) are others in the queue who are ripe for acquisition. Vodafone and Idea merger is also on track and as of 2018, there should be four major players including public-sector BSNL. Spectrum auctions in future should be limited amongst these four players, only with each bidder being given a resource cap to invest in a manner similar to IPL bidding. So, whereas they should be able to bid for the spectrum of their choice and their area of operation, they cannot invest astronomical sums to buy spectrum to destroy competition.

Making Fibre—Like Telecom Towers—a Common Shared Asset

A recent study by the Indian Council for Research on International Economic Relations (ICRIER) says that increase of mobile usage by 10% in India could help the GDP rise by 3.3%. This is a surprising insight as it is more than twice what advanced economies have been able to achieve through increased mobile penetration. This could be possible due to India's poor status in infrastructure development today. Improved communication would help speed up growth and development faster than it would in a comparatively developed economy.

However, to improve the rapid spread of digital India, reach of fibre network is critical. Only Reliance has a reasonably well laid out fibre optic network across the country. We must realise that India's data consumption rose sixfold to 120 crore GB per month only six months after the rollout of 4G services and launch of Reliance Jio, which in its first year has been able to capture 18.8% of mobile market share. This is largely because of its ability to support data on a network supported by optical fibre network and not just wireless. Reliance Jio has acquired the asset of Reliance Communications' (RCom) fibre optic cable network. Besides, Reliance as a petrochemical company has its own fibre optic cable manufacturing expertise, so it is in the best position to carry data.

So, its popularity is growing in metro cities where video downloads are faster with fibre optics infrastructure. Also, in two-tier or three-tier cities of India, where Reliance has its fibre network, its subscriber base is growing fast. Whereas government-backed BharatNet project is mired in a turf war between ministries to give clearance and a host of other problems, Reliance optical fibre network is streaming ahead. The BharatNet project was conceived way back in 2011 by UPA but the laying of cables started only in 2015. The expected stage of completion of phase one was December 2017 when 1,00,000 'gram panchayats' were to be connected with Wi-Fi backed by fibre optics network.

It is understood that over 2.4 lakh km of optical fibre was laid out under the project by November 2017 by three public-sector units under the supervision of BSNL. However, till date there is no confirmation of project completion because Wi-Fi connectivity is not available. According to BharatNet, Wi-Fi connectivity is currently available only in 14,569 gram panchayats, but consumers say that less than 10,000 villages have mobile connectivity and less than 5,000 have internet connectivity as of June 2018. The government has, however, moved ahead with laying the cables for phase two project, under which 2.5 lakh gram panchayats will be connected. This phase should be taken up only after phase one of the project is complete and telecom majors have tested the system and installed Wi-Fi connectivity to at least 80% of the connected villages.

It is not easy to share an asset with mobile service providers and the telecom tower industry will bear that out, especially because of the end connections and jurisdiction issues involved. Whereas Reliance Jio, Airtel, Vodafone and Idea have all agreed to use BharatNet fibre optic, there is no specific agreement or Public Private Participation (PPP) instrument on the specific use of the network. A PPP agreement needs to be drawn out between the government of India and telecom majors and a three-month trial period of use should be specified for last-mile connectivity and consumer interface and interconnectivity. Whereas shared asset is definitely commendable, investment should be utilised and effective and commercially feasible. Also, the project needs to be monetised by both parties in the PPP agreement before stage two is implemented.

Convergence Laws Needed for Mobile Companies' Piping Content

Over the past century content has been consumed in multiple forms such as books, newspapers, magazines, radio, television, etc. Each form has been distinctly different. The media was different in each case. Besides, it was produced and published by distinctly different entities. So, humans were consuming content from different sources, published in different media, and importantly, controlled by different entities. Now these are converging and thereby lies new concerns and need for new legislation, regulation and governance.

Things have become entirely different with the advent of technology during the last decade. Most of the people use devices to consume content today. Whether it is books or newspapers, music or cinema, television or video, or news or features, more than 60% of the people worldwide use smartphones as the primary device to consume content. This, in turn, places the control of content into the hands of three entities not remotely connected with content. They are the smartphone companies who control the hardware, the technology company who provides the software and the networking company or the pipeline company who sends the data or the voice from sender to receiver.

Convergence laws are important. This is because technology and pipeline companies are increasingly controlling content and content companies globally. American phone company American Telephone & Telegraph (AT&T) recently bought Cable News Network (CNN), Verizon bought Yahoo, AOL and *The Huffington Post.* Technology billionaire and Amazon owner Jeff Bezos owns *The Washington Post.* Indian billionaire Mukesh Ambani owns mobile service provider Reliance Jio and media channel Network18. This will be a future trend because of economies of scale. Being in control of the supply chain, they could make it difficult or maybe unusually expensive for competitors unless convergence laws are in place.

Besides, there are other issues like privacy that needs to be covered by such laws. Governance of pipeline companies is absent today because of lack of regulation.

But, it is not only software providers, like Google Android, who have got a control over your mobile phone. There are two other entities who can send you messages, delete messages, share your personal data and use them to sell miscellaneous products and services, tap your personal phone calls and even sell your personal data to others. They are phone manufacturers and service providers. A recent federal investigation suggested that Huawei and Zhongxing Telecommunication Equipment (ZTE), the Chinese device makers, could be stealing and storing critical data from the US by illegal tapping. They are capable of doing similar things in India too since they have been providing service technology to providers like Airtel from the very beginning of its operation that is, for 20-plus years now.

Though Google Android has admitted it and the Chinese phone makers are yet to be proven guilty, mobile service providers in India are known to frequently sell customer databases to corporates who want to sell products to the mobile phone users. Spam calls and messages that we get from banks, insurance companies, real-estate companies and educational institutions are all because personal databases with telephone numbers and locations are sold to them by some internet or mobile service provider. Mobile phone companies also give consumer companies, who buy their customer data services, an unlisted number to call from. So, if you or the regulator calls the phone number from where the spam call originated, you would be greeted with a message that says 'this number does not exist'. This makes convergence laws and governance of tech companies all the more important and necessary in the age of fake news.

CHAPTER 18
IT Sector:
Facing Global Headwinds

The IT sector in India is facing testing times. For 20 years it has been primarily an export-oriented industry. It chased niche global markets to grow in the IT services segment where it focused on coding and customisation of software services. It grew at 20% YOY in initial years and then around 15% after 2014. The growth now has petered down to a single digit. This has nothing to do with policies of the Indian government and is largely due to global headwinds. Still, for years, the IT and the BPO industry have accounted for over half of India's exports. So, the slowdown of growth in IT exports has resulted in a slowdown of overall exports and has led to pressure on the BOP.

The decline in growth was inevitable. There are several reasons for this. While Indian companies made inroads into coding, the IT services and IT-enabled services market could not enter the IT product development software market. Low-hanging fruits are always price-sensitive. So, when the competition started to nibble into the market, the only answer Indian IT majors had was to resort to cost-cutting. They did this through outsourcing or contract services. For years, outsourced work was being done by in-house subsidiaries or India-based H-1B visa-empowered pool of contractors. It was they who were doing the job at very competitive prices.

But, cutting costs to grow is not a really healthy way to exist in the long term. Yet most Indian IT companies chose to maintain their profit margins and play it safe. They shied away from taking risks in product development. The industry did not have a start-up culture before the arrival of e-commerce. This was an industry that was simply averse to taking risks to grow. They also were not keen on exploring the domestic Indian market or any other market besides the US and the EU. Data bears out this truth. Two-thirds of its revenues came from the US market and a quarter from the EU. Less than 10% of its revenue came from other markets and less than 5% came from product development.

Considering this play-safe attitude, it is surprising that healthy growth has continued for nearly two decades. But, there is also a bright side to this laid-back approach story. The reputation of the Indian industry has grown for being a trusted and dependable junior partner. Unlike the Chinese, here was an industry that was not trying too hard to grab cherry on the cake. So, while China dominated the hardware industry largely due to their control of rare earths market and manufacturing prowess, India remained large in peripheral areas of IT-related services.

Trust is a great factor in the data-sensitive software world. Slowly, Bengaluru developed into one of the best-known global IT hubs. Hyderabad, Chennai, Delhi National Capital Region (NCR) and Pune also became global IT destinations. This, despite the fact that Indian cities lacked woefully in developing their physical infrastructure when compared to China, Japan and South Korea—the other three big Asian IT hubs. Roads, logistics, connectivity and environment issues have been major bottlenecks that haunt India as a destination. Besides, Japan, China and South Korea were heavily into product development as they were manufacturing giants in their own right.

Trust and dependability have its own charm. Slowly, techies of Indian origin started finding themselves amongst the higher ranks of global companies due to skill, hard work and innovation. Today, Indians are present in large numbers in top positions in technology giants and some are at the very top. Sundar Pichai is chief executive officer (CEO) of Google, Satya Nadella is CEO of Microsoft, Shantunu Narayan is CEO of Adobe, Francisco D'Souza is CEO of Cognizant and Rajeev Suri is CEO and president of Nokia. There are some Indian entrepreneurs too who have created world-class businesses in the US. Sanjay Mehrotra co-founded SanDisk, valued over $15 billion, and has been its CEO since 2010. Laks Srini founded Zenefits, K.S. Sridhar founded Bloom Energy and Dhiraj Rajaram founded Mu Sigma—all three technology unicorns. Half a dozen India-based companies have also made it to the unicorn status apart from well-known e-commerce success stories. All these are silver linings in the horizon. India needs to leverage these strengths and create a global software ecosystem outside the US as China has created a hardware ecosystem based on their manufacturing prowess. But before we discuss that, let us explore where the industry is moving to and why.

Three Areas Indian Technology Companies Are Venturing into

The IT and the BPO sector, excluding e-commerce, earned revenues of $154 billion in 2017. Of this, BPO sector, euphemistically rechristened as Business Process Management (BPM) by NASSCOM, accounted for roughly $20 billion. This sector is expected to grow by around 8% to $167 billion as per initial estimates by the industry association. It also added 1,05,000 jobs to its impressive workforce of 3.97 million workers despite the economic slowdown. Compared to other businesses, India's presence is felt more in the global IT sector because it accounts for nearly 12% of the global IT software industry turnover of $1.3 trillion.

But, India's overseas markets had already started to shrink due to competition and the BPO sector faced serious challenges from south-east Asia. Additionally, President Trump's restriction on work visas showed that model of contracting and outsourcing back to India would be under severe threat. His insistence that companies who did business in the US hire more Americans queered the pitch for most of the Indian IT companies. Contracting jobs, as a result, fell sharply. More than 60,000 people have been retrenched in the top five Indian IT majors in the first six months of the financial year 2018–2019.

Indian companies have been restructuring their US operations to avoid sanctions and punitive action by Trump administration. Simply speaking, contract labour is on the way out and more white Americans are being hired in their US operations. All that has huge cost implications and operational expenses will rise for the US. Hence, belatedly they have been also trying to find a new operational area. Restructuring due to global headwinds has always been part of the IT sector evolution. But, this time, they do not have an option nor time on their side as they scramble to restructure.

The industry is today at an inflection point. It must change course and dive deep to keep its hold on global markets. The new areas being looked at by Indian technology companies are AI, big data and cybersecurity. Though few want to be quoted, significant amounts are being now invested into the development of value-added solutions. 'Almost 10% of the spending is going into developing AI solutions, which is huge, considering that we spend just 2% on research outside the existing business,' a vice president in product development division of a big Indian technology firm said in confidence.

AI Will Take Away Job Security but Will Increase Jobs

AI is the core area of focus, say people in the know, because it is what will cause loss of jobs. According to Brooklyn Institution, everyone—from retail giant Walmart to automaker Ford Motors—will be increasingly using AI to cut jobs aggressively in the next decade. The first to be hit may be the IT sector itself, especially the repeat and laborious coding jobs outsourced to India. 'Ongoing reductions in outsourced businesses (due to automation) will eventually result in a scenario where (only) 30% of the workforce will remain relevant,' says D.D. Mishra, research director at Gartner. So, Indian companies wanting to keep a hold on the outsourcing market are themselves investing in cutting jobs so that fewer number of people are needed to complete outsourced projects.

There is a lot of pressure to reduce outsourcing costs by overseas clients, especially in the US. Clients are asking their Indian vendors to both develop and also invest in automation tools. So, you are being asked to work and find innovative solutions that will actually make you redundant in the long run. In many cases, clients are funding their vendors on condition that 5% of the costs are reduced each year for the next few years. Automation and AI could endanger two-thirds of low-end IT sector jobs in India in the next few years. But, it will open up new avenues by improving efficiencies and adding scalability of operation. It will also give the opportunity for Indian companies to enter high-end research, funded as operational projects.

For example, AI-assisted fraud-detection techniques could assist the banking sector to analyse millions of transactions. They could even look for fault lines in round-trip trading. They could be used to analyse offshore banking transactions done with multiple beneficiaries, leading back to a few key beneficiaries. This could help banks save millions. Similarly, AI could help conduct smooth traffic-management through remote sensing, recording, tracking and penalising mechanism and relieve police force from mechanical duties. Indian television serials on crime are already regularly showing the use of drones and AI in search operations and summations. AI could eventually create better efficiencies to bring about more jobs than it takes away, confirms both Gartner and PwC.

In April 2018, as a guest on Lok Sabha TV's programme on job drought, I pointed out that we must now equip ourselves with new skills and be ready to take up assignments and short-duration jobs. We have to look for jobs that are not permanent in nature. In the age of AI, human labour will be replaced wherever they are found less efficient. I also told panellists what I had written 27 years ago in an article titled, 'Job Security Causes Underemployment', in my weekly column Taxpayers Money in *Financial Express*. The essence of the article is the same as the logic behind ushering in AI in 2018. Here are a few points highlighted from the August 1991 article. It shows how uncompetitive Indian industry was then due to job security and how removing labour unions in the 1990s actually improved the job situation. Even though the opinion was unpopular at the time, it pointed out how removing job security improves productivity and creates more jobs than it displaces. I had written in 1991:

> Wages and perquisites as a percentage of turnover in India are one of the highest in the world with 11% for the top 20 private-sector companies in India and 16% for the top 20 public-sector units. Though we have the lowest employee productivity rates in the world, we enjoy the privilege of having the highest number of holidays. With 20-odd festival and religious holidays, we are unique in terms of our secular multi-religious society. We also enjoy benefits of negotiated holidays of a socialist state that includes casual leave, earned leave, medical leave, maternity leave, education and training leave, leave for sports, movement leave, leave on tour, deputation leave, half-day leave and short leave. With a five-day

week in place, we could earn our full salaries without deduction while staying away from work for 200 days a year.

At that time, months before liberalisation, the economy was in dire straits and the turnover-to-capital ratio of the Indian industry was one of the poorest in the world at 3:2 for the private sector and 1:2 for the public sector. Resource utilisation was at its worst and companies both in the private and the public sector were over-staffed. There used to be the infamous overtime system those days where you would have to pay twice the wages for getting work done beyond scheduled hours. So, normally, workers slowed down the work during official duty hours and produced goods only if given overtime. But, since you could not fire people easily or even take them to task, workers became parasites and organisations became sick. As a result of low productivity, new jobs were not created and the economy was on verge of collapse at that time.

Fortunately, Narasimha Rao came in and liberalised the economy. Labour laws were changed and trade unions became toothless without government support. Industries were allowed to function without inspector raj and importantly, they were allowed to expand capacity without restrictive licensing laws. The economic recovery was slow and tedious but at the back of the revival was an attempt to improve employee efficiency and industry productivity. The same thing applies to streamlining of the IT industry today and reducing jobs with the help of AI. This is a unique opportunity and time when clients are willing to fund Indian companies to invest and incorporate AI. It would possibly reduce job security but go to improve productivity and create more employment opportunities.

Big Data Analytics Is the Next Biggest Thing for Policymakers

In the economic survey analysis of 2017, finance ministry reportedly started using data from GSTN network to understand trends in inter-state commerce. This is an interesting application for creating a predictive analytics model for forecasting tax receipts and future trends. Amazon uses such data modelling for its inventory management as well as for predicting future trends. But, while data is important, the expertise needed to handle big data and statistics is currently absent in the country and has to be developed.

In April 2018, RBI announced that it would be setting up a data sciences laboratory that would employ professionals with expertise in data analytics, data storage, statistics, economics, econometrics and finance. The division would deal with everything from banking supervision to inflation management and all aspects of data management that fall within its jurisdiction. That would be huge, because RBI is not only the bank supervisor but maintains all data of both the central government as well as all state governments. This actually means that RBI is the single institution that houses all data produced by all government departments in India. You can access all the data on the RBI website, though it is not in the best of shape. To say the least, the same data can be stored and presented in a 100 better ways.

Storing, classifying, using, searching and analysing data is a highly developed science today. All data today is computerised across India. It is data generated from and generated for the benefit of 1.3 billion Indians. Millions of computers are engaged in building that database on a daily basis. The data comes from diverse sources. Thousands of operators from block development offices, district offices, police stations, district collectors' offices, revenue offices upload data on a daily basis.

But, a large part of that data is faulty. The primary exercise that starts with data collection is outdated and fault-prone. The data collection procedure is neither documented nor audited. A lot of agricultural data, which I saw, that was ultimately sent for uploading on National Horticulture Board website were generated at a desk—without a preliminary visit to the fields. There was no laid-down procedure for data collection at the Block Development Office in a particular district in UP. There was no staff deputed for data collection. Nobody had a clue in the block about how to collect data or even the parameters of the data that was needed to be uploaded. An accountant from a nearby town arrived on first Sunday of every month and uploaded the data from a computer that was operated just once a month. Obviously, there was no site visit. And this is the standard that is applicable to many other offices where data is created from desk and just 5% addition to the figures of the previous year is the norm. So, to get big data right, we need to get the collection procedure sorted first.

All this development, from data collection to data analytics, will give the Indian IT sector tremendous opportunity to evolve itself and move ahead to create value-based solutions. Neither the government nor RBI can successfully move ahead on its own to tackle the complex world of big data without the help of India's technology companies. By creating an institution of data sciences, RBI would be merely enabling a process to store, research and analyse big data. It would be creating opportunities for India's biggest technology companies to harness that data for nation's use.

Cyber Crime Throws up Huge Opportunities

Developing anti-cybercrime expertise is a huge business of the future. The PwC report of 2018 claims that half the financial crimes in the UK reported in the year were cybercrimes. This is going to be the trend worldwide. Even as we move towards Digital India, incidences of cybercrimes will increase. Its reason is the huge amount of data that is being stored in clouds today and which is being transmitted telephonically through mobile phones to be placed on the internet. All that database is being sold openly without restraint. Despite a new personal data protection law, very little is being done about data protection in India. The government does not have the mechanism in place to ensure data protection. The violators are far too many and far too clever. Also activists are interested in scoring political brownies and the media does not report on day-to-day data breaches as elaborated below.

Many of us receive these Short Message Service (SMS) on our phone, one of which I am copying verbatim to explain the problem with our privacy laws. Here is a sample message that gives away an active database of a million mobile phone users for as little as ₹34,000:

> **Buy Bulk SMS Grow Your Business** 1 lakhs SMSes @₹7,000, 2 lakhs SMSes-@ ₹10,000 and 10 lakhs SMSes @ ₹34,000 WITH-ACTIVE-DATABASE. Guaranteed leads. Call @9650001327.

Hundreds and thousands of such SMSes are sent out each day by small marketing companies who partner with mobile operators in marketing customer databases. Despite laws to protect data, such transactions go on with impunity creating opportunities for cybercriminals to go fishing. Getting information about sensitive financial data is not difficult. Prying into bank statements sent through the internet is possible and several ethical hackers have demonstrated how it can be done. So, we need to understand that the elephant in the room is not Aadhaar but your mobile phone and there is no way you can expect privacy under the current laws and the way they are enforced.

Cyber security is developing into one of the most lucrative operational areas for technology companies. Infosys has reportedly shown interest in developing solutions to tackle cybercrime and others will soon follow suit. Cyber terrorism is another area that will see a lot of consumer dollars being spent. The cyber attack on the Saudi Reserve Bank and its biggest oil company Saudi Aramco a few years ago has made the gulf nation invest billions of petrodollars in cyber security. This is not going to be a one-off phenomenon.

Opportunities for Indian technology companies are many. It is not that they must only look towards the US for work. Digital India has opened and will open enormous opportunities in-house and so has e-commerce, aggregation business and many others. Banking and telecom software have been the core focus of Indian IT companies and both are growing hugely in India. So not all is lost for technology companies facing headwinds in North America. It is time for them to develop global solutions in the rapidly-evolving technology ecosystem and also take a good look at domestic markets.

Part IX

The Way Ahead

CHAPTER 19
Managing Future Risks

The impact of technology on modern-day life and governance is undeniable. We have seen massive changes in the past decade. We are going to see even faster changes in the next decade. It is no longer only the change and the speed of change that we must deal with. It's the acceleration of change that we will have to contend with in future. In short, it will not be about managing change, which inherently is difficult. It will be about managing scale, quality and accelerated change, which will be highly challenging. There are five risk-prone areas that need to be closely watched, because we will soon achieve the second level of disruptive innovation.

The first level of disruptive innovation was reached when computational costs dropped meteorically and data usage became easy and cheap. The first computers were operational in the 1950s. Data networks started transmitting information at 20 kilobytes (KB) per second by the 1990s. Two decades later the data transmission speed jumped by 50,000 times to 1 GB per second. The cost of data transit also fell 1,000 times, from \$1,200 per megabit in the mid-1990s to \$1.2 per megabit 20 years later.

The enormous increase in speed, along with the ease of data transmission at a very affordable cost helped almost all things to be connected through the internet. Soon every discipline had applications that had benefitted from IT. Medical science to metallurgy, textile to cement, agriculture to finance all benefitted from the disruptive changes that revolutionised the data world. The disruption spread to hundreds of real-world applications. From radiology and microsurgery to drug development and creation of artificial limbs every field of medical science saw dynamic changes. Similarly, automobile and airplane manufacturing saw complete IT integration and even services like hotel booking and cab booking got completely transformed. Old business models were severely disrupted as new IT-enabled business applications came into vogue.

Energy Prices Drop Could Bring the Second Level of Disruption

The second level of disruption is expected to happen in the next decade with the advent of renewable energy. Energy prices and availability, like data, affects not only one application but multiple industries. Be it medicinal science or agriculture, motor vehicles or spacecraft, the cost of energising and powering a machine or service has been always a major cause affecting its popularity. If energy costs plummeted, energy applications would increase and it would revolutionise the utility of each and every equipment on this planet.

But, energy costs have not fallen rapidly because humans have so long been dependent on fossil fuels. In the case of fossil fuels, particularly oil, the supplies were reduced whenever demand fell to ensure that prices gave producers adequate profits to run their national economies. That made fossil fuel prices volatile and industries tried to reduce energy consumption to stay ahead. But, all that is just about to change. Renewable energy power prices have dropped five times in the last five years to catch up with the price of fossil fuels. If this trend continues it would eventually break the back of the fossil fuel industry in the next few years.

This because two energy deficient nations, China and India, are increasingly generating and using solar power. That would cause a major shift in the costing as well as the development of renewable energy. Today solar and wind power tariffs at below ₹3 per Kilowatt-hours (kWh) are competing at par with thermal power generated by coal. If the prices fall to less than ₹1 per kWh, which it should in the next few years, it will become disruptive. It will cause millions of energy-dependent businesses and gadgets to change the way they do business. It will further reduce the cost of solar power and thereby increase its consumption further.

Soon we will be moving on to what is called the proverbial shifting sands. And we are not sure if the changes we are making today will make the life of citizens easy or difficult in five years' time. This is because technology and the energy industry will be ushering in changes faster than what we as humans can absorb. There are too many options, too many paths to choose from. And not all of them are right. It is paradoxical but what we think right today may turn out to be not so beneficial in the long run. An increasing number of natural disasters is prompting a discourse on whether continued human intervention is beneficial for humans. Floods, droughts, cyclones and earthquakes that we once thought were well under control of the human race through interventions have raised their ugly heads again with increasing frequency. We call them the effects of climate change.

Climate Change Risks Could Bring Challenges and Opportunities

Over the last two decades, there has been a flurry of natural calamities that have hit the world. Statistically, the first 20 years of this century has witnessed 400 to 500 natural disasters every year as against an average of 100 disasters annually in the previous century. The year 2000 recorded 526 natural disasters—the most ever in human history. As a matter of fact, the accelerated change started happening in and around 1950. Till that time, the annual disasters recorded by scientists never exceeded 20 per year. But 50 years later, yearly disasters had spiralled 20 times as per EM-DAT 2017, published by International Disaster Database, Belgium.

The data excludes man-made disasters like oil spills or wars or industrial accidents like Chernobyl or Fukushima but includes all natural disasters like droughts, floods, cyclones, earthquakes, volcanic activities, extreme weather, El Nino and wildfire. Climate change scientists claim that these natural disasters may not all be man-made but are assisted by human behaviour, industrial activity, increased carbon footprint and higher global temperatures. Hence the spike of activity after the 1950s. Excessive human intervention in nature is also considered by some scientists as a reason for triggering natural disasters.

For example, building of dams to check rampant rivers or harness its energy or reservoir capacity may be a good and time-tested idea. But, building over 50 dams in a small and narrow state like Kerala and cutting down the forests of the Western Ghats may not be a great idea. Dams were initially built to check floods. But for that, dams need to be partially emptied out before peak monsoon strikes - but no such exercise happens. In 1924, when Kerala witnessed the greatest flood of the century, it was due to torrential rain and a burst dam. In 2018, the dams did not burst because water was released before the situation got out of hand. But still, simultaneous release of water from 25 dams caused the flood waters to surge. The problem was not waters from Tamil Nadu but water released from Idukki dam, which is six times bigger than Mullaperiyar dam maintained by Tamil Nadu. Kerala State Electricity Board Ltd (KSEB) released Idukki dam's waters at the last minute because water was a resource which was being monetised. It did not want to release the stored dam waters prematurely that could have generated hydroelectricity worth ₹200 crore unless they were forced to. It so happened that it rained much more than expected and they had to open the dam on the 8 August when an orange alert was issued. But that was too late. The rain was relentless over the next two days. The Idukki dam waters had to be released as an emergency measure, flooding low-lying areas and affecting the much smaller Mullaperiyar dam. With both dams being forced to open the floodgates simultaneously, three districts were ravaged. The attempt to save ₹200 crore thus resulted in losses of over ₹20,000 crore for the state. The ruling party in Kerala has ordered a probe into the release of dam waters both by the state government as well as by neighbouring state Tamil Nadu.

The accelerated phenomenon of natural disasters is expected to increase in coming years. These risks will pose huge challenges. They will also create big opportunities. Only advanced predictive analytics with big data on weather forecasting could manage such complex situations. Few other problems will also surface. One is water-borne deficiencies and the second is water shortage. Presence of arsenic above permissible limits has been reported in several districts of UP, Bihar, Bengal and Jharkhand. Presence of Uranium in groundwater in states like Rajasthan is equally threatening. This is reported to have caused skin cancer, gall bladder and intestine cancer besides kidney ailments to thousands of people in the region. Water shortage is yet another major crisis in the offing. Acute water scarcity in Latur in Western Maharashtra necessitated supply of water from Miraj by train in 2017. Shimla water shortage of 2018 made headlines months later. The way we are consuming water, India could have more than one Cape Town each year. Water quality and quantity will remain a serious concern for India in the next few years. This trend could accelerate and lead to large-scale disaster and death. All these would need tech solutions.

Besides water, air pollution is fast moving to a crisis point. During the last decade, there have been strong warning signals. In 2010, Delhi and Agra entered WHO's list of top 10 polluted cities in the world. But we did precious little. On 8 November 2012, Delhi hit the headlines again with particulate matter (PM2.5) concentrations of 1,080 micrograms of particulate suspended matter per cubic metre, 40 times the permissible limit prescribed by WHO. By 2012 there were four north-Indian cities in the list, by 2014 there were seven and in 2016 all 10 of the most-polluted cities in the world were from north India. The big risk here is that things are steadily declining for the last seven years. Neither UPA nor NDA has been moving in the right direction to mitigate the crisis. Coal and petcoke use is on the rise and gas use is declining, which further accentuates the problem. If things continue like this, there will be a major outbreak of respiratory diseases in the cities of north India. There is no time to lose because for nearly a decade we are sliding and a precipice could be round the corner. Here again big data and analytics have a role to play.

Coping with Cybercrimes and Cyber Wars

There are several other areas of concern. Three of the world's big four audit firms have reported about the rise of cybercrimes. PWC, in its economic survey of 2018 in the UK, confirms that cybercrimes are increasingly becoming dominant. In a report on financial crimes, the auditing major says that a quarter of British firms they surveyed were victims of cybercrimes in the past two years. It also stated that one out of two financial crimes committed in Britain is an online crime. And that 55% of cybercrime incidents were committed by outside perpetrators. The findings of the survey are ominous and is a sign of caution for emerging economies that are going the digital way.

This means that criminals hacked into the computer networks to illegally access usernames and passwords of consumers. They then used those compromised identities and broke into supposedly secured systems of banks, credit card companies or payment gateways to withdraw billions of dollars from hundreds and thousands of consumers. Doing this in advanced nations like the UK is inherently more difficult than doing it in India. But, it is inherently possible only because consumers are lured into compromising their security during their online activities in an innumerable number of ways.

The fifteenth global fraud survey of consulting major Ernst &Young (E&Y) states, 'Organisations increasingly use digital technology to change the way they do digital business, which is heightening their exposure to fraud, corruption and other risks.' Over a TV panel discussion at NewsX in April 2018, Arpinder Singh, partner and national leader, Fraud Investigation and Dispute Services at E&Y told me that over the last five years, financial frauds have increased globally. He also said that there is clear evidence to show that one of the reasons why this is happening is because businesses are increasingly using technology solutions.

A follow-up discussion with several other software professionals in our Pan IIT group pointed to the reasons why this was happening. There is a global trend to use advanced software features and technology to drive in business-friendly solutions every day. It is a way to beat the competition and project your product or service as the most technologically advanced solution. New-age consumers lap it up and businesses go all out to achieve it. For example, voice recognition is the latest trending feature for login IDs. Everyone from Apple to Amazon, Google to Microsoft is spending billions of dollars in this race.

At the same time, cyber criminals and ethical hackers are working overtime, creating synthetic voices for deep fakes. This is a continuous ongoing parallel activity going on around the world. It is happening in all areas of emerging technologies—be it voice or facial recognition, biometric or fingerprint mapping. There are insights that the E&Y survey carried was not limited to one nation. They talked to 2,550 executives from 55 nations to reach their conclusions. India is one of those vulnerable nations and the increased thrust on digitisation will accelerate the process.

Consulting major McKinsey, working with World Economic Forum in a report published in 2014 titled 'The Rising Strategic Risks of Cyberattacks' said that organisations are today struggling to cope up with cyberattacks. While cybercriminals are working round the clock to breach secure systems to gain from financial frauds, 'hacktivists'—politically driven hacker activists—pierce online firewalls to make political statements. Talking to over 200 CxOs all over the globe, the McKinsey report had predicted that attackers will continue to increase their lead over corporate defences. And if that happens, there will be a backlash against digitisation and the pace of digitisation will suffer globally. India cannot have an exclusionist view of itself in this globally threatening scenario.

This is a major risk for nations like India trying to digitise at a quick pace. As a matter of fact, India is one country that is open to dual threats from hacktivists as well as financial criminals. There is an intense political and social media warfare between the left and the right groups currently raging in the country. Add to it the animosity with Pakistan and China. Besides, there is the jihadi terrorism in Kashmir and Maoist insurgency in four states, all of which together make the country a prime target for large-scale institutional hacking. It is also digitising at a fast pace with new and easy payment features for its citizens. Online payments to and from average citizen in India have doubled in the last four years and is growing annually at an astounding rate of 15% CAGR. This increasingly makes us susceptible to cybercrime as well as cyberattacks that have political motives.

Tackling Human Obsolescence Will Be a Challenge

With increased technology comes the risk of human obsolescence. With the advent of automation, robotics and AI, the prime question that comes to everyone's mind is what will happen to the jobs currently done by humans? Will humans become obsolete and redundant as labour-intensive and skill-oriented work gets increasingly done by machines both efficiently and at a lower cost? *Should we race towards machine learning and digitisation before looking at basic computerisation and retraining the masses?* This is a key question that populous nations like India must grapple with now before it becomes too late.

Machines are largely replacing unskilled labour and AI is replacing skilled labour. The mechanisation of shop floors, automation and robotics have been reducing jobs by thousands. We don't have a mechanism to track or retrain displaced labour. Combined harvesters and automatic power tillers and cultivators are cutting down on agriculture labour. MGNREGA gives just 100 days' employment a year to displaced agriculture labour. AI is already causing some disruptions in the technology world today, taking up coding and assembly jobs. There is no alternate strategy to retrain or create new job avenues for already skilled workers. Machines and AI are not only replacing unskilled labour but also technical and highly skilled workforce. The risk of human skills and know-how becoming obsolete in this fast-evolving technology-driven world is extremely high and needs to be addressed.

Jobs is part of a huge discourse today. It is not because jobs are not growing. It is because unemployment is growing. But, there is no data on the number of unemployed people and the new jobs we are creating. Nor is there any data on changing skill sets needed for being employed today. A large number of young Indians are getting educated each year. Whatever be the quality of education, quantitative churn out of Indian schools and colleges is huge. This passing out from educational institutions creates expectations. Nearly 3.5 crore (35 million) students enrol each year for graduation in India, of which 40 lakh (4 million) register for engineering and 10 lakh (1 million) for medical science. Even if two out of three students graduate, it means that we need to create two crore (20 million) jobs each year.

Apart from fresh jobs, there is a huge demand for reskilling. Most modern-day jobs need some IT skills and the capability to use gadgets. But, not all people are able to manage gadgets easily. Nearly 20 crore (200 million) people in India are above 60 years of age or senior citizens. They have not grown up in a gadget-dominated world and most are not comfortable handling digital devices. There are another 30 crore (300 million) people who are illiterate. For them, using gadgets is not easy either. While rapid digitisation will propel the nation ahead, it also will leave behind half a billion people in the race to benefit from technological improvements of the digital world. Just like economic or social disparity, this technological disparity must be removed.

Disruptive Technologies Will Help Winners Take All

There has never been an explosion of technology as it has been in the last decade. The reason can be attributed to start-up culture that started 20 years ago but is maturing now. As of August 2018, there were 263 unicorns having a total valuation of $850 billion in the world and nearly half of them are outside OECD nations. Each of them is innovating and trying to disrupt conventional business wisdom. Over 20 years ago, Google ventured into the start-up world, disrupting conventional business wisdom. Instead of selling a product or service, it gave it away for free. It also bought pay-per-click start-ups like Double Click to build its ad-based revenue model Google AdSense and AdWords. Google Search became a household name globally without being sold and Google raked in billions.

Today Uber, the highest-valued start-up at $60 billion, has disrupted businesses by bringing aggregation to the fore. It does not own cabs, it does not hire drivers. Still it commands the biggest fleet of transport vehicles globally and earns more revenue than any cab operator ever did in any part of the world. In short, today's start-ups are not investing in building the asset class of businesses they own but merely putting to use the existing surplus capacities and earning revenue from matching demand with supply. No wonder they are much more efficient than older businesses and can scale up their operations easily.

Uber's success has brought aggregation into contention in diverse businesses like food, retail goods, fashion, automobile spares, hotel rooms and grocery supplies. It is disrupting a lot of existing businesses that have built up capacities painstakingly over the years. They now find themselves well and truly beaten by nimble-footed, asset-light competitors. It has also cut down on capital investment hugely. More importantly, it has completely demolished the theory of monopolies and duopolies, driving up the prices of goods and services.

Finance Beyond Regulation May Be the Decade's Biggest Challenge

Last but not least, we must be careful of financial innovations. We have already seen what damage securitisation of mortgages did to the US housing market a decade ago. Decentralised trading permitted by commodity exchanges and national governments made regulators toothless. Now financial frauds are becoming increasingly difficult to track due to use of technology. The use of parking funds in offshore destinations is the first challenge. Thereafter, the use of round-trip trading in offshore deals makes it extremely difficult to pinpoint, co-relate and track source and ultimate beneficiary of funds. Machine learning can sift through piles of data but that itself is an art to master. Not all investigative agencies have the requisite technology or skill sets. So, it will become extremely difficult to track tax offenders and new-age taxes could be directed increasingly towards consumption and not towards income.

But, there are other challenges too. The biggest looming challenge is that of cryptocurrencies. Cryptocurrencies are in their early stages but though they do not have sanction and legitimacy as a currency, they are slowly becoming an accepted commodity. You can freely trade it in commodity exchanges of North America. That gives it a huge legitimacy and clearly shows that cryptocurrencies are here to stay. So, immaterial of what the governments say, cryptocurrencies will stay in the long run and cannot be wished away.

But it is not only efficiency that technology creates that we must applaud. We must also take note of inefficiencies that technology brings and keep away from them as far as possible, waiting till they turn into efficient and sustainable solutions. One such technology is blockchain technology. It is a technology in its formative stage that many are rushing to adopt. We cannot afford rushing into this because early investors in the industry will bear losses. The cryptocurrency business will at best be volatile. And these losses will be massive and will not be sustainable. So, we must know how to assess technology-risk and sift out those early first-generation technologies that are not so beneficial.

The blockchain technology is one such technology that we must view with scepticism. This again only because it is an extremely expensive, inefficient and risk-prone solution that is avoidable. Blockchain is inefficient for three reasons. Conceptually, the digital ledger is a technologically complex solution replacing paper ledger—which is a simple, easy to use, time-tested methodology for record keeping. So, there is a huge question whether the technology really adds value. Besides, it is an energy guzzler as it needs immense amounts of computing power for functioning. Its carbon footprint is extremely high. It is also a myth that digital solutions stored in the cloud can be secure or are hack-proof. The number of cryptocurrency heists and increasing cybercrimes go to prove the vulnerability of digital solutions.

The advent of cryptocurrencies will increasingly be a challenge to governments and regulatory bodies. So far it is largely controlled and used by techies who created them. But, as the world of high finance understands and adopts it in the global commodity markets, its use will spread. And with that will be created new and alternate channels of completely unregulated monetary transactions. This is not a risk for India alone but also for the rest of the world.

Risk Management Will Help in Better Decision-Making

As finance and technological risks mount, India needs to incorporate the institution of risk management in governance and decision-making. We need to understand what is the best solution and what is not the right solution after working out the numbers. This will help us wade through the complexities of technological and financial decision-making. For example, there is an inherent contradiction in many of our financial policies including those on securitisation, investment treaties with tax havens, FDI in multi-brand retail and many others. But, it is not only technological and financial decisions that need risk management. Many other decisions would do better with number crunching for an outcome check.

This can help the government avoid major losses and pitfalls of wrong decision-making. There are some bold decisions that have worked extremely well for the Modi government but there are some that have not. While demonetisation may not have achieved its purpose, UPI or digital payment system—an offshoot of demonetisation—has been a resounding success. US-based Fidelity National Information Services Incorporated said in its December 2017 report that of the 40-odd payment systems that it tracked and evaluated worldwide, UPI was the best. As a matter of fact, it was the only system to score full five marks out of five and is way ahead of Swiss' Interbank Clearing and Kenya's PesaLink that scored four and China's payment system that got only a score of two.

India has never done number crunching to check outcomes before a programme has been launched. That has been a major drawback because faults at the planning level cannot be deciphered without number crunching. So, we usually move ahead with a great idea without actually working on how we would reach the outcomes. Understanding and sorting out the implementation challenges are extremely important before the initiation of a project. The rural electrification project or the *Swachh Bharat* toilet-building projects are not new. They have all been done before. Only they have been done badly without a concern for outcomes. Now that all the issues are under political scrutiny, we are talking of ensuring that electricity reaches every home and that toilets are not only built but are functional and used. These are great learnings and have helped governance and better implementation, well after the political slugfest. It has proved that despite the daily protests in parliament and the streets, India is quickly adopting and changing the way it functions for the better.

Conclusion

This is a second book of the series on the *Roundup of the Indian Economy* dedicated once again to 'a new India that is efficient, compassionate and sustainable—free from doles and corruption'. Is it a far-fetched desire, a chimera or can it become a reality? Only time will give us the right answers.

Why Publishing around Elections Help

Like the last book, we are publishing this book just around the general elections. It has the work of complete four years of the Modi Government as recorded in public domain, the media and the annual reports of each ministry and in the reports of major global institutions. The bibliography gives details of references. The book shows how good and faulty decisions influence the economic well-being of the nation. It happily leaves out the election-year decision-makings that are taken with an eye on immediate votes. The timing of publication is such as to bring issues to the notice of voters before the elections. Why? Because the positive and the negative economic decisions of those who ruled the nation in the immediate past need to be seen. They also need to be compared with data from the previous regime. Only when we compare the present with the past do we come to know where we are headed.

Our study has nothing to do with politics but it does analyse economic decisions taken by the politicians. Unfortunately, neither the past nor the present government has delivered as promised. So this book, like our previous book, will have few political friends. We believe that none of the political parties in India have all the answers. They are all on a learning curve—just not ready to admit the same. Like PM Manmohan Singh,

PM Modi has tried his best to provide good governance, from his perspective. Unfortunately, he has succeeded only in parts and many decisions have been faulty. You cannot accuse him of policy paralysis but hyperactivity too needs to be avoided because it increases the mistakes you make. India remains an emerging nation, short on resources and not a surplus and mature democracy with plenty. A little bit of prudence would lead to lesser wastage of resources. These stretched resources lead to increased risks. For example, we did not invest enough in food parks that were needed for the agriculture sector but instead squandered resources on smart city projects that could have waited. Instead of first completing the rural water supply project that has been long pending, we pumped our resources into toilet building, knowing that *Swachh Bharat* cannot be successful without adequate water supply.

However, if it has risks, it also has opportunities. Both its democracy and politicians are evolving, getting some things right and some things wrong. So, we look at economic decisions, the possible causes and the outcomes.

Happily, Data Now Takes Centre Stage

The book is purely an economic analysis based on institutional data available, mostly from RBI or the government or international bodies such as IMF or World Bank. Though the authenticity of data is now frequently under question in political debates as it is often inconvenient for politicians, the fact that data has entered political discourse is itself a huge achievement. When my previous book with 30 data charts was published in February 2014, a major TV channel told me that they do not discuss economic data as it would cause fall of target rating point (TRP). A lot has changed in less than five years.

Today, many news channels, newspapers and websites are looking to create data stories and all that economic data is discussed threadbare. This was not the case when we penned our previous book in 2014. If we ignore the political slugfest that goes on in major news channels, we find that the discussion improves conversation on governance. Each and every decision of the government is under scrutiny by opposition, media and analysts—and the government defends these attacks with data and evidence to back its actions. This involves the citizens and makes politicians more accountable.

Readers across India, even if they are not students of economics, are increasingly starting to read and understand data stories. This is inevitable as the modern-day world revolves around data. But, problems exist with data, especially in India. It is not collected properly, it is not classified, stored or even presented accurately and it is often not authenticated with rigour and sanitised by regular audit checks. Besides, data fudging is an issue because government departments and even media houses are increasingly getting politicised. Political sides are being taken even by data statisticians and websites. Apart from this there is the issue of data accuracy and completeness. This is not a recent problem but a legacy issue. Not only is critical data of jobs and unemployment missing, but even solid waste data is prehistoric and unscientific. National Information Centre (NIC) data is neither user-friendly nor wide-ranged and the Department of Statistics data is not well organised. Besides, data should be open for all to access and not reachable only after logging in and sanitisation.

Inaccurate or insufficient data is going to make it difficult for us in the age of machine learning because algorithms of artificial intelligence (AI) are designed to recognise patterns in data to execute solutions. It is also important that data must be genuine and not politically motivated. Data integrity is paramount and checks and balance to ensure the same is needed. This is because wrong data can give totally wrong solutions in the age of AI.

The government and RBI are planning to use big data for inflation management. RBI data is more reliable, wide-ranged (includes central and state data) and accessible. This is because we need a single autonomous agency that is responsible for the storage, quality and analysis of all data.

What Happens If

India's general elections of 2019 are around the corner. There are three things that can happen: NDA—BJP and its allies—come back to power or UPA—Congress and its allies—dethrone them. There is also a possibility of a third-front formation that keeps out Congress and BJP and fights the election on its own. After the elections, if and only if they fail to win half the seats, do they ask Congress for support. This is post-poll alliance model adopted during both the assembly and the municipal elections in Karnataka where Janata Dal (United)(JDU) and Congress fought as frenemies—before the poll they were enemies and after the poll they became friends.

The frenemy model has several advantages and disadvantages. The advantage is that there is no seat-sharing by Samajwadi Party (SP), Bahujan Samaj Party (BSP), JDS or Trinamool with Congress. Cadres of these parties are bitterly against Congress because there are a lot of ideological differences. So, fighting elections separately gives the cadres more seats. For example, SP and BSP would not want to give more than a few seats to Congress in UP while Trinamool wants to put up its candidates for all seats in West Bengal. Rahul Gandhi would be hard pressed to satisfy Congress workers if a pre-poll alliance takes place with these parties. The minus point is that votes will get shared, giving BJP and NDA a clear advantage if this happens.

The bigger question is, however, what will happen to the economic decisions taken by this government if either of the following three combinations come to power: Congress as a junior partner in frenemy model; Congress as a senior partner in the UPA model; or BJP and the NDA returning to power. This is important because the Modi government has taken several positive steps and many retrograde decisions in each area. This is different from what the UPA did, which was more in the news due to inaction. For example, while removing subsidies on diesel and petrol by the NDA was a positive step, raising excise duties and VAT (in states) by more than three times was regressive.

There were many decisions taken by Modi government as readers of this book would have noted. A few were game-changing decisions—like rural banking, GST or digitisation—and they have set India on an irretrievable course. While some of them were great, some were disastrous. So, whether NDA returns to power or UPA ousts Modi government or whether the frenemies win the elections, we do not actually know what the future of all these decisions will be.

New India has to also remember that the Indian consumer is also a global citizen. The US-China trade war has to be dealt with now and we must react with our own initiatives to protect and enhance our business and jobs. Even though India is not directly involved, it is hugely affected.

An election in the distant US has affected jobs and crucial import tariffs in India. Another impending election in 2020 will affect the Indian economy positively or negatively.

NDA, to its credit did not reverse UPA decisions but took things forward, whether it was Aadhaar or rural electrification or toilet-building projects initiated by the UPA. They took the initiative and also tried to hog the limelight as they managed to complete the unfinished work in many cases. The fight between political opponents became bitter as the work came under scrutiny. The slugfest helped the completion of last-mile electrification of village homes and now could lead to better water supply in every rural home and toilet. Even MGNREGA is being revamped and restructured for better outcomes.

The big question is, how will the schemes initiated by Modi government be taken forward if UPA manages to oust NDA or if opposition groups with Congress as minor partner comes to power. Also, will NDA try to rectify the many mistakes it made, if it returns to power? If it is re-elected, will it be wise enough to review its own decisions? Or will it push forward full steam ahead— even with faulty schemes that cause hardship to people or loss to the exchequer?

There are no clear-cut answers to these questions and no easy solutions. But, a ray of light is high-decibel discussion around economic performance that was not happening before. As we evolve as a nation, if all citizens become aware of why the value of rupee is falling, why incomes and jobs are under pressure and why goods are becoming expensive, then we shall be able to pressurise our leaders to take decisions responsibly for the economic growth and prosperity or *achhe din* of every Indian. Narendra Modi, Rahul Gandhi, Navin Pattnaik, Mamata Banerjee, Naidu or Shivraj—it does not matter if the decision-making is uniformly responsible and the benefits flow to the people. We need to ensure that our politicians comply to responsible decision-making and work towards the nations' prosperity and not vote banks. And our votes work for the betterment of our democracy. So, we urge our readers to read, analyse and then vote to ensure better governance.

Bibliography

Chapter 1

Bandopadhyay, T. 'Life of Banks After Five Decades of Nationalisation.' *Livemint*, 16 July 2018, https://www.livemint.com/Opinion/kIecdkX8V2rERYPXCIjMiO/Life-of-banks-after-five-decades-of-nationalization.html (accessed 9 December 2018).

Baru, S. *How P. V. Narasimha Rao Made History*. New Delhi: Aleph Books, 2016.

Benegal, S. 'White Knight Verghese Kurien Made India Largest Producer of Milk.' *India Today*, 16 September 2017, https://www.indiatoday.in/magazine/news-makers/story/20170925-lal-bahadur-shastri-gujarat-amul-verghese-kurien-anand-operation-flood-1045163-2017-09-16 (accessed 9 December 2018).

Bhattacharya, S. *India's Coal Story*. New Delhi: Sage, 2017.

Chakrabarty, A. and Bannerjee, S. 'Coal Quandary.' *Down to Earth*, 17 August 2015, https://www.downtoearth.org.in/coverage/coal-quandary-46345 (accessed 9 December 2018).

Dasgupta, Y. 'Golden Quadrilateral Project Connecting Delhi Mumbai Kolkata and Chennai Crawling to a Finishing Line.' *The Economic Times*, 8 April 2013, https://economictimes.indiatimes.com/news/economy/infrastructure/golden-quadrilateral-project-connecting-delhi-mumbai-kolkata-and-chennai-crawling-to-finishing-line/articleshow/19436850.cms (accessed 9 December 2018).

Datta, P. 'How Atal Bihari Vajpayee's Economic Policy Paved the Way for India's Growth.' *Business Today*, 16 August 2018, https://www.businesstoday.in/current/economy-politics/atal-bihari-vajpayee-economic-policies-reforms/story/281364.html (accessed 9 December 2018).

Duggal, I. 'Why 6/6/66 Was a Devilish Day for the Rupee.' *Livemint*, 6 June 2016, https://www.livemint.com/Money/3wTK1Nm9I1fVeyHUIO5FAK/6-June-1966-A-date-to-remember-in-the-rupees-history.html (accessed 9 December 2018).

ET Online Bureau. 'Atal Bihari Vajpayee's Five Steps that Changed India for Ever.' *The Economic Times*, 25 December 2017, https://economictimes.indiatimes.com/news/politics-and-nation/atal-bihari-vajpayees-five-steps-that-changed-india-forever/articleshow/62240161.cms, (accessed 9 December 2018).

Friedman, M. and Friedman, R. *Free to Choose*. New York: Harcourt, Inc, 1990.

Ghosh, D. N. *No Regrets*. New Delhi: Rupa, 2015.

Khan, M. I. 'Operation Gibraltar: The Pakistani Troops Who Infiltrated Kashmir to Start a Rebellion.' *BBC*, 5 September 2015, https://www.bbc.com/news/world-asia-34136689 (accessed 9 December 2018).

Kumar, R. 'Putting Wheat in its Place, or Why Green revolution is Not What it Is Made Out to Be.' *The Wire*, 31 October 2016, https://thewire.in/76956/green-revolution-borlaug-food-security/?fromNewsdog=1 (accessed 9 December- 2018).

Laxminarayan, H. 'Indo-US Food Agreement and State Trading in Foodgrains.' *The Economic and Political Weekly*, 24 September 1960, 12 (39): 1441–1447, https://www.epw.in/system/files/pdf/1960_12/39/indous_food_agreementand_state_trading_in_foodgrains.pdf, accessed 9 December 2018.

Malhotra, I. 'Swallowing the Humilation.' *The Indian Express*, 12 July 2010, https://indianexpress.com/article/opinion/columns/swallowing-the-humiliation/ (accessed 9 December 2018).

Ninan, T. N. '1974—The Invisible Turning Point.' *Business Standard*, 30 October 2014, https://www.business-standard.com/article/companies/bs-40-1974-the-invisible-turning-point-114102701291_1.html (accessed 9 December 2018).

Ninan, T. N. 'Story of Two Devaluations.' *Business Standard*, 9 November 2012, https://www.business-standard.com/article/opinion/story-of-two-devaluations-113081601231_1.html (accessed 9 December 2018).

Ninan, T. N. and Mathai, P. G. 'World Bank Demanding 25 Percent Devaluation of Rupee Sparks of Controversy.' *India Today*, 15 June 1987, https://www.indiatoday.in/magazine/economy/story/19870615-world-bank-demanding-25-per-cent-devaluation-of-rupee-sparks-off-controversy-798941-1987-06-15 (accessed 9 December 2018).

Pande, S. 'Just the Right Image.' *Business Today*, 8 June 2014, https://www.businesstoday.in/magazine/case-study/case-study-strategy-tactics-behind-creation-of-brand-narendra-modi/story/206321.html (accessed 9 December 2018).

Rajan, R. G. *Fault Lines*. Noida, Uttar Pradesh: Collins Business, 2010.Ram Mohan, T. T. 'Indira Gandhi, the Reformer.' *The Economic Times*, 21 January 2010, https://economictimes.indiatimes.com/t-t-ram-mohan/indira-gandhi-the-reformer/articleshow/5482820.cms (accessed 9 December 2018).

RBI. IMF Data on India on GDP Growth, Fiscal Deficit and Current Account Balance. 2000–2018.

RBI. RBI Data on GDP Growth, Fiscal Deficit and Current Account Balance. 2000–2018.

RBI. RBI External Debt Reports. 2000–2018.

Sen, S. '50 Years On: PSBs Need More Autonomy to Fulfill Role.' *DNA India*, 2 August 2018, https://www.dnaindia.com/analysis/column-50-years-on-psbs-need-more-autonomy-to-fulfill-role-2644469 (accessed 9 December 2018).

Sen, S. *Neta, Babu and Subsidy: Economic Roundup 2000–2014.* New Delhi: Vitasta, 2014.

Sitapati, V. *Half Lion: How P. V. Narasimha Rao Transformed India.* New Delhi: Penguin, 2016.

Srivastava, S. 'Economic Milestone: Nationalisation of Banks (1969).' *Forbes*, 12 August 2014, http://www.forbesindia.com/article/independence-day-special/economic-milestone-nationalisation-of-banks-(1969)/38415/1 (accessed 9 December 2018).

Swaminathan, M. S. *50 Years of Green Revolution*. Chennai: Swaminathan Research Foundation, 2005.

Upmanyu, K. 'Decoding Indira Gandhi's Bank Nationalisation of 1969.' *The Quint*, 19 July 2018, https://www.thequint.com/news/india/indira-gandhi-bank-nationalisation-1969-morarji-congress (accessed 9 December 2018).

Chapter 2

BT Online Bureau, 'At Least 23,000 Dollar Millionaires Left India Since 2014: Report.' *Business Today*, Updated 17 March 2018, https://www.businesstoday.in/current/economy-politics/at-least-23000-dollar-millionaires-have-left-india-since-2014-report/story/273018.html (accessed 9 December 2018).

BT Online Bureau. 'CAG Reports Tabled in Parliament, Indict Government on Coal Block Allocation, Mega Power Projects, Delhi Airport Concession.' *Business Today*, 17 August 2012, https://www.businesstoday.in/sectors/energy/cag-reports-tabled-in-parliament-coal-blocks/story/187288.html (accessed 9 December 2018).

CAG. *Report No. 19 of 2010—Performance Audit of Issue of Licences and Allocation of 2G Spectrum of Union Government, Ministry of Communications and Information Technology.* 16 November -2010.

CAG. *Report of the Comptroller and Auditor General of India on Allocation of Coal Mine.*, 9 February 2012.

Chattopadhyay, S. '"Achhe Din" Giving BJP a Miss?' *Livemint*, 3 October 2016, https://www.livemint.com/Opinion/t9mfv88N7DMDWyoafDH6pO/Achhe-din-giving-BJP-a-miss.html (accessed 9 December 2018).

Das, S. 'Messiah Modi's Unclear Vision.' *Forbes*, 26 August 2014, http://www.forbesindia.com/article/column/messiah-modis-unclear-vision/38511/1 (accessed 9 December 2018).

ET Bureau. 'PM Modi's Promise of "₹15 Lakhs in Each Account" an Idiom: Amit Shah.' *The Economic Times*, 6 February 2015, https://economictimes.indiatimes.com/news/politics-and-nation/pm-modis-promise-of-rs-15-lakh-in-each-account-an-idiom-amit-shah/articleshow/46139139.cms (accessed 9 December 2018).

Express News Service, 'CAG Findings in 2G Spectrum Case.' *The Indian Express*, Updated 22 December 2017, https://indianexpress.com/article/india/cag-findings-in-2g-spectrum-case-quite-erroneously-2001-values-in-2008-report-said-a-raja-4993690/ (accessed 12 September 2018).

IMF. IMF Data on GDP Growth and Fiscal Deficit. 2000–2018, https://www.imf.org/external/pubs/ft/weo/2018/02/weodata/index.aspx (accessed 9 December 2018).

Jigeesh, A. M. 'CAG Says Raja Caused ₹1.76 lakhs Crores Loss in Scam.' *India Today*, 3 November 2010, https://www.indiatoday.in/2g-scam/investigations/story/cag-says-raja-caused-rs-176-lakh-cr-loss-in-scam-84990-2010-11-03 (accessed 9 December 2018).

John, N. 'Billions to Bust.' *Business Today*, 7 October 2018, https://www.businesstoday.in/magazine/cover-story/billions-to-bust/story/282440.html (accessed 9December 2018).

Marandi, R. 'India's Bad Loans Dwarf Bank Recapitalisation Plans.' *Nikkei Asian Review*, 30 May 2018, https://asia.nikkei.com/Business/Business-Trends/India-s-bad-loans-dwarf-bank-recapitalization-plans (accessed 9 December 2018).

Ministry of Coal. *Report of the Comptroller and Auditor General of India on e-Auction of Coal Mines, Compliance Audit Report No 20.* 2016, https://cag.gov.in/content/report-no-20-2016-%E2%80%93-union-ministry-coal-e-auction-coal-mines-compliance-audit (accessed 9 December 2018).

Pannu, S. P. S. 'Centre Earns Over ₹2 Lakhs Crores From e-Auction of Coal Blocks, Exceeds Expectations.' *India Today*, 2 May 2015, https://www.indiatoday.in/india/north/story/coal-blocks-centre-modi-government-e-auction-nda-251083-2015-05-02 (accessed 9 December -2018).

PTI. '2G Case: Delhi HC Notice to Raja, Kanimozhi on ED, CBI appeals.' *The Hindu Business Line*, 21 March 2018, https://www.thehindubusinessline.com/news/2g-case-delhi-hc-notice-to-raja-kanimozhi-on-ed-cbi-appeals/article23310584.ece (accessed 9 December 2018).

PTI. 'New IBC Provisions to Deepen Losses for Banks: Report', *The Hindu Business Line*, 24 November2017, https://www.thehindubusinessline.com/money-and-banking/new-ibc-provisions-to-deepen-losses-for-banks-report/article9971992.ece (accessed 9 December 2018).

PTI. 'RBI Set to Dump its Soft Approach, Will Now Play Hardball Over ₹8 Lakhs Crores Bad Loans.' *The Economic Times,* 16 July 2017, https://economictimes.indiatimes.com/industry/banking/finance/banking/rs-8-lakh-crore-npas May 20face-bankruptcy-proceedings-by March 202019-study/articleshow/59619016.cms (accessed 9 December 2018).

Rajgopal, K. 'Supreme Court Quashes Allocation of 214 Coal Blocks.' *The Hindu*, 24 September 2012, https://www.thehindu.com/news/national/supreme-court-quashes-allocation-of-all-but-four-of-218-coal-blocks/article6441855.ece (accessed 9 December 2018).

RBI. RBI Data on GDP Growth and Fiscal Deficit. 2000–2018, https://dbie.rbi.org.in/DBIE/dbie.rbi?site=home (accessed 9 December 2018).

RBI. RBI External Debt Report. 2000–2018, https://dbie.rbi.org.in/DBIE/dbie.rbi?site=home (accessed 9 December 2018).

Sen, S. 'Accounts Can Be Hacked, But Not Through Aadhaar.' *DNA India*, 13 August 2018, https://www.dnaindia.com/analysis/column-accounts-can-be-hacked-but-not-through-aadhaar-2649004 (accessed 9 December 2018).

Sharma, K. 'Will Modi Be Able to Beat What Seems Like Impending Political Isolation.' *WION*, 16 March 2018, http://www.wionews.com/india-news/opinion-will-modi-be-able-to-beat-what-seems-like-impending-political-isolation-36084 (accessed 9 December 2018).

Venkatesan, J. 'Coal Block Allocation Since 1883 Illegal: Supreme Court.' *The Hindu*, 25 August 2014, https://www.thehindu.com/news/national/supreme-court-cancels-all-coal-block-allocations/article6349454.ece (accessed 9 December 2018).

Chapter 3

BT Online Bureau, 'PM Modi Says 6 Lakh crore Loan Given to 12 Lakh People in Three Years.' *Business Today*, updated on 29 August 2018, https://www.businesstoday.in/current/economy-politics/pm-narendra-modi-mudra-loans-disbursed-to-12-crore-people/story/277971.html (accessed 9 December 2018).

Capital Market. '31.2 Crore Accounts Opened Under PMJDY with Aggregate Deposits of ₹75,502.09 Crores on 28 February 2018.' *Business Standard*, updated on 22 March 2018, https://www.business-standard.com/article/news-cm/31-20-crore-accounts-opened-under-pradhan-mantri January 20dhan-yojana-pmjdy-with-aggregate-deposit-balances-rs-75-572-09-crore-as-on-28-february-2018-118032200886_1.html (accessed 9 December 2018).

Chougule, A. L. 'Demonetisation—Political Gain, Economic Pain.' *Free Press Journal*, 12 September 2017, https://www.freepressjournal.in/editorspick/demonetisation-political-gain-economic-pain-ali-chougule/1135580 (accessed 9 December 2018)

ET Online. 'Modi Magic Still Holds: People Still Back Demonetisation: ET Online Survey.' *The Economic Times*, 8 November 2017, https://economictimes.indiatimes.com/news/economy/policy/modi-magic-holds-people-still-back-demonetisation-et-online-survey/articleshow/61547491.cms (accessed 9 December 2018)

Gupta, D. 'Are Banks Failing the Demonetisation Drive.' *India Today*, 13 December 2016, https://www.indiatoday.in/india/story/demonetisation-banks-it-raids-corruption-black-money-357287-2016-12-13 (accessed 9 December 2018).

Hindu Special Correspondent. '99.3% Demonetised Currency Returned—RBI.' *The Hindu*, 29August 2018, https://www.thehindu.com/business/Economy/993-of-demonetised-currency-returned-to-banks-rbi/article24808160.ece (accessed 9 December 2018).

Korunuma, Y. 'In Support of Demonetisation Despite the Hardship.' *Nikkei Asian Review*, 9 February 2017, https://asia.nikkei.com/Economy/In-support-of-demonetization-despite-the-hardship (accessed 9 December 2018).

London, T. and Hart, S. *Next Generation Business Strategies for the Base of the Pyramid*. London: FT Press, 2010.

Master Card Advisor, *Master Card Advisor: Cashless journey*. 2016, https://newsroom.mastercard.com/wp-content/uploads/2013/09/Cashless-Journey_WhitePaper_FINAL.pdf (accessed 9 December 2018).

Nair, V. 'India's Unbanked Population Halves to 233 million.' *Livemint*, 14 October 2015, https://www.livemint.com/Industry/v4zrym0BCjNvXg3qcUD30K/Indias-unbanked-population-halves-to-233-million.html (accessed 9 December 2018).

Parmar, B. 'Jan Dhan Scheme: LPG Subsidy Sees Zero-Balance Accounts Drop Below 50 Percent.' *The Hindu Business Line*, 10 August 2017, https://www.thehindubusinessline.com/money-and-banking/jan-dhan-scheme-lpg-subsidy-transfer-sees-zerobalance-acs-drop-below-50/article7522914.ece (accessed 9 December 2018).

Petroleum Ministry. Annual Reports, Ministry of Petroleum and Natural Gas. 2007–2018, http://petroleum.nic.in/documents/reports/annual-reports (accessed 9 December 2018).

Prahalad, C. K. *Fortune at the Bottom of the Pyramid: Eradicate Poverty Through Profits*. London: FT Press/Prentice Hall, 2009.

Rawat, D. S. and Chandok, V. C. 'The Black Money Act: Ignorance Is Not Bliss.' Grant Thorton, 2015, http://www.grantthornton.in/globalassets/1.-member-firms/india/assets/pdfs/assocham_black-money-report_v3.pdf (accessed 9 December 2018).

Rodrigues, J. 'Move Over Visa and Mastercard. Upstarts Are Gaining in Hot India Payments space.' *The Economic Times/Bloomberg*, 26 March 2018, https://tech.economictimes.indiatimes.com/news/mobile/move-over-mastercard-upstarts-are-gaining-in-the-hot-india-payments-space/63459845 (accessed 9 December 2018).

Sen, S. *Neta, Babu and Subsidy: Economic Roundup 2000–2014*, New Delhi: Vitasta, 2014.

Sinha, S. K., 'De-legalisation of Currency Erases INR1.5trn from FY17 GDP, Growth to Fall to Three-Year Low.' India Ratings and Research, 1 December 2016, https://www.indiaratings.co.in/PressRelease?pressReleaseID=25306&title=De-legalisation-of-Currency-Erases-INR1.5trn-from-FY17-GDP%2C-Growth-to-Fall-to-3-Year-Low (accessed 9 December 2018).

Chapter 4

Goods and Services Tax Network. GST Rules and System Statistics. Updated 4 November 2018, https://www.gstn.org/ (accessed 9 December 2018).

Lok Sabha. *Bill No. 192 of 2014 The Constitution (122 Amendment) Bill, 2014 (GST)*. 2014, https://www.thehindu.com/migration_catalog/article14544039.ece/BINARY/GST.9 December 2018.

PTI. 'GST Ceased Smuggling, but e-Waybill, Tax Slab Woes Remain.' *Business Standard*, 1 July 2018, https://www.business-standard.com/article/pti-stories/gst-ceased-smuggling-but-e-waybill-tax-slabs-woes-remain-ica-118070100486_1.html (accessed 9 December 2018).

Sen, S. 'Digital Raj Should Not Replace Inspector Raj and Audit Trails Must Not Lead to Raid Raj if Make in India Is to Happen.' *The Indian Express*, 3 October 2017, https://indianexpress.com/article/business/business-others/digital-raj-should-not-replace-inspector-raj-and-audit-trails-must-not-lead-to-raid-raj-if-make-in-india-is-to-happen-4872247/ (accessed 9 December 2018).

Sen, S. 'GST Council Gives Relief, but More Needs to Be Done for Make in India to Happen.' *The Indian Express*, 10 October 2017, https://indianexpress.com/article/business/gst-council-gives-relief-but-more-needs-to-be-done-for-make-in-india-to-happen-4883043/ (accessed 9 December 2018).

Sen, S. 'GST Evasion: 12 Provisions Under GST That Could Land you in Jail.' *The Indian Express*, 4 October 2017, https://indianexpress.com/article/business/gst-evasion-raids-12-provisions-under-the-gstr-act-that-could-land-you-in-jail/ (accessed 9 December 2018).

Sen, S. 'GST in "Smooth phase", Return Simplification High on Agenda: Hashmukh Adhia.' *The Indian Express*, 26 June 2018, https://economictimes.indiatimes.com/news/economy/policy/gst-in-smooth-phase-return-simplification-high-on-agenda-hasmukh-adhia/articleshow/64747553.cms (accessed 9 December 2018).

Sen, S. 'Simplifying GST: 40 Amendments in Three Months as Ease of Business Disappears, Tax Officer Arrives.' *The Indian Express*, 25 October 2017, https://indianexpress.com/article/business/simplifying-gst-40-amendments-in-3-months-as-ease-of-business-disappears-tax-officer-arrives-4905535/ (accessed 9 December 2018).

Sen, S. 'Simplifying GST: If Flipkart Can Manage Big Billion Days Why Can't GSTN Portal.' *The Indian Express*, 28 September 2017, https://indianexpress.com/article/business/economy/simplifying-gst-if-flipkart-can-manage-big-billion-days-why-cant-gstn-portal-4865615/ (accessed 9 December 2018).

Sen, S. 'Simplifying GST: If Make in India Has to Succeed, Ease of Business Has to Improve.' *The Indian Express*, 26 September 2017, https://indianexpress.com/article/business/economy/simplifying-gst-if-make-in-india-has-to-succeed-ease-of-business-must-be-improved-4862021/ (accessed 9 December 2018)..

Sen, S. 'Simplifying GST: Public Awareness of Massive GST Evasion Must Start Before Raids.' *The Indian Express*.' *The Indian Express*, 23 October 2017, https://indianexpress.com/article/business/simplifying-gst-public-awareness-of-massive-gst-evasion-must-start-before-raids-4902623/ (accessed 9 December 2018).

Sen, S. 'Simplifying GST: Reducing Data Entries, Educating Sales Tax Officers are key GST Measures to Make Make in India Succeed.' *The Indian Express*, 27 September 2017, https://indianexpress.com/article/business/simplifying-gst-reducing-data-entries-educating-sales-tax-officers-are-key-gst-measures-to-make-make-in-india-succeed-4863440/ (accessed 9 December 2018).

Sen, S. 'Simplifying GST: The Dishonest Indian Still Cheats with Full GST, Half GST and No GST Bills.' *The Indian Express*, 16 October 2017, https://indianexpress.com/article/business/economy/simplifying-gst-the-dishonest-indian-still-cheats-with-full-gst-half-gst-and-no-gst-bills-4892834/ (accessed 9 December 2018).

Sen, S. 'Simplifying GST: The Six Big Positives of GST Implementation that Makes the Pain Worthwhile.' *The Indian Express*, 27 October 2017, https://indianexpress.com/article/business/banking-and-finance/simplifying-gst-the-6-big-positives-of-gst-implementation-that-makes-the-pain-worthwhile-4909356/ (accessed 9 December 2018).

Sen, S. 'Simplifying GST: With Massive Tax Refunds Pending Clearance Will the Tax Inspector Have a Field Day..' *The Indian Express*, 26 October 2017, https://indianexpress.com/article/business/economy/simplifying-gst-with-massive-tax-refunds-pending-clearance-will-the-tax-inspector-have-a-field-day-4907462/ (accessed 9 December 2018).

Sen, S. 'Three Key Issues that Needs to Be Sorted Out Before GST2 Kicks in.' *The Indian Express*, 6 October 2017, https://indianexpress.com/article/business/three-key-issues-that-need-to-be-sorted-out-before-gstr2-kicks-in-4877057/ (accessed 9 December 2018).

Sen, S. 'Why Can't You Revise Returns in GSTR if You Can Revise Returns Under the Income Tax Act.' *The Indian Express*, 5 October 2017, https://indianexpress.com/article/business/why-cant-you-revise-returns-in-gstr-if-you-can-revise-returns-under-the-income-tax-act-4875350/ (accessed 9 December 2018).

Chapter 5

Abraham, T. 'Goa Mining Industry in the Pits as Ban Takes Effect.' *Hindu Business Line*, 16 March 2018, https://www.thehindubusinessline.com/news/goa-mining-industry-in-the-pits-as-ban-takes-effect/article23274568.ece (accessed 9 December 2018).

BT Online Bureau. 'CAG Reports Tabled in Parliament, Indict Government on Coal Block Allocation, Mega Power Projects, Delhi Airport Concession.' *Business Today*, 17 August 2012, https://www.businesstoday.in/sectors/energy/cag-reports-tabled-in-parliament-coal-blocks/story/187288.html (accessed 9 December 2018).

CAG. *Report No 19 of 2010 of the Comptroller and Auditor General of India on Performance Audit on issue of Licences of 2G Spectrum of Union Government.* 16 November 2010.

CAG. *Report of the Comptroller and Auditor General of India on Allocation of Coal Mines.* 9 February 2012.

CAG. *Report of the Comptroller and Auditor General of India on Allocation of Coal Mines.* 9 February 2012, https://cag.gov.in/content/report-no-20-2016-%E2%80%93-union-ministry-coal-e-auction-coal-mines-compliance-audit (accessed 9 December 2018).

Express News Service. 'Tangedco in Fix for Coal Sourcing from Indonesia.' *The New Indian Express*, 26 January 2018, http://www.newindianexpress.com/states/tamil-nadu/2018/jan/26/tangedco-in-fix-for-coal-sourcing-from-indonesia-1763632.html (accessed 9 December 2018).

IEA. International Energy Agency Reports. 2012–2018.

Khedekar, N. 'Northern Grid Power Failure.' *Firstpost*, 2 August 2014, https://www.firstpost.com/tech/news-analysis/northern-grid-power-failure-what-went-wrong-3605053.html (accessed 9 December 2018).

Ministry of Coal. Annual Reports of Coal India Ltd. Coal India Ltd., 2012–2018.

Nambiar, P. '63,395 Mining Clearances Pending with State Governments.' *Livemint* 4 June 2014, https://www.livemint.com/Politics/nuyoouWgH2WDWNJ8m2xGEN/63395-mining-clearances-pending-with-state-governments.html (accessed 9 December 2018).

Pannu, S. P. S. 'Centre Earns Over ₹2 Lakh Crores From e-Auction of Coal Blocks, Exceeds Expectations.' *India Today*, 2 May 2015, https://www.indiatoday.in/india/north/story/coal-blocks-centre-modi-government-e-auction-nda-251083-2015-05-02 (accessed 9 December 2018).

PTI. 'S. Bhattacharya Appointed CMD of Coal India.' *The Times of India*, 24 December 2014, https://timesofindia.indiatimes.com/business/india-business/S-Bhattacharya-appointed-CMD-of-Coal-India/articleshow/45631587.cms (accessed 9 December 2018).

Rajgopal, K. 'Supreme Court Quashes Allocation of 214 Coal Blocks.' *The Hindu*, 24 September 2012, https://www.thehindu.com/news/national/supreme-court-quashes-allocation-of-all-but-four-of-218-coal-blocks/article6441855.ece (accessed 9 December 2018).

Sen, S. 'How and Why the Indian Power Grid Collapsed.' *The Economic Times*, 29 August 2012, https://economictimes.indiatimes.com/blogs/Whathappensif/how-and-why-the-indian-power-grid-collapsed/ (accessed 9 December 2018).

Sen, S. *Neta, Babu and Subsidy: Economic Roundup 2000–2014*. New Delhi: Vitasta, 2014.

Sengupta, D. 'Coal India Misses Production Target for 2017–18 by 15 mt.' *The Economic Times,* 2 April 2018, https://economictimes.indiatimes.com/industry/indl-goods/svs/metals-mining/coal-india-misses-production-target-by-15-mt/articleshow/61455237.cms (accessed 9 December 2018).

TNN. 'Mining Legacy: Almost 93 Gaping Pits.' *The Times of India*, 20 October 2012, https://timesofindia.indiatimes.com/city/goa/Mining-legacy-Almost-93-gaping-pits/articleshow/16885928.cms (accessed 9 December 2018).

Chapter 6

Blackmon, D. 'Horizontal Drilling: A Technological Marvel Ignored.' *Forbes*, 28 January 2013, https://www.forbes.com/sites/davidblackmon/2013/01/28/horizontal-drilling-a-technological-marvel-ignored/#4ad4949c6f11 (accessed 9 December 2018).

Geezer, A. R. 'Oil Prices Drop as Market Collapses.' *The European Tribune*, 15 December 2014, https://www.eurotrib.com/story/2014/12/13/84155/976 (accessed 9 December 2018).

Lok Sabha TV. 'Public Forum: India's Oil Strategy.', 16 February 2017, https://www.youtube.com/watch?v=EPFHszQtpa0 (accessed 9 December 2018).

Ministry of Petroleum and Natural Gas. Ministry of Oil and Natural Gas Annual Reports on Petroleum and Natural Gas Prices, Production and Imports. 2008–2018, http://petroleum.nic.in/documents/reports/annual-reports (accessed 9 December 2018).

Ministry of Petroleum and Natural Gas. Petroleum and Natural Gas Prices, Production and Imports. Petroleum Planning and Analysis Cell, 2008–2018, http://ppac.org.in/content/149_1_PricesPetroleum.aspx (accessed 9 December 2018).

PTI. 'India Plans to Bring Down Emission Level of Old Power Plants to National Standards: Official.' *The Economic Times*, 7 July 2018, https://economictimes.indiatimes.com/industry/energy/power/india-plans-to-bring-down-emission-levels-of-old-power-plants-to-national-standards-by-2022-official/articleshow/64897023.cms (accessed 9 December 2018).

Rapier, R. 'The Irony of President Obama's Oil Legacy.' *Forbes*, 15 January 2016, https://www.forbes.com/sites/rrapier/2016/01/15/president-obamas-petroleum-legacy/#18d8d404c10f (accessed 9 December 2018).

Ray, S. 'Why Indians Will Continue to Pay High Oil Prices Despite Lower Global Rates.' *The Hindustan Times*, 22 September 2017, https://www.hindustantimes.com/india-news/why-are-indians-paying-high-oil-prices-blame-messy-centre-state-finances/story-n61K9d25ip10MJtnK2znqM.html (accessed 9 December 2018).

Sen, S. 'Government Needs to Cap Oil Prices with Tax Rebates, Not Subsidies.' *DNA India*, 4 June 2018, https://www.dnaindia.com/analysis/column-govt-needs-to-cap-oil-prices-with-tax-rebates-not-subsidies-2621759 (accessed 9 December 2018).

Sen, S. 'Oil: Opportunity or Threat.' *Think Pragati*, 18 May 2018, https://www.thinkpragati.com/opinion/4553/oil-opportunity-or-threat/ (accessed 9 December 2018).

Sen, S. 'Real Time Satellite Mapping Key to Addressing India's Pollution Problems.' Observer Research Foundation, 3 February 2018, https://www.orfonline.org/expert-speak/real-time-satellite-mapping-key-to-addressing-india-pollution/ (accessed 9 December 2018).

Sen, S. 'There is Something in the Air Tonight.' *Think Pragati*, 25 May 2018, https://www.thinkpragati.com/opinion/4651/theres-something-in-the-air-tonight/ (accessed 9 December 2018).

Sen, S. 'Will ONGC's HPCL Acquisition Lead to Long-Awaited Integrated Supply Chain?' IANS/*Business Standard*, 27 January 2018, https://www.business-standard.com/article/companies/will-ongc-s-hpcl-acquisition-lead-to-long-awaited-integrated-supply-chain-118012700252_1.html (accessed 9 December 2018).

Sen, S. 'Pollution Test: India can learn from China's experience.' *DNA India*, 10 May 2018, https://www.dnaindia.com/analysis/column-pollution-test-india-can-learn-from-china-s-experience-2613411 (accessed 9 December 2018).

Singh, S. P. 'India to Save ₹2 Lakh Crores on Crude Imports as Oil Hits 11-Year Low.' *Business Standard*, 10 December 2015, https://www.business-standard.com/article/economy-policy/india-to-save-rs-2-lakh-cr-on-crude-imports-as-oil-hits-11-year-low-115120900956_1.html (accessed 9 December 2018)

Chapter 7

Cala, A. 'Renewable Energy in Spain Is Taking a Beating.' *The New York Times*, 8 October 2013, https://www.nytimes.com/2013/10/09/business/energy-environment/renewable-energy-in-spain-is-taking-a-beating.html (accessed 9 December 2018).

Chalasani, J. P. 'Wind Needs a Bigger Boost.' *Business Today*, 30 December 2017, https://www.businesstoday.in/magazine/the-hub/wind-needs-a-bigger-boost/story/298972.html (accessed 9 December 2018).

Chandrasekharan, K. 'Solar Tariffs Rise in Gujarat Reverse Auction.' *The Economic Times*, 29 March 2018, https://solarquarter.com/index.php/world/93-web-in-india/9669-solar-tariffs-rise-in-gujarat-reverse-auction (accessed 9 December 2018).

Das, K.N. and Varadhan, S. 'Solar Energy Boom Turns to Bust for Indian Manufacturers.' *Reuters*, 5 June 2017, https://in.reuters.com/article/india-solar/solar-energy-boom-turns-to-bust-for-indian-manufacturers-idINKBN18W0KV (accessed 9 December 2018).

ET Bureau. 'India Adds Record Wind Power Capacity of 5400MW in 2016–17.' *The Economic Times*, 3 April 2017, https://energy.economictimes.indiatimes.com/news/renewable/india-adds-record-wind-power-capacity-of-5400mw-in-2016-17/57981956, 9-Dec.

Heal, G. 'Oil Demand and Prices Set to Drop Dramatically as New Technologies Take Hold.' *CNBC*, 3 May 2018, https://www.cnbc.com/2018/05/03/oil-demand-and-prices-to-drop-as-solar-wind-energy-take-hold.html (accessed 9 December 2018).

Jai, S. 'Government Weighs Reverse Auction VS Conventional Bidding for Renewable Projects.' *Business Standard*, 30 June 2018, https://www.business-standard.com/article/companies/govt-weighs-reverse-auction-vs-conventional-bidding-for-renewable-projects-118063000385_1.html (accessed 9 December 2018).

Kondratieva, K. 'Competitive Bidding Positive for Wind Industry in the Long Run.' *The Hindu Business Line*, 30 July 2017, https://www.thehindubusinessline.com/economy/competitive-bidding-positive-for-wind-industry-in-the-long-run/article9794173.ece, 9-Dec.

Maisch, M. 'NTPC Looking for Off Taker for 250 MW Kadapa Solar Park After APSPDCL Refuses to Sign PPA.' *PV Magazine*, 28 July 2017, https://www.pv-magazine.com/2017/07/28/ntpc-looking-for-off-taker-for-250-mw-kadapa-solar-park-after-apspdcl-refuses-to-sign-ppa/, 9-Dec.

PTI. 'India Third-Largest Solar Market in the World: Mercom Communications.' *Business Standard*, 15 May 2018, https://www.business-standard.com/article/current-affairs/india-third-largest-solar-market-in-the-world-mercom-communications-118051500643_1.html (accessed 9 December 2018).

PTI. 'India to Comfortably Achieve 100 GW Solar Energy Target by 2022: Government.' *The Economic Times*, 7 August 2018, https://economictimes.indiatimes.com/industry/energy/power/india-to-comfortably-achieve-100-gw-solar-energy-target-by-2022-government/articleshow/65307570.cms (accessed 9 December 2018).

Sanjay, P. 'Indian Solar Installations Grew by 123% to Reach a Record 9.6 GW in 2017.' Mercom, 22 February 2018, https://mercomindia.com/indian-solar-installations-market-update/ (accessed 9 December 2018).

Sharma, S. 'Solar Tariffs in India Have Fallen by 73% Since 2010: Mercom Capital.' *Livemint,* 24 March 2017, https://www.livemint.com/Industry/xkdwxNscR9K6omngOwOaAN/Solar-tariffs-in-India-have-fallen-by-73-since-2010-Mercom.html (accessed 9 December 2018).

Stacey, K. 'India Defends Solar Panel Makers From Chinese Rivals.' *The Financial Times*, 22 January 2018, https://www.ft.com/content/a6599b78-f9cc-11e7-9b32-d7d59aace167 (accessed 9 December 2018).

Chapter 8

Arun, M. G. 'India Abandoned: Foreign Investors Are Leaving Indian Shores Like Never Before, Creating an Investment Drought.' *India Today*, 5 August 2013, https://www.indiatoday.in/magazine/the-big-story/story/20130805-foreign-investors-leaving-indian-shores-arcelormittal-posco-764965-1999-11-30 (accessed 9 December 2018).

Dash, J. 'Indian Aluminium Exports Jump by 36% on High Global Demand.' *Business Standard*, 4 July 2018, https://www.business-standard.com/article/markets/indian-aluminium-exports-jump-36-in-2017-18-on-high-global-demand-118070300845_1.html (accessed 9 December 2018).

FE Online. 'Mining Giant Rio Tinto to Close Diamond Project in Madhya Pradesh Amid Environmental Concerns.' *The Financial Express*, 20 August 2016, https://www.financialexpress.com/industry/rio-tinto-to-close-diamond-project-in-madhya-pradesh-amid-environmental-concerns/352702/ (accessed 9 December 2018).

Mazumdar, R. 'Aluminium Consumption in India to Grow From 3.3 million to 5.3 Million Tonne.' *The Economic Times*, 7 October 2016, https://economictimes.indiatimes.com/industry/indl-goods/svs/metals-mining/aluminium-consumption-in-india-to-grow-from-3-3-million-tonne-to-5-3-million-tonne/articleshow/54738630.cms (accessed 9 December 2018).

Ministry of Mines. *M. B. Shah Commission Report* 25 November 2014, https://mines.gov.in/ViewData/index?mid=1333 (accessed 9 December 2018).

Ministry of Mines. *Mines and Minerals Annual Report.* 2008–2018, https://mines.gov.in/ViewData/index?mid=1385 (accessed 9 December 2018).

Mishra, A. 'Rule of Thumb.' *Business Today*, 15 September 2013, https://www.businesstoday.in/magazine/features/orissa-niyamgiri-rejects-vedanta-entry-impact-reasons/story/197972.html (accessed 9 December 2018).

Mohanty, M. 'Ras Al Khaimah Investment Authority Sends India Arbitration Notice.' *The Economic Times*, 12 January 2017, https://economictimes.indiatimes.com/industry/indl-goods/svs/metals-mining/ras-al-khaimah-investment-authority-sends-india-arbitration-notice/articleshow/56504957.cms (accessed 9 December 2018).

Patel, D. 'Mines and Minerals: Iron Ore, Gold Production Rises, But Bauxite Falls.'.' *The Indian Express*, 5 April 2018, https://indianexpress.com/article/business/business-others/mines-minerals-iron-ore-gold-production-rises-but-bauxite-falls-5123676/ (accessed 9 December 2018).

Patnaik, S. 'Bauxite Mining Back in the Limelight.' *The Hindu*, 11 June 2018, https://www.thehindu.com/news/cities/Visakhapatnam/bauxite-mining-back-in-the-limelight/article24131227.ece (accessed 9 December 2018).

PTI. 'Goa Government Mum on Recovery of Losses From Illegal Mine Owners.' *The Hindu Business Line*, 13 September 2012, https://www.moneylife.in/article/goa-government-mum-on-recovery-of-losses-from-illegal-mine-owners/28458.html (accessed 9 December 2018).

Sen, S. 'Is Mining Doomed in India?' *Think Pragati*, 28 June 2018, https://www.thinkpragati.com/think/4954/is-mining-doomed-in-india/ (accessed 9 December 2018).

Sen, S. *Neta, Babu and Subsidy: Economic Roundup 2000–2014*. New Delhi: Vitasta, 2014..

Sukumar, C. R. 'Anrak Moves NCLT After Andhra Pradesh Government Declines Bauxite Supply.' *The Economic Times*, 14 August 2017, https://economictimes.indiatimes.com/industry/indl-goods/svs/metals-mining/anrak-moves-nclt-after-andhra-pradesh-government-declines-bauxite-supply/articleshow/60054040.cms (accessed 9 December 2018).

Tare, K. 'Goa Illegal Mining All Set to Take a Political Toll With Top Congress Leaders Linked to the Scam.' *India Today*, 8 October 2011, https://www.indiatoday.in/magazine/investigation/story/20111017-goa-illegal-mining-scam-miners-congress-leaders-digambar-kamat-margao-747942-2011-10-08 (accessed 9 December 2018).

TNN. 'Coal Scam: Madhu Koda Sentenced to Three-Year Jail Term.' *The Times of India*, 16 December 2017, https://timesofindia.indiatimes.com/india/coal-scam-madhu-koda-sentenced-to-3-year-jail-term/articleshow/62093513.cms (accessed 9 December 2018).

Vishnoi, A. 'Rio Tinto's Madhya Pradesh Diamond Mining Project Runs Into Forest Hurdle.' *The Economic Times*, 10 December 2015, https://economictimes.indiatimes.com/industry/indl-goods/svs/metals-mining/rio-tintos-madhya-pradesh-diamond-mining-project-runs-into-forest-hurdle/articleshow/50114323.cms (accessed 9 December 2018).

Woodman, J. 'India's Rejection of Vedanta's Mining Project is a Victory for Tribal Rights.' *The Gaurdian*, 14 January 2014, https://www.theguardian.com/global-development/poverty-matters/2014/jan/14/india-rejection-vedanta-mine-victory-tribal-rights (accessed 9 December 2018).

Chapter 9

Arora, R. 'Highway Construction Hits Record 10,000 km in FY 18.' *The Economic Times*, 2 August 2018, https://economictimes.indiatimes.com/news/economy/infrastructure/highway-construction-hits-record-10000-km-in-fy18/articleshow/63586665.cms (accessed 9 December 2018).

FB Bureau. 'Domestic Air Passenger Traffic Grows to 17 %.' *The Financial Express*, 25 September 2018, https://www.financialexpress.com/infrastructure/airlines-aviation/domestic-air-passenger-traffic-grows-17-to-11-35-million-in-august/1325472/ (accessed 9 December 2018).

India Today Desk. '14 of World's Most Polluted 15 Cities in India, Kanpur Tops WHO list.' *India Today*, 2 May 2018, https://www.indiatoday.in/education-today/gk-current-affairs/story/14-worlds-most-polluted-15-cities-india-kanpur-tops-who-list-1224730-2018-05-02 (accessed 9 December 2018).

Ministry of Housing and Urban Affairs. Annual Reports. 2011–2017, http://mohua.gov.in/publication/annual-reports.php (accessed 9 December 2018).

Ministry of Petroleum and Natural Gas. Annual Reports. 2008–18, http://petroleum.nic.in/documents/reports/annual-reports (accessed 9 December 2018).

Petroleum Planning and Analysis Cell. Annual Reports. 2008–2018, http://www.ppac.org.in/View_All_Reports.aspx (accessed 9 December 2018).

Sen, S. 'CrunchTime for Waste Management.' *TerraGreen*, August 2013 issue.

Sen, S. 'If 80% Water Consumption in India Is for Agriculture, Why Is it So Unregulated and Inefficient?' Observer Research Foundation, 3 May 2018, https://www.orfonline.org/expert-speak/if-80-water-consumption-in-india-is-for-agriculture-why-is-it-unregulated-and-inefficient/ (accessed 9 December 2018).

Sen, S. 'India's Drying Panghats.' *Woman's Era*, June 2016 (Second) issue..

Sen, S. 'India's Smart City Dream Needs Sub City Infrastructure.' *CEO World Magazine*, 17 October 2018, https://ceoworld.biz/2018/10/17/indias-smart-city-dream-needs-sub-city-infrastructure/ (accessed 9 December, 2018).

Sen, S. 'Pollution Test: India Can Learn From China's Experience.' *DNA Today*, 10 May 2019, https://www.dnaindia.com/analysis/column-pollution-test-india-can-learn-from-china-s-experience-2613411 (accessed 9 December 2018).

Sen, S. 'Something in the Air Tonight.' *Think Pragati*, 25 May 2018, https://www.thinkpragati.com/opinion/4651/theres-something-in-the-air-tonight/ (accessed 9 December 2018).

Sen, S. 'Sustainable Mining of World's Landfills.' *Alive*, September 2016 issue.

Sen, S. 'The Solid Waste Management Conundrum.' *TerraGreen*, December 2017 issue.

Sood, J. 'Nitin Gadkari Raises the Bar With New Road Tender, Construction Targets.' *Livemint*, 18 April 2018, https://www.livemint.com/Politics/nZsLJHrmwuJGsoYBoZbVIL/Nitin-Gadkari-sets-ambitious-target-for-road-construction.html (accessed 9 December 2018).

TNN. 'Centre to Fight Arsenic in Groundwater in States.' *The Times of India*, 8 March 2017, https://timesofindia.indiatimes.com/india/centre-to-fight-arsenic-in-groundwater-in-states/articleshow/57526787.cms (accessed 9 December 2018).

UNI. 'Groundwater in 16 States Contaminated with Uranium as per WHO Norms, Government Tells RSS.' 6 August 2018, http://www.uniindia.com/~/ground-water-in-16-states-is-contaminated-with-uranium-as-per-who-norms-govt-tells-rs/Parliament/news/1311104.html (accessed 9 December 2018).

Chapter 10

Aulakh, G. 'Samsung to Invest ₹5,000 Crores to Expand Noida Plant.' *The Economic Times*, 6 June 2018, https://economictimes.indiatimes.com/tech/hardware/samsung-to-invest-rs-5000-crore-to-expand-noida-plant/articleshow/59008448.cms (accessed 9 December 2018).

Burugula, P. and Ghosh, J. 'FPI Holdings from Singapore, Mauritius Surge 25% Before Data Implementation.' *Business Standard*, 20 May 2018, https://www.business-standard.com/article/markets/fpi-holdings-from-singapore-mauritius-surge-25-before-dtaa-implementation-117051901050_1.html (accessed 9 December 2018).

CarAndBike Team. 'Auto Sales: Indian Auto Industry Registers Over 12% Growth in FY 2018.' *NDTV*, 10 April 2018, https://auto.ndtv.com/news/auto-sales-indian-auto-industry-registers-over-12-per-cent-growth-in-fy-2018-1835483 (accessed 9 December 2018).

ET Online. 'A Scary Glimpse of How China's Obor Can Ruin Small Countries.' *The Economic Times*, 12 July 2018, https://economictimes.indiatimes.com/news/defence/a-scary-glimpse-into-how-chinas-obor-can-ruin-small-countries/articleshow/60173526.cms (accessed 9 December 2018).

FE Online. 'BHEL Posts Net Loss of ₹877 Crores in FY 16.' *The Financial Express*, 7 April 2016, https://www.financialexpress.com/industry/bhel-posts-net-loss-of-rs-877-crore-in-fy16/233636/ (accessed 9 December 2018).

FE Online. 'Three Years of Modi Rule: FDI Inflows Jump to 60 billion in 2016–17.' *The Financial Express*, 19 May 2017, https://www.financialexpress.com/economy/3-years-of-modi-rule-fdi-inflows-jump-to-60-billion-in-2016-17-from-36-billion-in-2013-14/676518/ (accessed 9 December 2018).

HBL Bureau. 'Management of Strategy Led to Losses in BHEL: CAG.' *The Hindu Business Line*, 8 August 2017, https://www.thehindubusinessline.com/companies/mismanagement-of-strategy-led-to-losses-in-bhel-cag/article9807122.ece (accessed 9 December 2018).

Jaiswal, S.. *Foreign Direct Investment in India and Role of Tax Havens*, Centre for Budget and Governance Accountability, 2017, http://www.cbgaindia.org/wp-content/uploads/2017/12/Foreign-Direct-Investment-in-India-and-Role-of-Tax-Havens.pdf (accessed 9 December 2018).

Jay, J. 'Xiaomi to Oppo: How Chinese Smartphone Players Have Evolved in India.'.' *The Indian Express*, 1 May 2017, https://indianexpress.com/article/technology/mobile-tabs/xiaomi-to-oppo-how-chinese-smartphone-players-have-evolved-in-india/ (accessed 9 December 2018).

Nayar, L. and Das, R. U. 'Now We Will Know the Real Foreign Investment into India.' *Outlook India*, 12 May 2016, https://www.outlookindia.com/website/story/now-well-know-real-foreign-investment-into-india/296886 (accessed 9 December 2018).

PTI. 'BHEL Net Profit Plunges 62% to ₹1,314 Crores in FY 15.' *Livemint* 6 April 2015, https://www.livemint.com/Companies/ZPwBQJ5ve3f1NhS0uzboOO/BHEL-net-profit-plunges-62-to-Rs1314-cr-in-FY15.html (accessed 9 December 2018).

PTI. 'China Accounts for 89% of India's Total Solar Cells Import.' *Business Standard*, 1 August 2018, https://www.business-standard.com/article/economy-policy/china-accounts-for-89-of-india-s-total-solar-cells-imports-in-2017-18-118080100849_1.html (accessed 9 December 2018).

Sen, S. 'Calm Down: Banks Are Bleeding, but There Is Enough Cash to Get Through.' *DNA India*, 31 March 2018, https://www.dnaindia.com/analysis/column-calm-down-banks-are-bleeding-but-there-is-cash-to-get-through-2620406 (accessed 9 December 2018).

Sen, S. 'Three Uncertainties that Has Made Make in India Difficult.' Observer Research Foundation, 4 July 2018, https://www.orfonline.org/expert-speak/42173-three-uncertainties-that-has-made-make-in-india-difficult/ (accessed 9 December 2018).

Sen, S. *Neta, Babu and Subsidy: Economic Roundup 2000–2014.* New Delhi: Vitasta, 2014.

Singh, I. P. 'Farmers Carpet Jalandhar Roads with Potatoes.' *The Times of India*, 16 December 2011, https://timesofindia.indiatimes.com/city/chandigarh/Farmers-carpet-Jalandhar-roads-with-potatoes/articleshow/11126976.cms (accessed 9 December 2018).

TNN. 'India Moves to 100th Spot in Ease of Doing Business.' *The Times of India*, 31 October 2017, https://timesofindia.indiatimes.com/city/chennai/india-moves-to-100th-spot-in-world-banks-ease-of-doing-business-rankings/articleshow/61373766.cms (accessed 9 December 2018).

Chapter 11

B. R., Rohith. '₹500 Crores Corpus Fund Approved.' *The Times of India*, 27 May 2015, https://timesofindia.indiatimes.com/city/bengaluru/Rs-500-crore-corpus-fund-approved/articleshow/46714139.cms (accessed 9 December 2018).

Bhosale, J. 'Global Prices Shoot up by 30% to 40% Due to Drought Fears in India.' *The Economic Times*, 11 June 2015, https://economictimes.indiatimes.com/news/economy/agriculture/global-pulses-prices-shoot-up-by-30-to-40-due-to-drought-fears-in-india/articleshow/47628443.cms (accessed 9 December 2018).

Ghaswalla, N. A. 'Domestic Demand, Exports Spice Up Masala Market.' *The Hindu Business Line*, 30 April 2014, https://www.thehindubusinessline.com/markets/commodities/Domestic-demand-exports-spice-up-masala-market/article20762443.ece (accessed 9 December 2018).

Ghosh, S. 'Surge in 2015 Pulse Prices Was a Result of Cartellisation.' *The Wire*, 6 July 2017, https://thewire.in/economy/surge-in-2015-pulse-prices-was-a-result-of-cartellisation (accessed 9 December 2018).

Padmanabhan, Anil. 'The Curious Case of Rising Onion Prices.' *Livemint* 24 August 2015, https://www.livemint.com/Opinion/tZuQGCgP3Ldcf5fPITMHcI/The-curious-case-of-rising-onion-prices.html (accessed 9 December 2018).

Pegg, D. 'Paradise Papers Prompt Criminal Complaint Against Glencore.' *The Guardian*, 21 December 2017, https://www.theguardian.com/business/2017/dec/21/paradise-papers-prompt-criminal-complaint-against-glencore (accessed 9 December 2018).

PTI. 'Crashing Garlic Prices Cause Discontent Among MP Farmers.' *India Today*, 7 May 2018, https://www.indiatoday.in/pti-feed/story/crashing-garlic-prices-cause-discontent-among-mp-farmers-1228425-2018-05-07 (accessed 9 December 2018).

PTI. 'Pulse Price Continues to Rise. Tur Dal Hits ₹200/kg.' *Hindustan Times*, 19 October 2015, https://www.hindustantimes.com/business/pulse-prices-continue-to-rise-tur-dal-hits-rs-200-kg/story-l1djOa0zIlv4nfKPJVgRwL.html (accessed 9 December 2018).

Quazi, A. H. 'Low Garlic Prices Leads to Losses for Farmer in Hadauti Region.' *Hindustan Times*, 29 March 2018, https://www.hindustantimes.com/jaipur/low-garlic-prices-leads-to-losses-for-farmers-in-hadauti-region/story-dejp5AAueiCjDY9yeh0W6J.html (accessed 9 December 2018).

Sen, S. 'Kitchen Under Siege.' *Woman's Era*, July 2015 issue.

Sen, S. 'Potato Farming: India Makes a Hash of it.' *The Hindu Business Line*, 2 November 2014, https://www.thehindubusinessline.com/opinion/potato-farming-india-makes-a-hash-of-it/article20901025.ece1 (accessed 9 December 2018).

Chapter 12

Acharya, N. 'Punjab, Haryana and Andhra Corner 50% MSP Rice Procurement.' *Business Standard*, 7 July 2018, https://www.business-standard.com/article/economy-policy/punjab-haryana-and-andhra-pradesh-corner-50-msp-rice-procurement-118070600243_1.html (accessed 9 December 2018).

Chandrasekhar, G. 'MSP Alone Cannot Lift the Farm Sector.' *The Hindu Business Line*, 5 July 2018, https://www.thehindubusinessline.com/opinion/msp-alone-cannot-lift-the-farm-sector/article24342441.ece (accessed 9 December 2018).

Dasgupta, M. 'BJP Government Has a Lot of Ground to Cover in Delivering Poll Promises.' *Hindustan Times*, 25 January 2018, https://www.hindustantimes.com/india-news/bjp-govt-has-lot-of-ground-to-cover-in-delivering-promises-made-in-2014/story-90ZTu03wAYis9JrUWc0qhO.html (accessed 9 December 2018).

Krishnamurthi, L. and Khandelwal, S. 'Agriculture Journal: China Versus India by the Numbers.' *Wall Street Journal*, 20 September 2011, https://blogs.wsj.com/indiarealtime/2011/09/20/agriculture-journal-china-versus-india-by-the-numbers/ (accessed 9 December 2018).

Sen.S, If 80% Water Consumption in India is for Agriculture Why is It Not Regulated, ORF, 3 May 2018, https://www.orfonline.org/expert-speak/if-80-water-consumption-in-india-is-for-agriculture-why-is-it-unregulated-and-inefficient/ (accessed 9 December 2018).

Sen. S, Efficient Irrigation For Solving India's Water Crisis Terragreen July 2018 issue http://terragreen.teriin.org/index.php?option=com_terragreen&task=category&category_id=20&issueid=133 (accessed 9 December 2018).

Sen. S, Can Walmart Flipkart Deal Ease The Woes Of Indian Farmers, Down To Earth, June 2018 issue https://www.downtoearth.org.in/news/agriculture/can-the-walmart-flipkart-deal-ease-the-woes-of-indian-farmers--60878 (accessed 9 December 2018).

Srivatsva, S. 'Israeli Technology to Transform Indian agriculture.' *The Economic Times*, 22 November 2017, https://economictimes.indiatimes.com/tech/internet/israeli-technology-to-transform-indian-agriculture/articleshow/61752914.cms (accessed 9 December 2018).

Chapter 13

Chitravanshi, R. 'Centre to Fund Social Audits Under MGNREGA Scheme.' *The Economic Times*, 26 September 2017, https://economictimes.indiatimes.com/news/economy/finance/centre-to-fund-social-audit-units-under-mgnrega-scheme/articleshow/60847380.cms (accessed 9 December 2018).

Jitendra. 'NDA Introduces Changes in MGNREGA.' *Down to Earth*, 17 August 2015, https://www.downtoearth.org.in/news/nda-introduces-changes-in-mgnrega-45189 (accessed 9 December 2018).

Livemint. 'MGNREGA: A Tale of Wasted Efforts.' 6 February 2014, https://www.livemint.com/Opinion/BDqu4xhDywL6n1cUXlpa5K/MGNREGA-A-decade-of-wasted-efforts.html (accessed 9 December 2018).

PTI. 'Government Converges MPLAD and MGNREGA to Create More Durable Assets.' *The Economic Times*, 23 June 2012, https://economictimes.indiatimes.com/news/economy/policy/govt-converges-mplad-mgnrega-to-create-more-durable-assets/articleshow/11605108.cms (accessed 9 Deccmber 2018).

PTI. 'Reported Corruption in MGNREGA Just Tip of the Iceberg: Parliamentary Panel.' *The Hindu Business Line*, 29 August 2011, https://www.thehindubusinessline.com/economy/policy/reported-corruption-in-mgnrega-just-tip-of-iceberg-parliamentary-panel/article23056732.ece (accessed 9 December 2018).

Qazi, M. 'Water-Stressed India Stares at Harder Crisis.' *Asian Age*, 4 June 2018, http://www.asianage.com/india/all-india/040618/water-stressed-india-stares-at-harder-crisis.html (accessed 9 December 2018).

Roy, V. C. 'MNCs Eye Harvester Market in Punjab.' *Business Standard*, 20 January 2013, https://www.business-standard.com/article/companies/mncs-eye-harvester-market-space-in-punjab-112022100071_1.html (accessed 9 December 2018).

Roy, V. C. 'MNCs Thrive on Indian Harvester Market.' *Business Standard*, 17 December 2012, https://www.business-standard.com/article/economy-policy/mncs-thrive-on-indian-harvester-market-112121702028_1.html (accessed 9 December 2018).

Sen, S. *Neta, Babu and Subsidy: Economic Roundup 2000–2014*. New Delhi: Vitasta, 2014.

The Hindu. 'Bengal Tops in Rural Job Scheme, TN Is Second.' 11 March 2018, https://www.thehindu.com/news/national/bengal-tops-in-rural-job-scheme-tn-is-second/article23041918.ece (accessed 9 December 2018).

World Bank. 'India Groundwater: A Valuable but Diminishing Resource.' 6 March 2012, http://www.worldbank.org/en/news/feature/2012/03/06/india-groundwater-critical-diminishing (accessed 9 December 2018).

Chapter 14

Archana, K. C. 'Nine Innovative and Eco-Friendly Toilets that Can Help India Over its Sanitation Woes.' *India Times*, 31 August 2017, https://www.indiatimes.com/news/india/9-innovative-eco-friendly-toilets-that-can-help-india-overcome-its-sanitation-woes-328865.html (accessed 9 December 2018).

Bhaduri, A. and Desai, P. 'Millions Wait for Toilets and Water.' India Water Portal, 2 September 2018, http://www.indiawaterportal.org/articles/millions-wait-toilets-and-water (accessed 9 December 2018)

Fourthlion. 'What Is Working in SBM Grameen, and What Isn't?' *Livemint* 2 October 2015, https://www.livemint.com/Politics/T8GCbsb34MEbjuCWmkraaL/What-is-working-in-SBM-grameen-and-what-isnt.html (accessed 9 December 2018).

Himatsingka, A. 'Swachh Bharat Mission: Getting People to Use Toilets is Next Big Challenge.' *The Economic Times*, 17 February 2018, https://economictimes.indiatimes.com/news/politics-and-nation/swachh-bharat-mission-getting-people-to-use-toilets-is-next-big-challenge/articleshow/62955975.cms (accessed 9 December 2018).

Khanna, P. 'Nirmal Bharat Abhiyan Failed to Achieve its Desired Targets: CAG.' *Livemint*, 16 December 2015, https://www.livemint.com/Politics/ghYnnKN03hSqre4cwSrwqN/Nirmal-Bharat-Abhiyan-failed-to-achieve-its-desired-targets.html (accessed 9 December 2018).

Makkar, S. 'Three Years of Swachh Bharat: States May Be Inflating Number of Toilets Built.' *Business Standard*, 2 December 2017, https://www.business-standard.com/article/economy-policy/rush-on-to-meet-swachh-bharat-mission-target-after-3-yrs-117100200018_1.html (accessed 9 December 2018).

Ministry of Drinking Water and Sanitation. *Annual Report 2017–18*. https://mdws.gov.in/sites/default/files/Annual_Report_2017-18_English.pdf (accessed 9 December 2018).

Mukherjee, A. '₹9,890 Crores Unspent Under Swachh Bharat, Finds Parliamentary Panel.' *DNA India*, 20 July 2018, https://www.dnaindia.com/india/report-rs-9890-crore-unspent-under-swachh-bharat-finds-parliamentary-panel-2639362 (accessed 9 December 2018).

Paliwal, A. 'Next Gen Toilets.' *Down to Earth*, 17 September 2015, https://www.downtoearth.org.in/news/next-gen-toilets-39004 (accessed 9 December 2018).

Pragati. 'India's Sanitation Story.' 16 August 2014, http://pragati.nationalinterest.in/2014/08/indias-sanitation-story/ (accessed 9 December 2018).

Sanan, D. 'Swachh Bharat Mission: Another Futile Toilet Chase.' *Down to Earth*, 21 September 2016, https://www.downtoearth.org.in/blog/governance/swachh-bharat-mission-another-futile-toilet-chase--55758 (accessed 9 December 2018).

SBM Grameen. 'Why Twin Pit Toilets?' 5 February 2018, https://sbmgramin.wordpress.com/2018/02/05/why-twin-pit-toilets/ (accessed 9 December 2018).

UNDP. *Human Development Report 1986*. 1986.

UNDP. *Human Development Report 1990*. 1990, http://hdr.undp.org/en/reports/global/hdr1990 (accessed 9 December 2018).

UNDP. *Human Development Report 1998*. 1998, http://hdr.undp.org/sites/default/files/reports/259/hdr_1998_en_complete_nostats.pdf (accessed 9 December 2018).

UNDP. *Human Development Report 1999*. 1999, http://hdr.undp.org/sites/default/files/reports/260/hdr_1999_en_nostats.pdf (accessed 9 December 2018).

UNDP. *Human Development Report* 2016. 2016, http://hdr.undp.org/sites/default/files/2016_human_development_report.pdf (accessed 9 December 2018).

Chapter 15

Business Today Desk. '*India Today* Conclave: Jayant Sinha Defends Government's Employment Initiatives, Congress Says No Jobs on Ground.' *Business Today*, 9 March 2018, https://www.businesstoday.in/buzztop/buzztop-feature/india-today-conclave-2018-jayant-sinha-defends-jobs-sachin-pilot-no-jobs/story/272305.html (accessed 9 December 2018).

Capital Market. 'Liquidity Crunch Impacting Credit Flow to MSME Sector: CII.' *Business Standard*, 15 November 2018, https://www.business-standard.com/article/news-cm/liquidity-crunch-impacting-credit-flow-to-msme-sector-cii-118111500646_1.html (accessed 9 December 2018).

FE Online. 'Don't Use EPFO Data as a Proxy for Jobs' Creation—Here is Why.' *The Financial Express*, 22 November 2018, https://www.financialexpress.com/opinion/dont-use-epfo-data-as-a-proxy-for-jobs-creation-here-is-why/1389492/ (accessed 9 December 2018).

Gardner, S. 'Wall Street Does Not Value Having Employees and that Is Changing Everything About the US Workplace.' *Business Insider*, 25 January 2018, https://www.businessinsider.com/companies-dont-like-having-full-time-employees-2016-6?IR=T (accessed 9 December 2018).

Ghosh, S. K. and Ghosh, P. 'Payroll Reporting Works.' *The Hindu*, 27 January 2018, https://www.thehindu.com/opinion/op-ed/payroll-reporting-works/article22492132.ece (accessed 9 December 2018).

Jha, S. 'Government Starts Monthly Job Data, May Junk Labour Bureau's Quarterly Survey.' *Business Standard*, 29 April 2018, https://www.business-standard.com/article/economy-policy/govt-starts-monthly-job-data-may-junk-labour-bureau-s-quarterly-survey-118042800649_1.html (accessed 9 December 2018).

Madhavan, N. 'Can India Capitalise on US-China Trade War.' *The Hindu Business Line*, 8 November 2018, https://www.thehindubusinessline.com/opinion/can-india-capitalise-on-us-china-trade-war/article25446070.ece (accessed 9 December 2018).

Nag, A. 'Farm Exports to Trade War Hit China Key to India Cutting Deficit.' *The Economic Times*, 10 October 2018, https://economictimes.indiatimes.com/news/economy/foreign-trade/farm-exports-to-trade-war-hit-china-key-to-india-cutting-deficit/articleshow/66144482.cms (accessed 9 December 2018).

Nair, R. 'Modi Government Amends Labour Rules to Encourage Contract Jobs.' *Livemint*, 21 March 2018, https://www.livemint.com/Home-Page/WpuNaIcqbRbsLUgXbkgIPM/Govt-extends-facility-of-fixed-term-employment-for-all-secto.html (accessed 9 December 2018).

PTI. Job Creation in New Sectors Not Visible in Economic Data, Says Jayant Sinha.' *The Financial Express*, 9 March 2018, https://www.financialexpress.com/economy/job-creation-in-new-sectors-not-visible-in-economic-data-says-jayant-sinha/1093029/ (accessed 9 December 2018).

Sen, A. 'India Tells China: $63 Billion Trade Deficit Untenable.' *The Hindu Business Line*, 12 July 2018, https://www.thehindubusinessline.com/economy/macro-economy/63-b-trade-deficit-untenable-india-tells-china/article24401094.ece (accessed 9 December 2018).

Sen, S. 'Can India Benefit from the US-China Trade War.' Observer Research Foundation, 28 May 2018, https://www.orfonline.org/expert-speak/can-india-benefit-from-the-us-china-trade-war/ (accessed 9 December 2018).

Sen, S. 'To Avoid a Political Slugfest the Transparency of Employment Data is Crucial.' *Hindustan Times*, 6 June 2018, https://www.hindustantimes.com/analysis/to-avoid-a-political-slugfest-the-transparency-of-employment-data-is-crucial/story-lzmHoartyxlBd4Gz6OM5DI.html (accessed 9 December 2018).

Sen, S. 'US-China Trade War an Opportunity for India to Boost Soya Production.' *Down to Earth*, 4 April 2018, https://www.downtoearth.org.in/news/agriculture/chance-in-crossfire-60047 (accessed 9 December 2018).

Shukla, A. 'Niti Aayog to Furnish Reliable Job Data in October.' *The New Indian Express*, 24 December 2018, http://www.newindianexpress.com/business/2018/feb/09/niti-aayog-to-furnish-reliable-job-data-in-october-1770591.html (accessed 9 December 2018).

Sinha, S. '9.5 Lakh Jobs Created in July, Show EPFO Data.' *The Hindu Business Line*, 20 September 2018, https://www.thehindubusinessline.com/economy/95-lakh-jobs-created-in-july-show-epfo-data/article24998698.ece (accessed 9 December 2018).

Sood, V. 'Top Seven IT Firms Including Infosys, Wipro to Lay Off at Least 56,000 Employees this Year.' *Livemint*, 12 May 2017, https://www.livemint.com/Industry/4CXsLIIZXf8uVQLs6uFQvK/Top-7-IT-firms-including-Infosys-Wipro-to-lay-off-at-least.html (accessed 9 December 2018).

Suneja, K. 'China to Reduce Tariffs on 8549 Types of Goods from India, Four Other Asian Countries.' *The Economic Times*, 28 June 2018, https://economictimes.indiatimes.com/news/economy/foreign-trade/china-to-reduce-tariffs-on-8549-types-of-goods-from-india-4-other-asian-countries/articleshow/64767620.cms (accessed 9 December 2018).

Wakefield, J. 'Foxconn Replaces 60,000 Factory Workers with Robots.' *BBC*, 25 May 2016, https://www.bbc.com/news/technology-36376966 (accessed 9 December 2018).

Wang, Y. 'Tesla Will Be Challenged Like Never Before in China—Here's Why.' *Forbes*, 27 August 2018, https://www.forbes.com/sites/ywang/2018/08/27/tesla-will-be-challenged-like-never-before-in-china-heres-why/#5be24e9710e1 (accessed 9 December 2018).

West, D. M. *What Happens If Robots Take the Jobs? The Impact of Emerging Technologies on Employment and Public Policy*. Brookings Institute, October 2015, https://www.brookings.edu/wp-content/uploads/2016/06/robotwork.pdf (accessed 9 December 2018).

Chapter 16

Balaji, S. 'Why Indian Entrepreneurs Are Looking Beyond America to Fulfil Their Startup Dreams.' *Forbes*, 10 January 2018, https://www.forbes.com/sites/sindhujabalaji/2018/01/10/why-indian-entrepreneurs-are-looking-beyond-america-to-fulfill-their-startup-dreams/#412edc175b0a (accessed 9 December 2018).

BI India Bureau. 'India Is the Fastest Growing Start-Up Ecosystem in the World: NASSCOM.' *Business Insider*, 30 October 2014, https://www.businessinsider.in/india-is-the-fastest-growing-startup-ecosystem-in-the-world-nasscom/articleshow/44982544.cms (accessed 9 December 2018).

Chanchani, M. 'Venture Capital Firms' $2 Billion Fund Hunt No Walk in the Park.' *The Economic Times*, 23 February 2018, https://economictimes.indiatimes.com/small-biz/startups/newsbuzz/venture-capital-firms-2-billion-fund-hunt-no-walk-in-park/articleshow/63037044.cms (accessed 9 December 2018).

Department of Industrial Policy and Promotion. *Annual Report*. 2017–18, https://dipp.gov.in/publications/annual-report (accessed 9 December 2018).

Ghosh, N. 'Why Indian Startups Are Relocating to Singapore.' *Livemint*, 23 October 2015, http://epaper.livemint.com/epaper/viewer.aspx.J, Anand. 'Accel Partners Reveal Why it Had Invested in Flipkart at a Time it Had No Backers.' The VCCircle Network, 10 May 2018, https://www.vccircle.com/flipkarts-first-vc-backer-reveals-why-it-invested-when-no-else-wanted-to/ (accessed 9 December 2018).

Kashyap, K. 'The Richest Indian-Owned Company Is Emerging as a Pivotal Player in India's Startup Ecosystem.' *Forbes*, 17 May 2018, https://www.forbes.com/sites/krnkashyap/2018/05/17/the-richest-indian-owned-company-is-emerging-as-a-pivotal-player-in-indias-startup-ecosystem/#45c002b04720 (accessed 9 December 2018).

Katakam, A. 'The Dotcom Bubble.' *Frontline*, 10 June 2000, https://frontline.thehindu.com/static/html/fl1712/17120950.htm (accessed 9 December 2018).

Lim, J. X. 'Indian Startups, Here's How You Can Expand to Singapore.' *Business Standard*, 2 November 2017, https://www.business-standard.com/article/companies/indian-startups-here-s-how-you-can-expand-to-singapore-117110200991_1.html (accessed 9 December 2018).

PTI. 'Over 1,000 Tech Start-Ups Added in 2017: NASSCOM.' *The Hindu Business Line*, 9 January 2018, https://www.thehindubusinessline.com/info-tech/over-1000-tech-startups-added-in-2017-nasscom/article9939247.ece (accessed 9 December 2018).

PTI. 'Start-Ups in India See 108% Growth in Funding, Receive $4.2 Billion in 2018, Says NASSCOM.' *The Financial Express*, 28 October 2018, https://www.financialexpress.com/economy/startups-in-india-see-108-growth-in-funding-receive-4-2-billion-in-2018-says-nasscom/1361322/ (accessed 9 December 2018).

Sai, M. 'Modi's MUDRA Scheme Raining Loans on Women and Religious Minorities.' *Business Standard*, 30 May 2018, https://www.business-standard.com/article/economy-policy/modi-s-mudra-scheme-raining-riches-on-women-and-religious-minorities-118053000376_1.html (accessed 9 December 2018).

Sen, S. '50 Years On: PSBs Need More Autonomy to Fulfil Role.' *DNA India*, 2 August 2018, https://www.dnaindia.com/analysis/column-50-years-on-psbs-need-more-autonomy-to-fulfill-role-2644469 (accessed 9 December 2018).

Sen, S. 'Bansal Divests Risk Move Flipkart to Singapore for Growth.' *The Economic Times*, 13 May 2013, https://economictimes.indiatimes.com/blogs/Whathappensif/bansal-s-divest-risk-move-flipkart-to-singapore-for-growth/ (accessed 9 December 2018).

Sen, S. 'Can the Walmart-Flipkart Deal Ease the Woes of Indian Farmers?' *Down to Earth*, 19 June 2018, https://www.downtoearth.org.in/news/agriculture/can-the-walmart-flipkart-deal-ease-the-woes-of-indian-farmers--60878, Dec-18.

Sen, S. 'Three Uncertainties that Has Made Make in India Difficult.' Observer Research Foundation, 4 July 2018, https://www.orfonline.org/expert-speak/42173-three-uncertainties-that-has-made-make-in-india-difficult/ (accessed 9 December 2018).

Singal, A. 'Has India Become the Hub of Startups, Courtesy IIT?' *Entrepreneur India*, 13 August 2018, https://www.entrepreneur.com/article/318373 (accessed 9 December 2018).

Verma, S. 'Flipkart Buys Back Logistics Arm from WS Retail.' *Livemint*, 22 September 2015, https://www.livemint.com/Companies/DadIlWWt07oLLh3rdS8YUN/Flipkart-buys-back-logistics-arm-from-WS-Retail.html (accessed 9 December 2018).

Chapter 17

Saran, R. 'Bengal CM Jyoti Basu Made India's First Cell Phone Call to Telecom Minister Sukh Ram in 1995.' *India Today*, 26 December 2005, https://www.indiatoday.in/magazine/cover-story/story/20051226-bengal-cm-jyoti-basu-made-indias-first-cell-phone-call-to-telecom-minister-sukh-ram-in-1995-786399-2005-12-26 (accessed 9 December 2018).

The Hindu Business Line. 'Reliance Stages Grand Entry with Three Mobile Offers.' 27 December 2002, https://www.thehindubusinessline.com/2002/12/28/stories/2002122802340100.htm (accessed 9 December 2018).

PTI. '29,000 New Mobile Towers Installed to Check Call Drops: Ravi Shankar Prasad.' *The Economic Times*, 23 December 2015, https://economictimes.indiatimes.com/industry/telecom/29000-new-mobile-towers-installed-to-check-call-drops-ravi-shankar-prasad/articleshow/50294714.cms (accessed 9 December 2018).

Sen, S. 'Consumers Lose Billions in Call Drop Scam.' *Alive*, October 2015.

Sinha, B. 'Telcos a Cartel that Earns ₹250 Crores a Day, Denies Proper Services: TRAI.' *Hindustan Times*, 22 April 2016, https://www.hindustantimes.com/business/telecom-cartel-earns-rs-250-crore-a-day-but-doesn-t-invest-attorney-general-on-call-drops/story-CYtWXrg0vZ3cr2INWFVVvJ.html (accessed 9 December 2018).

Sen, S. 'Torrent of Call Drops Make Digital India Sound Like a Joke. One Answer: Segregate Voice from Data.' *The Times of India*, 29 March 2018, https://epaper.timesgroup.com/Olive/ODN/TimesOfIndia/shared/ShowArticle.aspx?doc=TOIDEL/2018/03/29&entity=Ar02601&sk=4AACBD5D&-mode=image# (accessed 9 December 2018).

Business Today. 'Not Just You, PM Modi Too Faces Call Drops! And, He Wants Telcos to Solve the Problem Fast.' 27 September 2018, https://www.businesstoday.in/sectors/telecom/pm-narendra-modi-faces-call-drops-mobile-telecom-operators-dot/story/282919.html (accessed 9 December 2018).

Gibbs, S. 'What Is Wi Fi Calling and Will it Solve My Mobile Phone Black Spot?' *The Guardian*, 7 April 2015, https://www.theguardian.com/technology/2015/apr/07/what-is-wi-fi-calling-mobile-phone-black-spot (accessed 9 December 2018).

Kashyap, K. 'India's Smartphone Makers Are Planning on Pushing Out Their Chinese Competitors.' *Forbes*, 28 June 2017, https://www.forbes.com/sites/krnkashyap/2017/06/28/indias-smartphone-makers-are-planning-on-pushing-out-their-chinese-competitors/#b0798c22fd73 (accessed 9 December 2018).

Aulakh, G. 'Handset Makers May Invest ₹6,000 Crores for More Local Inputs.' *The Economic Times*, 20 February 2018, https://economictimes.indiatimes.com/tech/hardware/handset-makers May 20invest-rs-6000-crore-for-more-local-inputs/articleshow/62992495.cms (accessed 9 December 2018).

Aulakh, G. 'Samsung to Invest ₹5,000 Crores to Expand Noida Plant.' *The Economic Times*, 6 June 2017, https://economictimes.indiatimes.com/tech/hardware/samsung-to-invest-rs-5000-crore-to-expand-noida-plant/articleshow/59008448.cms (accessed 9 December 2018).

Mukherjee, W. 'Vivo to Invest ₹4,000 Crores in India.' *The Economic Times*, 29 November 2018, https://economictimes.indiatimes.com/tech/hardware/vivo-plans-to-invest-over-rs-4000-crore-in-india/articleshow/66871796.cms (accessed 9 December 2018).

Bhupta, M. 'Bharti Airtel, Vodafone and Idea Control 74% of Market.' *Business Standard*, 14 June 2016, https://www.business-standard.com/article/companies/bharti-airtel-vodafone-idea-control-74-of-market-116061301029_1.html (accessed 9 December 2018).

ET Telecom. 'Total Mobile Subscribers Stands Over 1 Bn in March. Airtel Leads with 29.37% Market Share.' *The Economic Times*, 2 March 2018, https://telecom.economictimes.indiatimes.com/news/indias-total-mobile-subscriber-base-stands-over-1-bn-in-march-airtel-leads-with-29-37-market-share/64001454 (accessed 9 December 2018).

Manzar, O. 'Has BharatNet Fulfilled its End Task of Providing Functional Internet?' *Livemint,* 17 May 2018, https://www.livemint.com/Opinion/5THaiuocuuIhQxZeClVs4K/Has-BharatNet-fulfilled-its-end-task-of-providing-functional.html (accessed 9 December 2018).

Sen, S. 'Reliance Makes Another Media Move.' *Indian Printer and Publisher*, December 2018 issue, https://indianprinterpublisher.com/publishing/reliance-makes-another-media-move/ (accessed 9 December 2018).

Laghate, G. 'Mukesh Ambani's Reliance Set to Get Controlling Stake in Hathway, DEN.' *The Economic Times*, 16 October 2018, https://economictimes.indiatimes.com/industry/telecom/telecom-news/mukesh-ambanis-reliance-set-to-get-controlling-stake-in-hathway-den/articleshow/66230504.cms (accessed 9 December 2018).

Dhapola, S. and Rajan, N. 'UIDAI Aadhaar Helpline Number in People's Contacts: Google Admits it Is to Blame.' *The Indian Express*, 6 August 2018, https://indianexpress.com/article/technology/tech-news-technology/people-find-uidai-helpline-number-added-to-their-contacts-body-says-it-is-wrong-5290239/ (accessed 9 December 2018).

Sen, S. 'Accounts Can Be Hacked, but Not Through Aadhaar.' *DNA India*, 13 August 2018, https://www.dnaindia.com/analysis/column-accounts-can-be-hacked-but-not-through-aadhaar-2649004 (accessed 9 December 2018).

DOT. Annual Reports. Ministry of Communication, 2017–2018, http://www.dot.gov.in/reports-statistic/2471 (accessed 9 December 2018).

IANS. 'JPC Asks CAG to Explain How 2G Loss is ₹1.76 Lakhs Crores.' *Hindustan Times*, 19 May 2011, https://www.hindustantimes.com/delhi-news/jpc-asks-cag-to-explain-how-2g-loss-is-rs-1-76-lakh-crore/story-W08V9gzTSahBnXMP9ACRVN.html (accessed 9 December 2018).

The Hindu. 'Sukh Ram Convicted in One More Case.' 31 July 2016, https://www.thehindu.com/news/national/other-states/sukh-ram-convicted-in-one-more-case/article2640081.ece (accessed 9 December 2018).

India Today. 'India's Biggest Spectrum Auction Fetches ₹1.1 Lakhs Crores.' 25 March 2015, https://www.indiatoday.in/india/story/spectrum-auction-ends-fetches-rs-rs-1.10-lakh-crore-telecom-ministry-245890-2015-03-25 (accessed 9 December 2018).

PTI. '1.1 Lakh Gram Panchayats Given Optical Fibre Connectivity: Government.' *The Economic Times*, 8 February 2018, https://economictimes.indiatimes.com/tech/internet/1-10-lakh-gram-panchayats-given-optical-fibre-connectivity-government/articleshow/62833908.cms (accessed 9 December 2018).

Chapter 18

Bhakta, P. 'How Local Companies Will Gain from RBI's Tough Stance on Data Localisation.' *The Economic Times*, 12 October 2018, https://tech.economictimes.indiatimes.com/news/startups/how-local-companies-will-gain-from-rbis-tough-stance-on-data-localization/66177688 (accessed 9 December 2018).

ET Bureau. 'RBI to Form Regulatory Sandbox for Fintech, Set Up Data Science Lab.' *The Economic Times*, 21 September 2018, https://economictimes.indiatimes.com/industry/banking/finance/banking/rbi-to-form-regulatory-sandbox-for-fintech-set-up-data-science-lab/articleshow/65894188.cms (accessed 9 December 2018).

Ganesh, V. 'Automation to Kill 70% of IT Jobs.' *The Hindu Business Line*, 9 January 2018, https://www.thehindubusinessline.com/info-tech/automation-to-kill-70-of-it-jobs/article9960555.ece (accessed 9 December 2018).

Ganesh, V. 'Indian IT Exports See Signs of Growth.' *The Hindu Business Line*, 30 August 2018, https://www.thehindubusinessline.com/info-tech/indian-it-exporters-see-signs-of-growth/article24823421.ece (accessed 9 December 2018).

Mendonca, J. and Pramanik, A. 'How Indian IT Companies Are Trying to Survive as Outsourcing Business Declines.' *The Economic Times*, 7 June 2018, https://economictimes.indiatimes.com/tech/ites/how-indian-it-companies-trying-to-survive-as-outsourcing-business-decline/articleshow/64499542.cms (accessed 9 December 2018).

Ministry of Electronics and Information Technology. Annual Reports. From 2014 to 2018, http://www.dot.gov.in/reports-statistic/2471 (accessed 9 December 2018).

Pramanik, A. 'Asia Second in Innovation, Thanks to Bengaluru and Singapore.' *The Economic Times*, 15 December 2017, https://economictimes.indiatimes.com/small-biz/startups/newsbuzz/asia-second-in-innovation-thanks-to-bengaluru-and-singapore/articleshow/62077706.cms, Dec-18.

Pramanik, A. 'NASSCOM Sees Single-Digit Growth for India's IT Sector.' *The Economic Times*, 21 February 2018, https://economictimes.indiatimes.com/small-biz/startups/newsbuzz/nasscom-sees-single-digit-growth-for-indias-it-sector/articleshow/63007866.cms (accessed 9 December 2018).

PWC. *Global Economic Crime Survey 2018*. 2018, https://www.pwc.co.uk/forensic-services/assets/gecs/global-economic-crime-survey-2018-uk-findings.pdf (accessed 9 December 2018).

Rodrigues, J. and Speciale, A. 'How Central Banks Are Using Big Data to Help Shape Policy.' *Bloomberg*, 19 December 2017, https://www.bloomberg.com/news/articles/2017-12-18/central-banks-are-turning-to-big-data-to-help-them-craft-policy (accessed 9 December 2018).

Sen, S. 'Job Security Causes Underemployment.' *The Financial Express*, 17 September 1991.

Sen, S. 'Will AI Help Create More Jobs?' Observer Research Foundation, 23 September 2018, https://www.orfonline.org/expert-speak/44485-will-ai-help-create-more-jobs/ (accessed 9 December 2018).

Singh, S. 'Will Artificial Intelligence Take Over Jobs?' *The Economic Times*, 23 January 2018, https://economictimes.indiatimes.com/tech/ites/will-artificial-intelligence-take-over-jobs/articleshow/62610145.cms (accessed 9 December 2018).

Chapter 19

Bhargava, Y. 'India Third-Most Vulnerable to Cyber Crimes.' *The Hindu*, 5 April 2018, https://www.thehindu.com/news/national/india-third-most-vulnerable-country-to-cyber-threats/article23437238.ece (accessed 9 December 2018).

Brady, R. 'Are We Ready for an Artificially Intelligent Future?' *Tech Crunch*, 15 June 2015, https://techcrunch.com/2016/05/29/human-obsolescence-are-we-ready-for-an-artificially-intelligent-future/ (accessed 9 December 2018).

Cox, J. 'Financial Institutions Say the Biggest Threat of Financial Crimes Stems from Cyberspace.' *The Independent*, 29 May 2017, https://www.independent.co.uk/news/business/news/cyber-crime-financial-institutions-risk-bank-investment-management-finance-attack-wannacry-a7761381.html (accessed 9 December 2018).

Down to Earth. 'Blunder 999.' 19 September 2018, https://www.downtoearth.org.in/news/idukki-dam/blunder-999-34609 (accessed 9 December 2018).

Dutta, P. K. 'Three Years of Narendra Modi Government: Job Creation Is at the Lowest.' *India Today*, 18 May 2017, https://www.indiatoday.in/india/story/narendra-modi-job-creation-unemployment-977811-2017-05-18 (accessed 9 December 2018).

EM-DAT. EM-DAT The International Disaster Database. 1950–2017, https://www.emdat.be/ (accessed 9 December 2018).

Ernst & Young. *15th Global Fraud Survey*. 2018, https://www.ey.com/Publication/vwLUAssets/EY_Global_Fraud_Survey_2018_report/$FILE/EY%20GLOBAL%20FIDS%20FRAUD%20SURVEY%202018.pdf (accessed 9 December 2018).

Glasner, J. 'Global Unicorn Exits Hit Multi-Year High in 2018.' *Crunch Base*, 15 August 2018, https://news.crunchbase.com/news/global-unicorn-exits-hit-multi-year-high-in-2018/ (accessed 9 December 2018).

Mooney, C. and Dennis, B. 'Hurricanes, Wildfires Made 2017 the Most Costly US Disaster Year on Record.' *The Washington Post*, 8 January 2018, https://www.washingtonpost.com/news/energy-environment/wp/2018/01/08/hurricanes-wildfires-made-2017-the-most-costly-u-s-disaster-year-on-record/?noredirect=on&utm_term=.f0012fd9b482 (accessed 9 December 2018).

PTI. 'Fear that Artificial Intelligence Will Take Up Both Skilled and Unskilled Jobs: Raghuram Rajan.' *The Economic Times*, 23 March 2018, https://economictimes.indiatimes.com/jobs/fear-that-artificial-intelligence-will-take-up-both-skilled-unskilled-jobs-raghuram-rajan/articleshow/63432627.cms (accessed 9 December 2018).

PTI. 'Nearly 1.2 Crores Jobs Created in 10 Months Till June: CSO Report.' *The Times Of India*, 24 August 2018, https://timesofindia.indiatimes.com/business/india-business/nearly-1-2-crore-jobs-created-in-10-months-till-june-cso-report/articleshow/65534695.cms (accessed 9 December 2018).

Punj, S. and Arun, M. G. 'Welcome to Jobless Growth: Why India is Facing an Unemployment Crisis.' *India Today*, 2 May 2016, https://www.indiatoday.in/magazine/cover-story/story/20160502-employment-scenario-job-crunch-jobless-growth-economy-828782-2016-04-20 (accessed 9 December 2018).

Rajesh, S. V. 'Kerala: What Will Happen if Idukki Dam Shutters Are Lifted?' *The Week*, 30 July 2018, https://www.theweek.in/news/india/2018/07/30/kerala-idukki-dam-shutters-lifted.html (accessed 9 December 2018).

Sample, I. 'AI Will Create "Useless Class" of Human, Predicts Bestselling Historian.' *The Guardian*, 20 May 2016, https://www.theguardian.com/technology/2016/may/20/silicon-assassins-condemn-humans-life-useless-artificial-intelligence (accessed 9 December 2018).

Sen, S. 'Improved Disaster Management Saves Kerala Despite Lack of Preparedness.' Observer Research Foundation, 10 September 2018, https://www.orfonline.org/expert-speak/43901-improved-disaster-management-saves-kerala-despite-lack-of-preparedness/ (accessed 9 December 2018).

Sen, S. 'Trade in Extra Legal Currency: Will Bitcoins Unleash Fresh Round of Volatility in Today's Commodity Markets.' *Down to Earth*, 14 February 2018, https://www.downtoearth.org.in/news/economy/trade-in-extralegal-currency-59657 (accessed 9 December 2018).

The Economist. 'Natural Disasters Made 2017 a Year of Record Insurance Losses.' 11 January 2018, https://www.economist.com/finance-and-economics/2018/01/11/natural-disasters-made-2017-a-year-of-record-insurance-losses (accessed 9 December 2018).

World Economic Forum. *Global Risks Report.* 2017, http://reports.weforum.org/global-risks-2017/part-1-global-risks-2017/ (accessed 9 December 2018).

Index

About the Authors

Sandip Sen is an author, journalist and a TV commentator. He has worked for *The Indian Express, Delhi Press* and *IPP* as an editor and has authored two books. He has been published by national newspapers such as *The Times of India, DNA, Hindustan Times, Hindu Business Line, The Economic Times, Financial Express,* besides think tanks like CSE, TERI and ORF for more than a decade. Prior to journalism, he worked for 10 years in the energy industry and 22 years in manufacturing.

Aarohi Sen is a principal at Accenture. He is a thought leader researching on the impact of digital technologies on large industrial enterprises. He joined Accenture in 2007 and has worked on ideas of innovation, the future of IT and manufacturing operations. He has been a contributor to leading business periodicals such as *The Harvard Business Review, The European Business Review, Fortune and Mint.* The views expressed in the book are his own and not of Accenture.

www.ingramcontent.com/pod-product-compliance
Ingram Content Group UK Ltd.
Pitfield, Milton Keynes, MK11 3LW, UK
UKHW040228290926
15471UKWH00001B/63

9 789387 457935